www.afcinc.org

Reaching **Chinese intellectuals** for **Christ** in this generation

www.afcinc.org

Queen of the Dark Chamber

–Christiana Tsai

Her sickbed was turned into her pulpit,
and her dark chamber
was made her mission field.
God's power was perfected in her weakness,
and the Good News was preached
from where she was to the ends of the earth.

Foreword by Rev. Billy Graham
and Rev. Moses Chow

Christiana Tsai

I
Queen
of the
Dark
Chamber

Contents

Chapter 1

The School of Adversity

IT WAS THE TWELFTH DAY of the second month, and all over China, people were celebrating the Birthday of the Flowers, by tying red strips of cloth on the trees and bushes. These red strips fluttering gaily in the breeze were their birthday greetings to the new flowers.

My father, however, had no time for such celebrations. He was busy at his desk in the Viceroy's Yamen (Governor's administration building) when a servant entered and saluted him, "Great Master, I have good news to report. You have a new daughter and the madam is well."

"Another daughter!" my father sighed. "That makes eighteen children in all. Too many! Too many!"

"Too Many" became my baby name. Though their first greeting was not enthusiastic, my parents did not neglect me. They sent around the customary red eggs to all our relatives and friends to tell them of my arrival. When I was one month old, these relatives and friends came to visit me, bringing gifts of embroidered caps, baby shoes, bibs, and similar articles. Then they enjoyed a feast including a dish of chicken noodle soup. Noodles are a symbol of long life and are always served on birthdays.

In spite of the fact that my parents thought eighteen children were too many, erelong another sister arrived, and they gave her the baby name of "Full House." She was followed by number twenty, who was also a sister, so they called her "Running Over." All my sisters were good-looking, but I was considered rather plain. Yet it was I, alone, "Too Many," who left the high ancestral walls to enter a mission school, crossed the ocean to America, and now have the honor of writing to you.

Hangchow, near the coast of central China, is my old family home. Here the Tsai family have lived for generations and here are the graves of my ancestors. Hangchow is one of the beauty spots of China, famed for its flowering hills, picturesque West Lake, historic temples, storied pagodas, and the swift-flowing Chientang River that sweeps its southern walls and then empties into the long narrow neck of the Hangchow Bay. There the river crashes into the high spring and fall tides as they surge in, forming a wave of foaming water which advances for miles back up the river and submerges both banks along the way. This phenomenon is called the Hangchow Bore. So great is the beauty of Hangchow that there is a common saying, "Heaven is above; Hangchow and Soochow are below."

My grandfather was born in the early part of the nineteenth century, when the Manchu emperors still ruled China. After he passed the government examinations required for a high literary degree, he received an appointment to the governorship of the important Province of Kwangtung in the south. So he left his wife, six sons and a daughter in Hangchow, and made the long journey south to take up his new post. Alas, no sooner had he reached it than he was stricken with disease and died. When my grandmother heard the news, she was stunned. She sat like a statue for days. Her sons tried in vain to move her, get her to speak, eat, or go to bed. She only sat staring in front of her. Now with no visible means of support, she must raise six sons and a daughter. She, who had been trained to ease, must toil night and day. She must dismiss the servants, sell the house, and pawn all the fine garments. Her family must learn to eat rice gruel and cabbage. But she resolved, come what may, all her sons would be scholars, in the family tradition.

My father was the second son, and many a time he told us of his childhood poverty. "How do you think I got my education?" he would ask my brothers, when they complained of hard work.

"We did not even have a teacher or the books we needed. I had to walk through wind and swirling snow for miles to borrow a book, and agree to return it after a certain number of days. Then we boys, after a day's hard work, would sit together around the table and copy from the borrowed book. In the center of the table was a small cup of oil, with a floating wick, giving a very dim light. When we were hungry, we would eat a handful of cold, left-over rice from the basket. In the winter months our hands were so numb we could hardly hold our pens. You don't know what hardship is!"

Somehow the family managed to get along. The boys were largely self-educated; the elder taught the younger. When they grew to manhood, they prepared to take the literary examinations that opened the way for civil service, just as their father and grandfather had done. The daughter, of course, was not allowed to study. She was only a girl and must learn to do the housework.

Three children in old-fashioned clothes

My father and his older brother passed the first degree examinations in Hangchow, and later went to Nanking to take the examinations for the next degree. On the day appointed, the two brothers appeared at the Examination Halls. Both were dressed in long blue cotton gowns and short black coats. Their hair was neatly braided in long queues and they wore black skull caps; each carried a basket containing fruit, pens, ink, a bowl, and chopsticks.

Gaily colored awnings hung over the entrance. At the gate two attendants roughly searched the young men for hidden papers or books. They entered an open courtyard where crowds of students and attendants milled around. A high tower overlooked the many long rows of examination cells which extended on four sides from the tower. Each row contained about a hundred cells, opening into a narrow aisle, and exposed to the weather in front.

The two brothers were very nervous and kept close together to bolster their courage. They were assigned separate cells where they laid down their baskets. The cells were the size of telephone booths, and each contained a narrow board to sit on, a niche in the wall for a light, a nail to hang the basket, and another board for a table.

Soon the examiners summoned them to the courtyard, called the roll and gave each student his roll of paper. This was all the paper he was allowed, so he carefully hid it in the pocket of his gown. Toward evening, the examiners went to the street gates and with great ceremony closed and sealed them. This was a signal that the examinations were to begin. For three days and nights no one could go out or come in for any reason whatever.

In the tower overhead, an examiner appeared and beat a gong to call the students to assemble in the courtyard. They gazed up and saw him wave a banner. He called out in a loud voice: "O ye spirits of the dead! Look upon these students gathered here! If any has offended you in word or deed, do you now punish the offender and avenge the wrong." The nervous students, who believed in evil spirits, shivered with fear, some nearly fainting. The gong

Examination cells and tower

was sounded again, and the students went to their own cells.

An attendant, holding a lighted lantern with the subject of the essay written on the sides, passed slowly down each aisle, giving the students time to see the title clearly. During the three days and nights, the students could neither lie down to sleep or speak to anyone; an attendant paced up and down the aisle to guard against any cheating.

At mealtimes when the gong sounded, each took his bowl and chopsticks out to the courtyard, where there were great steaming caldrons of rice gruel. He dipped out what he wanted, noisily wolfed it down, and then turned back to the cell. The strain of preparation, anticipation and prolonged concentration was so great that there were always a few students who died under the ordeal, and their bodies were passed out through a secret door in the wall.

When the essay was finished, each signed his name on the designated flap, sealed it and handed the paper to the examiner. Then when the gates were opened, they went out, too weary to speak, anxious only for a place to lie down for a few hours. The examinations were strictly impartial. The subjects always demanded thorough knowledge of Confucian Classics. The Board of Examiners read each essay and judged it on its own merits before they unsealed the author's signature. Appointments were often given to those who received the highest grades. This system of examinations had been in operation in China since A.D. 600.

One day a messenger handed an official notice to my grandmother stating that my father had passed the examination! Grandmother had no money to give the messenger for bringing the good news, so she took her best coat to a neighbor for a deposit, and borrowed money. She and Father were very happy, but my uncle was so disappointed that he went to his room and wept. Soon another messenger arrived with a notice saying that uncle too had passed. Another coat was taken to the neighbors, and more money borrowed to pay the second messenger, and the family sat down to celebrate the great occasion, shabby but proud.

Every member of the family eventually won an important political post. My eldest uncle became Vice-Governor of Hopei Province, living at Tientsin; and my father Vice-Governor of Kiangsu, living at Nanking. Later he became Acting-Governor, and held many other important offices. My third uncle became a high official (Taotai) in Peking; my fourth uncle, Mayor of Paotingfu; my fifth uncle, Mayor of Yangchow; and my sixth uncle, Mayor of Siangyang, in Hupch. As for the despised little girl, she married an official having the highest rank of all—instructor of the Emperor himself! Such are the sweet uses of adversity!

Many years later my father became head of the Examination Halls in Nanking. He used to don his gorgeous robes, put on his cap with a peacock feather hanging down behind and a red button on top (the insignia of the highest official degree), and set out in his green sedan chair with eight bearers. Liveried horsemen preceded and followed him.

Examination halls-5,000 cells for students

Father always had a deep affection for the poor and did much for them. One night during the examinations he decided to see what was going on below. He took off his official robes, put on an attendant's gown, and went downstairs. In the darkness of the courtyard he heard someone sobbing. He found a student huddled on a step, crying as if his heart would break. "What is the matter?" Father asked. "Who are you?"

"My name is Hung, and I am from Wusih. My widowed mother is too poor to send me here, but some friends loaned money for me to come. My essay slipped out of my gown and fell into the night soil! Alas, now I have no more paper and I dare not return and tell my mother I have lost the chance! It would break her heart! I can only kill myself." My father was moved with compassion. "I have a roll of paper which I do not need," he said. "I will get it for you, and you can rewrite your essay. Wait here for me." When he returned, the young man looked in his face, recognized him as the Chief Examiner and kowtowed before him. "Sir," he cried, "I shall remember you with gratitude all my life. You have saved me and my mother!"

The next incident after passing his examinations was a strange marriage. In China engagements are often made when both parties are young, and arranged without either the boy or girl seeing each other. Sometimes the parents arrange them even before the children are born. So it happened that at an early age my father was engaged to a young woman whom he had never seen and who lived far to the north, in Peking. As there were no mails in these days, they had had no news of her for some years; my grandmother urged him to go up to Peking, marry his bride, and bring her home.

The journey to Peking took several months and was very tiresome and difficult. He was surprised to find on arrival that she had been dead two years, and her coffin was there waiting for him! According to Chinese custom, she was his wife and he must bring her coffin back to Hangchow and bury her in his family graveyard. Now his first wife was dead, so he must marry again. He married a girl from Hangchow who bore him seven children, and then she too died. After her death he went to Peking again and married a beautiful young lady, with whom he fell deeply in love. This woman, my mother, was not only beautiful, but very capable and a great help to him in his work. She was slender, with delicate features, and an ivory-tinted complexion. Her jet black hair was brushed smoothly back into a knot at the neck, and fastened with gold and jade hairpins. She bore him fifteen children. But her burdens as wife and mother, and mistress of a vast household, were so great, that she urged my father to take a concubine to share the responsibilities with her. The latter bore him two children, so in all he had twenty-four children,—quite a family, even in China, where big families are common.

After my father had had various political offices, and had been stationed in several cities, he went to Nanking, where he lived from 1870 to 1910.

A city gate

Chapter 2

Inside High Walls

PEKING, "Northern Capital," lies in the dusty plains of North China. Within its high walls the Manchu Empress Dowager lived in indescribable splendor, ruling over her vast empire. Nanking, "Southern Capital," lies in the green fields and hills of the Yangtse Valley and has been the political trouble spot in Central China. After the Manchus were overthrown, Nanking served as capital under various governments during the last half century. It lies on the southern banks of the Yangtse, about two hundred miles from its mouth. Its lofty city walls curve with the natural contours of the land, enclosing an immense city area, while its nine city gates with their storied towers look down on the stream of burdened coolies, creaking wheelbarrows, speeding ricksha men, battered carriages, and gleaming cars passing through its portals. Each conveyance pictures in a way the kaleidoscopic events that these ancient walls have witnessed in recent times.

It was in Nanking that I was born, seventh in line of daughters, and so was called "Miss Seven." Who could have dreamed that I was to see Nanking throw off the yellow Manchu gown, put on a Republican suit, then change to a Japanese uniform, and later go back again to the Republican outfit?

It was through these city gates that my father passed in his green sedan chair as Vice-Governor of the Province of Kiangsu. It was outside these walls, in a little houseboat, that the pioneer missionaries waited until they could find a home to live in. In their wake came an ever-growing stream of missionaries. The churches, schools, seminaries, colleges, hospitals, and homes scattered over the city are material evidence of their devoted work, while the changed lives and society around them continue to show the enduring spiritual results. From the river and the hills around, the revolutionaries besieged the city in 1911 and drove out the Manchus, opening the way for Sun Yat Sen, father of the Chinese Republic, to come in as the first president of China. Through these same gates, sixteen years later, Chiang Kai-shek entered and made Nanking his capital. In 1937, after only ten years of this rule, a Japanese army blasted a corner of the wall and entered the city, raping, burning, and looting with great ferocity. The Japanese were defeated eight years later, and Chiang Kai-shek re-entered the gates of Nanking.

How well I remember our home on the Street of the King's Favorite! It was an amazing labyrinth of halls, courtyards, dwellings and gardens surrounded by high walls. Let me take you there. We will enter an imposing gateway flanked by stone lions, pass through brass-studded lacquered doors, on each side of which are long benches where the retainers sit, and find ourselves in a courtyard that opens into a lofty hall. The hall is furnished in stiff, carved tables and chairs, and the walls are hung with immense scrolls. Passing through a door at the back, we find ourselves in another courtyard, with still another hall back of that. But there are two doorways set on either side of the courtyard, and we will enter one of these which is quaintly shaped like a round moon. Inside is a beautiful hall with scarlet and gold pillars, latticed doors, delicately painted ceiling, and carved rosewood furniture. Here we find Father interviewing a guest. When he wants to dismiss the guest, he merely raises his teacup, and the retainers call out, "The guest is leaving."

So from courtyard to hall we wander, from surprise to fresh surprise. Here is a garden with pavilion and climbing roses. There is a library where my brother is reading a book. Next we come to a pond with a rockery and weeping willows, where some children are playing and watching the yuan-yang ducks swimming around. Beyond is a gaily painted theatre where we have plays on special occasions, and next to that a lotus pond with an overhanging balcony where we will drink tea and eat nuts. Each doorway is a different shape—a moon, a leaf, a fan, a vase. Each window set in the wall is a different design of tiles. Everywhere are flowering trees and plants.

If we turn in another direction, we will come upon the living apartments of the family. Most of them are in rows of seven rooms with latticed doors, but we must enter from the middle room, which is the family hall. In front is a square table with stools around it where some children are eating breakfast. On each side of the hall are bedrooms. The beds are immense canopied structures of polished wood inlaid with mother-of-pearl and neatly piled with brightly colored quilts.

He raises his cup and the servants call, "The guest is leaving."

Each of these halls and gardens had a special name such as, Ancestral Hall, Wisteria Arbor, Magnolia Study, White Crane Pagoda, Bamboo Grove, Fairy Fox Pavilion, etc.

Tsai family's garden

And now let me introduce you to my family.

During my early childhood, there were still eight unmarried children at home. Each of us had two special servants, and one of them always accompanied us wherever we went. The nurse stayed with the child for at least three years and was a mother to him. My nurse stayed with me for sixteen years, and we were devoted to each other.

One of the gates of the Tsai's family

One important item of etiquette for Chinese children is to learn to speak politely to others, especially to their elders. Instead of saying "Good Morning" or "Good Night," or "Good-by," we addressed people simply by their titles, such as "Father," "Mother," "Great Elder Brother," "Second Elder Brother," "Sixth Younger Sister," "Great Uncle," "Second Sister-in-law," etc. We were never allowed to use our given names for each other as this was not considered polite. So for practice I had to

On February 12, 1890, (during the reign of Guangxu Emperor of the Qing Dynasty) Christiana Tsai was born, the 18th child in her family in Nanjing. Typical of a highly-ranked government official in the old days, the Tsais had a lavishly-built house with many servants, male and female.

go around and address the animals, "Sister Cat," "Brother Dog," and "Brother Horse." We had two men teachers for the boys, two women teachers for the girls, a music teacher, and a sewing teacher. Because my father wanted us to know Chinese history, he employed two storytellers to instruct us.

Foot-binding for girls began when they were six years of age. Though Father had forbidden it, Mother was practical and knew that society still considered it necessary for every well-born girl to have bound feet if she were to get a husband. She ordered that my feet be bound, but my nurse took pity on my tears and at night often loosened the bandages and gently rubbed my feet. So my feet didn't become smaller and smaller every year as my elder sisters' did, and on New Year's Day I was not allowed to wear embroidered red shoes. "Look at your big boats!" my mother cried. "You'll never get married; you can wear only black shoes."

Eight of my brothers were married and their wives and children lived with us, each in a separate apartment with their own servants. My married sisters, of course, went to live with their husbands' families. Then there were about twenty cousins, children of my uncles, living with us. The men cousins were married and lived with their families and servants in their own apartments. Each of the sisters-in-law and cousins-in-law had her own maid to comb her hair, attend to her wardrobe and to her various needs.

In the kitchen there was a head cook with fifteen assistants who served meals to each family in their own quarters. They fed all the servants as well, for these servants all lived within our walls in rooms assigned to them. There was a head gardener with his assistants, and there was an apartment especially for tailors who did all our sewing. There were many chair-bearers and grooms for the horses. At night two watchmen went about beating drums, and two king thieves were paid to keep other thieves away. They always frightened us at night by leaping up on the roofs and whistling to warn other thieves that they were there.

In charge of these were head-servants who had their own assistants, and a treasurer who paid the bills. Mother was in charge of all,—sons, daughters, daughters-in-law, nieces-in-law, grandchildren and servants. The head servants reported to her and she gave orders through them. She had to administer all the discipline and keep order in this great family. The secret of her success was that, though she exacted formal obedience, she gave each family freedom to live their own lives in privacy and according to their own desires.

Every morning after breakfast each son and daughter, daughter in-law and cousin went to the apartment of Father and Mother to address them. They simply said, "Father! Mother!" and then went away unless they received some special orders.

Father was a tall, thin man who was always solemn and dignified. Every evening when he returned home in his green sedan chair, liveried servants would line up on both sides of the main entrance, holding up bright-colored lanterns. As he stepped out of the chair, a servant preceded him to the private entrance calling, "The great one has arrived." That was the signal for us children to line up and address him, and he always acknowledged our salutations with a nod. Little Jade, the concubine, then came forward, took off his embroidered official gown, and put on a garment suitable for the house. We children seldom saw him except on these formal occasions.

Dressed up for the New Year

Chapter 3

Golden Days

CHINA NEW YEAR was the happiest time of the year for us children. But it was also a great ordeal because we were afraid of committing an error in etiquette and being reprimanded. We believed that all the countless ceremonies must be carried out punctiliously if we were to have good luck throughout the year—any slip might bring bad luck. At least a month in advance the servants began cleaning the house from top to bottom, and preparing great quantities of food. There is a saying in China, "Whether you are rich or poor, you must all scrub and be clean to greet the New Year."

A week before New Year, some of the adults gathered in the kitchen to send the Kitchen God to Heaven. A picture of him was pasted on the wall of the kitchen all year, and he was supposed to watch over the family doings. They kowtowed and burnt incense and placed an offering of candy before him, after which the picture was torn down and burned. We believed that the candy would give him a sweet taste in his mouth, and hoped that he would report only good things about us when he got to Heaven.

By New Year's Eve all preparations had to be complete and all debts paid. Good wishes were written on wide strips of red paper and pasted on the doors. Everyone bathed and put on his new clothes. The men all had queues in those days, and they wore black skull caps and fur-lined, satin gowns. The women and children wore short fur-lined or padded silk jackets, and red embroidered skirts and shoes. The women wore velvet or satin head bands, encrusted with pearls or jade ornaments, to keep their ears warm, and we children wore tasseled caps and silver lockets. We each carried a little covered brass stove containing a red hot charcoal briquette hid in ashes, to keep our hands and feet warm, for our houses were not heated.

After Father and Mother had given each of us gifts of money to put under our pillows for good luck, we all went to the Ancestral Hall to worship our ancestors. Paintings of our ancestors hung on the walls, and before each picture was a bowl, a cup, chopsticks, and a spoon for that person's spirit to use. Long tables were covered with steaming food—whole roast pigs, ducks, chickens, fish, and so on—offerings for the spirits. We all knelt in order of rank and kowtowed, after which the servants brought yellow bags of paper money, one for each ancestor, and gave them to Father, who burned them one by one in a great brass urn, and threw a cupful of wine on the ashes in farewell. When the ceremony was over, we all went to the great hall for the feast. We seldom slept at all on New Year's Eve. In the morning of the New Year the doors were all opened, a barrage of firecrackers set off, and we were free to do what we liked for eighteen days, except that we must still worship our ancestors each day of that period.

Every New Year we called in a fortuneteller to "calculate our fortunes" for the year. Blind people generally become fortunetellers because the Chinese say that since they cannot see this world they must be able to see the unseen world. The fortuneteller was led in by a little boy, and he carried a sounding brass disk which he tapped as he went along. He calculated our fortunes on the basis of eight characters—the year, the month, the day and the hour of birth. Chinese calculate time in cycles of sixty years, and each cycle is subdivided into periods of twelve years, each of which is called after an animal. I was born in the year of the tiger, the twelfth day of the second month, at ten o'clock at night. Since I was born in the year of the tiger at night time, and a tiger goes out to hunt prey at night, the fortuneteller said I would be diligent and never lack for food, but girls born on the twelfth day of the second month, the birthday of the flowers, turn out to be either the very best or the very worst among women. So they are not likely to get married. A man's family would rather take the chance of avoiding a wicked wife than of getting a paragon.

With such a fortune, Mother was never able to contract an engagement for me. When I was a few years old, a wealthy family from a city in the north sent a go-between to our homes to seek an engagement for one of their sons. She described the advantages of marrying into that family, and my mother inquired from other sources concerning them. After several months of talking back and forth, Mother agreed to match our fortunes and handed my eight characters written on red paper to the go-between. She took it to the boy's family and they called in a fortuneteller to see whether his eight characters and mine would portend a happy marriage. Since they couldn't be sure which way I would turn out, they decided not to contract the engagement. Had that part of the procedure been fortuitous, the next step would have been to place our eight character strips together under the incense burner which stood before his ancestral tablets for a period of three days. If no misfortune occurred to the family during that time, that is, if nothing were broken, not even a bowl or a chopstick, they would know that I would never break his good fortune and our marriage would be propitious. Once an engagement is agreed upon, the boy's eight characters and those of the girl are written in special red and gold folders. Possession of these folders is equivalent to having a marriage license.

These foolish superstitions reveal how slender is the thread of happiness that binds two lives together, and how blindly people grope in the face of the unknown future to escape the tragedies that lurk beside their pathway. In fact, we Chinese have a proverb that though a bride may ride in a red embroidered sedan chair, she may have picked up an unlucky ticket after all. But this incident also shows that a loving heavenly Father guards His child in all circumstances, working all things together for good, and using even a blind fortuneteller's prognostications for my advantage.

In the ninth month, when chrysanthemums were at their height, the gardener arranged hundreds of pots in geometric designs beside the garden walks and inside the Colored Glass Hall, before the whole family—father, mother, children, sisters-in-law, cousins, their wives, and grandchildren—all dressed for the occasion met together to celebrate the Chrysanthemum Festival. No one can appreciate the beauty of these flowers who hasn't seen the great varieties of color, size, and form that can be grown. We first walked around enjoying them while the servants set chairs and carved teapoys among the pots. Then we sat down, each to his own teapoy, and ate steamed crabs. Everyone had a board, tiny hammer, a pick, and a hook to crack the shell and extract the delicious meat. In the meantime, the cook was busy at a great caldron of boiling soup. Into it he dropped bits of fish, chicken, mushrooms, leeks, cabbage, water cress, and other delicacies. Finally he put in a bowlful of pure white chrysanthemum petals.
We all had a drink of this broth called "Chrysanthemum Pot."

When the eating was over, we all sat in silence while each one composed a short poem for the occasion. We read them in turn, and Father awarded the honors. Seventh Brother and Sixth Sister were generally the best poets; I never even got honorable mention. In this way we carried out the ancient tradition of Chinese poets.

Of course, there were other festivals during the year, but most of the time we either played in the gardens or studied with our teachers, for Father wanted his daughters also to be educated. The lotus pond was big enough to have a little boat, and with a servant to pole us around, we could pick the lotus flowers and eat the seeds from the lotus pods. My brothers had horse races in the big orchard, while we girls hid in the Buddhist temple and watched excitedly. We enjoyed the Hall of Western Culture where there were strange upholstered leather chairs on casters, and we thought it was great fun to roll them around the room. We never thought of sitting on them, for we hardly considered them chairs.

We lived in a fabulous fairyland and beautiful and costly things were given to us, but we were rarely allowed outside the high walls. Prisoners in the palace, we dreamed of the world outside. Going to a school just for girls, where a foreign woman would teach me English and piano was my castle in the air.

But there was one day in a year when the doors were opened for us, and our eager eyes drank in the magic sights and sounds of the outside world.

There was an amusement place by the Confucian Temple, in the south part of the city, where we enjoyed an excursion once every summer. For nights before, I hardly slept. In the morning of the great day I dressed in my summer silks and jewelry, and stepping into a sedan chair curtained with silk gauze, went to the shore of a famous canal skirting the temple grounds. Here my father had hired two immense pleasure boats—amazing affairs with fancy railings and carved windows. We all got on these boats and were poled back and forth in the widest part of the canal. The cooks and servants followed in smaller boats with the food, for this was a day of great feasting. First they served us appetizers, tea, and soup with tiny meat balls, steamed dumplings, spring rolls, ham and nut biscuits, date and nut cookies, and the like. At noon we had a real feast, with a first course of eight cold dishes, such as minced ham, sliced duck, smoked fish, and alkaline eggs. Then followed six hot dishes, brought in one at a time, such as shrimp and peas, shredded pork and bamboo shoots, liver and water chestnuts. Next followed hot dishes such as bird's nest soup, sharks' fins, eight-precious-fruit pudding, and last of all, four huge platters with a whole roast duck, a whole stewed chicken, a whole large fish, and a big roast of pork. Of course, we took only a nibble from each plate and barely touched the last course.

Dinner lasted about two hours, and while we were eating, dozens of singing girls came on to dance and sing for us, magicians did their tricks, and there was a Punch and Judy show. In the afternoon we children climbed into small boats and were poled down the canal to a large peach orchard, where we could pick all the peaches we wanted. In later years, there was a foreign-style restaurant where we went in the evening, to eat foreign food. The menu always consisted of beef soup, meat sandwiches, cold sausage, pudding, cocoa, bread, butter, and jam. This was nothing short of marvelous to us, but we didn't dare touch the knives or forks for fear of cutting our mouths, so we ate everything with a large spoon. We were also entranced by a foreign shop in the restaurant where we could buy leather pocketbooks, tiny bottles of perfume, and jars of hard candy.

When my mother was forty years of age, we had a double ceremony, celebrating her birthday and Third Brother's marriage to the granddaughter of Li Hung-chang, a well-known ambassador to the United States. Troups of noted actors were hired to perform in our private theatre continuously for three days. Three days before the wedding the bride's trousseau arrived, carried by many servants. Chairs, tables, stools, tubs, cradles, chests, cupboards, trunks, boxes, rolls of silk, satin, velvet and tapestry, jewelry, porcelainware, kitchenware, silver, scrolls, vases, and screens, formed a procession over a mile long. As each servant with his article came to our entrance, eight of our secretaries stood on each side of the gateway to receive him. Those on one side called the name of the article, and those on the other checked the item on their list. Then the articles were taken to the bride and groom's apartments, and we had to pay a fabulous sum in tips.

On the day of the wedding, all the doors were opened from the brass-studded ones on the street, to the last hall at the back; all screens were removed, allowing a view from the front clear to the back. Archways of bamboo, festooned with green and scarlet silk streamers, were erected. At the front entrance were two rows of our tallest menservants, dressed in long official gowns, their chests crossed with scarlet and green sashes. Beyond the servants, my brothers and cousins stood in a double line to welcome the men guests. Farther in, my sisters and sisters-in-law stood to welcome the women.

When a man guest arrived, his chair-bearers set him down at the entrance, and one of our servants came forward to receive his big red calling card. Then, holding this card high over his head with one hand, he led the guest down the aisle to the men of the family, who greeted him before he was taken to the theatre and seated with the other guests. When a woman guest arrived, her chair was carried on past the men to where the women of the family greeted her and had her escorted to an upstairs balcony of the theatre, where the women watched the play through bamboo curtains.

Late in the day, after all the lanterns were lighted, we heard the trumpets and knew that the great, red bridal sedan-chair was arriving. But, strange to say, the gates were shut and barred, and no one was there to welcome her. The bearers had to set the chair down while the bride's relatives paid a big sum to our servants to open the doors and let her in. This little device was supposed to teach her patience in her new home. When the doors were opened, her chair was brought to the front hall, where the groom stood to welcome her. At the same moment, an earsplitting barrage of firecrackers was set off. Her two bridesmaids pulled back the curtains, and she stepped out in her elaborately embroided scarlet and green satin gown, heavy pearl-encrusted headdress and veil. The bride and groom now bowed together to heaven and earth, and next bowed to each other, after which the groom went with the bride to the bridal apartment and removed her veil.

From there the couple went to the big hall where the whole family stood to welcome the bride before escorting the couple to the Ancestral Hall where everyone kowtowed before the ancestral tablets. The bride and groom next kowtowed to Father and Mother, and then in turn to the rest of us, from the eldest to the youngest. Returning to the bridal chamber they sat together on the bed behind an embroidered curtain, and exchanged cups of wine. There was a big feast for the guests who teased the bride.

Father and Mother and the other elders each gave the bride an expensive gift, and she in turn gave separate gifts to every member of the family, and money to each of the servants. The cost of weddings and funerals has put many a family in debt for life.

Chapter 4

Roots of Bitterness

OUR HOME on the Street of the King's Favorite was a small-scale copy of the sumptuous summer palace of the Manchus in Peking. We were Chinese and, though we didn't know it, were living in the twilight of the Manchu dynasty. These rulers had conquered China in 1644 and forced the Chinese to wear the queue as a sign of subjection. Then they followed the invariable course of tyrants; after establishing a mighty empire, they gave themselves up to enjoying the luxuries they had squeezed from the poor. A brilliant, crafty old woman, the Empress Dowager, sat on the Dragon Throne at Peking. She had gained her power by devious means and held tenaciously to the old order of things. So, while the court rioted in splendor in the palace, the common people, in despair, began rioting in the country, in an effort to overthrow their foreign rulers. The Manchu and Chinese officials were blindly self-satisfied and abysmally ignorant of the Western world, so they resisted all efforts to establish trade and diplomatic relations with the West.

England, France, and America coveted the vast potential trade of China and were determined to exploit her resources. Unfortunately, in the case of England, they forced the sale of opium on China. When one of the Chinese officials, a Mr. Ling, resisted by burning a whole cargo of opium, the English backed up their demands with gunboats, won the so-called "Opium War," and demanded important treaty ports with extraterritorial privileges as indemnity. So the progressive West won the diplomatic, military, and economic victories over the reactionary East, and reduced the Chinese nation to political impotence, and embittered the whole country for generations to come. Though the Empress Dowager was largely responsible for these defeats, the people, resentful of all foreigners, frequently rioted in an effort to drive them out, not only the Manchus but also the Westerners.

Kwang Hsu was the young heir to the Manchu throne, and he was an enlightened liberal who had the real good of the nation at heart. His wise advisers had helped him prepare a program of reform. The Empress Dowager opposed this, so they plotted to dethrone her. One of the conspirators turned traitor and went to the Empress while she was sitting in the theatre and whispered the details of the plot in her ear. There in the sight of all, she listened and her face never moved a muscle. She gave orders to imprison Kwang Hsu. So the last effort to reform the government was nipped in the bud: Kwang Hsu remained a prisoner for life and the Empress Dowager triumphed for a time.

All over China there was increasing resentment against foreigners. Pioneer missionaries suffered much persecution during those years. The Chinese people had long ago organized in mutual protection societies to avenge their wrongs. The Green Society generally used peaceable means, but the Red Society used violence. The Red had greater power over northern China, and the Green in southern China. The Red Society, the Big Sword Society, and the Boxer Society were all similar organizations. They became the media through which the common people expressed their resentment of their oppressors, whether native, Manchu, or Western.

My father was charitable and loved the poor. At the end of every month we used to see a line of poor widows, each holding a receipt book, coming to receive their monthly support. On the hot summer days he ordered two five-gallon jars of fresh tea to be placed in front of our street door, for use of the tired passers-by. He provided free medicine for travelers who became ill. On windy, snowy nights, groups of servants would be sent out to look for the poor in different parts of the city and to give them rice tickets and tickets for a set of winter clothes. When a poor person was sick and had no money to see a doctor, or died without money to buy a coffin, my parents encouraged us children to take out our savings, or New Year's money, to help them.

My father was a liberal, and a conscientious leader as well. He sternly forbad Mother to accept any bribes whatsoever. When he had to decide the fate of any man, whether to condemn him to death or set him free, he often spent the whole night pacing up and down in his study. He was friendly to Westerners and risked his life to save them. He later lost his fortune in unsound investments by listening to the advice of some Europeans.

Charles Leaman, the first Protestant missionary to buy land and establish work in Nanking, arrived in 1874. He wore Chinese clothes and had his hair braided into a queue. But since the Chinese always seized a man by his queue, Mr. Leaman had it cut off and attached to his cap. He carried his money, consisting of pieces of silver, sewed into the lining of his sleeveless jacket, which he wore inside his long gown. When he needed some money, he would take a penknife, slit open the jacket, take out a piece, weigh it, and purchase what he needed. At the change of the seasons, he pawned his old garment to buy a new one. He could find no place to rent in Nanking, for the people were afraid of foreigners. He had to sleep wherever he could find a corner, and eat the food of the common people. During the day he sat in the teashops and talked with the men who came to drink tea and discuss their various affairs. Three times a day he went out on the streets to preach. Foreigners were so little known here that the people thought he was a Chinese from the coast.

He married Miss Lucy Crouch, a South China missionary, also of the Presbyterian Church. They went to Nanking where they carried on a pioneer work and devised means to get land for a chapel and a home. Magistrates were unwilling to sell or rent to foreigners, so in the meantime, Mr. and Mrs. Leaman and their little daughter Mary spent many months living in a small houseboat on the canal outside the city walls.

Finally they bought some land, a former battle ground, which the Chinese considered unlucky for they thought it was haunted by the spirits of the dead. "If you want this land," the magistrate had said, "you can go and live with the devils there." Here they built two houses, a church, and a school. More missionaries arrived, and a third house was built. This was the beginning of the first Presbyterian mission station at Four Flagstaffs.

Mrs. Leaman had been a teacher in Canton's well-known True Light School which was founded by her dear friend, Miss Noyes. She had studied the far-reaching possibilities of a truly Christian girls' school, and longed to start one in Nanking. Boys in China often got an education, but girls rarely learned to read. Here in Nanking, neither the girls nor their parents saw the value of a woman learning to read, so they were not interested in going to school when Mrs. Leaman advertised. For three months no girl dared enter the compound, then one day a little girl came in. Mrs. Leaman let her play around for the first few days so she would get used to things, and then suggested they start learning to read. The girl refused immediately, saying, "I only came to eat and play; I don't want to study!" And she went away.

The next pupil was the gateman's daughter, and she had to be paid to study! No one at that time would have dreamed that in the lifetime of the Leaman's two daughters, Mary and Lucy, the school would have an enrollment of sixteen hundred students! Nor did anyone foresee that there would soon be dozens of girls' schools right in Nanking. Often in recent years I have seen the students of this school, in celebration of Founder's Day, dramatize those early days. It was very real to them, but at the same time from their sophisticated point of view, very amusing!

There were a number of riots against foreigners in those early years. The people feared and hated the "foreign devils," and spread many rumors about them. One day they seized Mr. Leaman, bound him with ropes, and were going to throw him into a canal. Friends ran to tell Mrs. Leaman. Carrying baby Lucy, and leading Mary, she arrived at the scene just in time to save him. Another mob, led by members of the Big Sword Society, decided to kill the foreigners one night. As they marched toward the Leaman home, rattling their great swords, a big storm came up and they were delayed. Christian Chinese friends warned the Leamans, who hurriedly got into sedan chairs and escaped through the back door, just as the rioters rushed in the front way.

In the meantime, the wily Empress Dowager, hoping to save herself from the rebels, had persuaded the Boxer Society that the Westerners were the cause of China's troubles. She incited them to start a nationwide anti-foreign, anti-Christian massacre. All foreigners in the country were to be killed. Bands of Boxers tortured and murdered both foreign and Chinese Christians. My uncle, Mayor of Pao-ting-fu, died just at this time, and there was a terrible massacre in that city. Forty-six missionaries were killed in one day! Many years later I stood on the very spot where they died, facing their graves. A prominent American speaker read to the group a letter written by one of them to her son in America, just before she died. She told him of their suffering and danger, and yet urged him to prepare and come to China as a missionary to take up their work after they were gone. "And now," said the speaker, "that boy is on his way to China." That was the true spirit of Christ who prayed for His enemies while He was hanging on the cross.

In Nanking, Father received the Empress' order to kill all the foreigners in his jurisdiction. He was Acting-Viceroy while the Viceroy was absent, and knowing that his superior also opposed this order, he decided to disobey it. He changed the words "kill all foreigners" to "protect all foreigners." This was a dangerous step to take, for if his insubordination had been discovered, he and all his family would have been killed. Then he came home and told Mother, "I will not kill these innocent people, and we may all be killed for disobeying the Empress' order. You must take the whole family and go hide in the country." When word of this was passed around, everybody began to weep, until Mother said, "That would be impossible! What could I do alone with this big family on my hands?" In the end we did not run away, and all the foreigners and Christians were spared in our area. We, too, were safe, as the Empress Dowager never received word of Father's insubordination; an international army captured Peking at this time, and she herself was forced to flee.

Chapter 5

The Deceitfulness of Riches

To AN UNTHINKING PERSON, this picture of wealth and ease would mean that our family was very happy. But underneath the peaceful life was a feeling of pessimism. We knew by experience the vanity of life and the deceitfulness of riches. For Father, who made it all possible, it was the success of a self-made man, trained in the school of adversity. From childhood he had developed his power by hard work, and in later years the money we spent had been acquired, not by corruption in office, but by honest business investments.

We children, cradled in luxury, had nothing to do but enjoy his wealth. We had no incentive for hard work, wherein we might have found some happiness and strength; we became haughty, wasteful, and idle. My elder brothers especially, used Father's money in gambling, carousing, and loose living. My sisters, who had married into wealthy, influential families, often came home in tears, complaining of their cruel mothers-in-law and selfish sisters-in-law. Many of the family smoked opium and our rooms reeked with its sickening sweet smell. Once when I was in severe pain, my sister brought me an opium tray and urged me to smoke. Though at other times I had refused, I yielded once. But the sudden way in which the pain stopped warned me there would be danger if I repeated this panacea, so I determined never to touch it again. Many opium smokers first contract the habit in order to relieve pain, only to find that they are later powerless to break away.

Third Brother was the worst profligate in the family. He loved to dress in flashy clothes and ride fine horses. If a groom offended him, instead of dismissing the man, he sent him to the magistrate for a public beating, until my father put a stop to that. Since he dared not invite his companions to our home, he would steal out at night. When Father set a man to watch before his door, Brother climbed through a side window and got away. In the morning, when the guard opened the door, he found the curtains of the bed closed and shoes beside the bed, but when he looked inside, it was empty.

Since Father now refused him more money, Brother devised tricks to secure it. One day he went to a goldsmith's shop where Mother traded, and told them she had sent him to buy six gold bracelets and charge them to her account. The owner knew his bad reputation and suspected that this was a trick, so he sent a clerk home with him to collect the money. Arriving at the door, Third Brother smoothly told the clerk to wait at the entrance till he got the money from Mother. The clerk waited all day, but Brother never showed up. Finally the clerk told the gateman to inform Mother why he was waiting. Mother got the message and sent for Brother. Needless to say he had taken the bracelets out a back door, pawned them, and had already spent the money. When Father heard this, he was beside himself with rage, and picking up a big knife, rushed to Brother's apartment, seized him by the queue and threatened to kill him. Mother heard the noise, rushed in screaming and seized Father by his queue. The servants heard the confusion, and came in and separated the three.

One of my sisters had married the son of an even wealthier official, whose residence was like a king's palace. This official was a libertine who had accumulated his wealth by taking bribes. He had twelve beautiful concubines to each of whom he gave an extravagantly furnished apartment, but no matter how late the hour, these concubines could not close their doors and retire until he had placed the signal of a lighted lantern over the apartment of the one with whom he had decided to stay. His son, my brother-in-law, was an even greater rascal than Third Brother.

At the beginning of the revolution in 1911, we were forced to flee from Nanking, and Third Brother went to Shanghai carrying a suitcase of gold and jewelry belonging to his wife. He asked his brother-in-law to lend him a carriage, so he could take the gold to a goldsmith's shop and exchange it for money. This request was readily granted, and Third Brother set out on his errand. When they approached an open space, the driver suddenly slowed down, and a masked robber sprang from behind a wall, flung open the door of the carriage, seized the suitcase, and made off. Third Brother called the driver to his assistance, and jumped out to give chase, calling "Help! Help!" But the driver, who was paid to help the robber, did not follow. Third Brother ran until he was exhausted, and a crowd of people ran after him to help in the chase, but the thief had disappeared. A policeman arrived and questioned my brother, while the crowd listened, but nobody had seen the thief or knew where he had gone. Two children at last came forward and said they had seen a man sitting on a suitcase in front of one of the doorways in their alley. So the thief was caught, and we knew from the behavior of the driver that it was the brother-in-law who had hatched the plot in order to lay his own hands on the gold.

These are just two out of many stories I could tell, but they show that in these great households where people are without Christ, the evil that goes on is unimaginable.

As for me, I was a timid, overprotected child, hiding behind my nurse when strangers appeared, and covering my face with her apron when anyone spoke to me. Everyone who grows up in such a household is constantly hearing stories of the evil all around, and getting involved in the innumerable plots and counterplots of this ingrown society. What I saw and heard frightened me, so when I was able to discern between good and evil and knew I was growing up, I shrank from the adult role and pondered a great deal on the vanity of life. All our family constantly sent for the Buddhist monks to chant and perform masses in the temple in our house. We had an aged Buddhist instructor, too, and he taught me to read the Buddhist classics, to say their prayers, to burn incense before their idols. I even took vegetarian vows to eat no meat, not even eggs, for twenty-five days out of each month. Buddhism, which is a religion of escape from the realities of life, only deepened my pessimism, and I applied for entrance into a Buddhist convent near us; but the Lord, who had planned my life, though I did not know it, took pity on me and prevented my taking this step.

There came a change in our family affairs. Troubles fell on us thick and fast, followed by repeated financial reverses. My father and mother had always been great lovers, and they used to talk over their family problems and come to an agreement before they acted. Of course, their greatest problem was how to provide for their huge family. My mother wanted to invest our money in some land along the Yangtse River front, just outside the city wall. "That land is cheap now and is certain to become valuable very soon as the river trade develops. Don't you see the British steamers are opening up trade here on the Yangtse? Nanking will soon become a great river port," she said.

"How can we be sure of that?" my father replied. "That water front is only a mud-walled fishing village now, with a single hulk anchored by the shore where the river steamers tie up. Surely the British will not be able to develop more trade than that. We dare not gamble on our future. There are some Europeans who have been coming to see me who have traveled all over China, and tell me there are immense beds of coal lying close to the surface of the ground in South Anhwei Province. All they need is some capital for development, and these mines will yield fabulous sums. We Chinese have destroyed all our forests by cutting down the trees for fuel. If we can sell people coal instead of wood, our family will be secure for life." Such was the line of argument, and my father prevailed. Circumstances proved later that he was wrong and she was right. He bought three coal-rich mountains and organized a mining company. The man he depended on to run the company was ignorant, and frittered the money away in unwise expenditures. We never mined any coal. There the mountains stand to this day, and I know not who has mined them. As for the river front, that land later proved very valuable.

Our main source of income was now lost, and other catastrophes followed. Just as Job was one day rich and content, and the next day poor and sick, so my father lost one investment after another. First came a telegram saying a big store in a distant city had been burned; then another message telling of the loss of another store. Next a private steamer which we owned was sunk in the river. Had my father known the Lord, he might have learned to say with Job, "The Lord gave, and the Lord hath taken away; blessed be the name of the Lord." The result was that though he still kept his official position, my father lost his health and became so sick that we thought he would die. In such an emergency, the Chinese custom is to make superstitious preparations for the funeral.

I remember watching the servants clean all the hanging glass lanterns, and open all the doors. Outside the front door appeared a large paper sedan chair for him, paper chair-bearers, a paper horse, and boxes of paper ghost money. Lighted incense sticks were placed in all the incense burners, and the sweet-smelling smoke made the air blue. In the garden, carpenters were making a huge coffin out of fragrant wood, and in the big reception hall were high piles of colored silk quilt covers, the children's gifts to him. My older sisters were busy sewing large pearls to the corners of his hat and embroidered gowns, to serve as lights to guide his way in the other world. We children were each given a bundle of incense sticks, told when to light them, and when to kneel down and cry in farewell. For at the instant he breathed his last, all the doors must be opened for the spirit to go out, the lanterns lit, the paper models burned, and we must light our incense sticks, kneel down and wail in farewell. These preparations were the sign that he was expected to die at any moment.

Suddenly, my mother appeared and called Fifth Brother and me, saying, "You two are to go to the big Buddhist Temple and make a vow to the idol of the City King, promising that every one of you will give your father a year from your own life if the god will prolong his life beyond the allotted span."

This temple, with all its fierce-looking idols was a terrifying place for a young girl. I remember how I shivered as we bowed to the ground before the great idol, while the tremendous bell boomed, the drums beat, and the chief monk in his yellow robes read aloud the names of the children who had vowed to give a year to our father. Coming home I decided that I must do something further to save my father's life. Chinese books are full of stories of children who have sacrificed themselves to help their parents, for filial devotion is a cardinal virtue with the Chinese. I had read in a book somewhere of a child who had saved his father's life in a heroic way, so I decided to follow his example. But to make it efficacious, I vowed that for a hundred days I would not tell anyone what I had done.

I had no idea of hygiene, so in my room I took a pair of rusty scissors, set my teeth into my forearm, pulled up the flesh and hacked off a good-sized piece. I then spread some ashes from the incense burner on the wound to stop the bleeding, tied my arm with a soiled handkerchief, and pulled my sleeve down to cover it up. Fortunately, I did not sever an artery and bleed to death. I then put the flesh in a pot and went out to the kitchen. The cook asked if he could help me, but I only shook my head. I put the flesh in water and cooked it; then took the soup to Father and begged him to drink it. As I raised his head, it fell back on my fresh wound, causing me excruciating pain. He drank the liquid and did recover, not because of the soup, but because the good Lord, whom I did not know, saw my love, heard the unspoken prayer, and healed him.

The wound got well slowly and I suffered a great deal, but I kept my arm covered so no one would know. The hundred days passed and my vow was accomplished. Later, Father and Mother found out what I had done and were deeply moved at my love for them.

The green sedan chair

Chapter 6

Out into the World

A MELANCHOLY UNREST filled my heart, and nowhere could I find peace. I had won my parents' affection, but it did not satisfy me. My father saw I was not happy, so he used to take me every Sunday to the theatre to see Chinese plays; but I did not like them. I often played mah-jongg all night long, and it was uncanny how I always won; but this had no fascination for me. I drank our Chinese wine which has given happy dreams to many, but it could not drive away my sadness. In our family orchestra, with my brothers and sisters, we played Chinese instruments in our garden pavilion every summer evening, but music seemed but "a clanging brass and tinkling cymbal" to me. I immersed myself in Buddhism and kept my vegetarian vows, but this only inclined me the more to pessimism. I found with the preacher in Ecclesiastes that everything was "vanity and vexation of spirit." All this outward display of wealth and pomp engendered in me something like a festering sore, for it increased my troubles rather than dispersed them.

The only solution that I could see was for me to go away from home; but I did not dare suggest this to my parents, so I poured out my heart to my nurse. "I want to attend one of those foreign missionary schools where they teach English and piano."

"But aren't you afraid they will make you 'eat Christianity'?" she asked.

"I don't want their Christianity, but I'd rather be an educated spirit than a stupid person," I reiterated again and again. She passed my confidence on to one of my brothers, and he in turn told my parents. They saw my unhappiness and arranged for me to attend a fashionable Christian girls' school in Shanghai. The registration fee was paid, the trunks were packed, and I was ready to go when my father called me to him. "I have been thinking about your leaving home and going alone to this strange city so far away. I am afraid you might get sick, so I've decided not to allow you to go." I dared not argue with him, but I was sick with disappointment. However, I did not give up hope, and the next semester I brought up the subject again. Three times I paid my registration fee, packed my trunks and prepared to go, only to be disappointed at the last moment. It was such an unheard-of thing for a young girl to leave her home and go away to school that even though they loved me, my parents could not bring themselves to the point of carrying it out.

I still did not give up hope. I suggested to Mother as a compromise, "Let me go to this mission girls' school here in Nanking. There I will be near home and you can know what happens to me." She agreed to this, and one wonderful day I dressed up in new clothes, got into my sedan chair, and went across the city to the Leamans' home, and the Ming Deh Girls' School at Four Flagstaffs. The chair-bearers let me down at the gate, and I walked into the mission compound. There were three plain foreign-style residences and a schoolhouse, set in a lawn shaded by trees and crossed by flower-bordered walks. It all looked so neat and clean. In the Leaman's house I was impressed by the carpeted floors and clean whitewashed walls, with the sunshine streaming in through the curtains at the windows. For the first time an indescribable peace stole into my heart. A tall, thin American lady, who turned out to be Mrs. Leaman's daughter Mary, came in. She wore a grey dress with black borders, and there was something in her quiet manner and kind voice that radiated peace. Here was the inner light, serenity, and strength that I had been seeking for.

"I want to register in your school so I can learn to speak English and play the piano," I said. She looked at my fashionable clothes and embroidered shoes and saw I was from a rich family.

She asked, "What is your name? Who are your parents? Where do you live?"

"My father's name is Tsai Sung Hua. We live at Millstone Street and I am called Tsai Ling Fang."

"Mr. Tsai, the Acting-Viceroy?" she asked in astonishment. I nodded. But she looked very serious and I grew fearful as she said, "We would be very glad to have you come and learn English and piano, but we cannot take you in as a boarder. Our school is very poor, and many of the students are orphans. Our food is very coarse, and our students do the housework. I fear you would not enjoy living here since you are used to better things."

"Oh, yes! I would," I insisted. "I don't mind coarse food and poor people. I want to learn English."

"But did your mother give you permission to come to our school?"

"Oh, yes, indeed she did," I answered.

"Well, we have a rule that the parents must come here themselves and give us their permission for you to study. Can you ask your mother to come?" she asked.

"I can try," I answered. So I went home and asked my mother. She was angry at first. Why should she, a Viceroy's wife, go across the city to see those poor missionaries? But I pleaded with her and she finally consented.

The next day she got into her green sedan chair, I followed in mine, and with an escort of horsemen, we appeared at the Ming Deh Girls' School gate. There was a great commotion at the entrance, and intense excitement among the girls as we entered the house. But my mother was very gracious and Miss Leaman was very polite, so I was finally registered as a day student; Miss Leaman still insisted that they could not take the responsibility of having me live there with the poor orphans. At home my mother bought a private ricksha and hired a ricksha man just to take me across the city to school.

My first English lesson was a story about "A Deer at the

Brook," and then I had an organ lesson. Some days later Miss Leaman said, "Don't you want to join our English Bible class?"

"No," I answered emphatically.

"But you can't be really educated if you don't know this Book," she explained. I didn't answer her, but in my heart I thought, "Not educated, if I don't read the Bible? What do you think about our Confucian classics? Are our Chinese scholars not educated?" However, I reluctantly agreed to join them, for though I wanted none of their Christianity, an extra English class was welcome. During the lesson period, while Miss Leaman read, "Verily, verily I say unto you," I fumed in my heart, saying to myself, "What is all this nonsense about 'Verily, verily I say unto you'? I don't understand what she is talking about."

At Christmas time I was invited to attend the service in the church, but I did not understand the meaning of Christmas. I gazed curiously at the colored paper flags strung across the church, at the bamboo trees against the walls, at the worshipers in their coarse blue cotton gowns covering their heavy padded garments. Occasionally I caught a word from the pastor, whose long sermon was incomprehensible to me. Bewildered, I turned to the students beside me. "What are they saying?" I asked one on my right. "What does that mean?" I asked the other on the left. But they were trained not to speak in church, so they only shook their heads. Then Miss Lucy Leaman came up behind me and whispered politely, "We are having worship now."

"Worship?" I thought. "I see no one to worship."

After the service, as I was stepping into my ricksha, Miss Lucy hurried down to the gate and thrust a paper parcel into my hands, and with no word of explanation she left me. I knew nothing of Christmas presents and wondered what she was giving me. I opened the parcel and found a Chinese Bible, which I disdained to read. This was my first Christmas!

The kindness of the missionaries impressed me profoundly.

Mrs. Charles Leaman, Founder of Ming Deh Girls' School

Every day on my way home I used to pass a ricksha coming the other way. A tall foreign lady with curly hair sat in it, and she always bowed to me and smiled. This gratuitous kindness puzzled me, too, for we Chinese are taught to speak politely to others but never think of smiling at strangers. I found out later that this was Miss Ellen Dresser, a missionary returning from her work in the southern part of the city. To this day that winning smile is one of my treasured memories, for it is the genuine evidence of God's indwelling love which never fails to convey its message of cheer.

My family saw that no harm had come to me from attending school, but because the long daily rides across the city were very tiring, they decided to send me to another school in the city of Soochow, where I could stay as a boarder. This school was especially for girls from wealthy homes, so better food and service were provided. The gates of home had opened, and I left the high walls of my childhood and passed out into the wide, wide world.

Ming Deh Girls' School, the first girls' school in Nanjing, was established in 1884 (the tenth year during the reign of Emperor Guangxu) and was a girls-only school. The founders were missionaries Mr. and Mrs. Charles Leaman of the Presbyterian denomination. When Miss Tsai enrolled in Ming Deh, Miss Mary Leaman was the President. She was the daughter of Mr. and Mrs. Charles Leaman.

In 1925, Ming Deh Girls' School adopted a new school system with separate departments of high, middle, and elementary schools and kindergarten. This photo witnesses the first group of children in the kindergarten. One of the the chairs they sat on was brought to Miss Tsai's dark chamber and seated many visitors.

Chapter 7

The Light of the World

WITH THE OVERTHROW of the Manchus and the establishment of the Republic of China in 1911, western education, modern inventions, and Christianity had come to China to stay. The antiforeign riots were a thing of the past. Men's queues were forcibly cut off, and foot-binding and opium smoking abolished by law. The Standard Oil Company of America had put kerosene lamps into people's homes. The ricksha copied from Japan was far speedier than the sedan chair. Nanking had some roads at least twenty feet wide now, and people went by horse and carriage on the longer trips to the river front. The British and American Tobacco Companies were sending their salesmen into villages and cities to sell cigarettes.

But more disturbing to the Chinese peasants than all these was a railroad opened from Shanghai to Nanking, a distance of about two hundred miles. The carriers, wheelbarrow coolies, donkey boys, boatmen, and farmers saw in this railroad a threat to their living, and determined to get rid of this devilish invention. Rumors spread that the god of the locomotive demanded human sacrifices. Eighth Brother was an executive for this railroad, and he suggested that we take the trip to Soochow by the new train. So Second Sister-in-law and I arrived at the Nanking Railroad Station, and slightly awestruck, we passed the crowds of curious and angry people who were staring at the "little houses that run on wheels." The train had no sooner started from the station than a shower of bricks and stones shattered the windows. Not far out of Nanking the train came to a halt, as some peasants were lying on their faces on the tracks, determined to stop the "fire wagon" with their lives. The conductors and railroad personnel got off the train and reasoned with them for a long time before they moved. In later years, the Shanghai-Nanking Railway was said to have had the greatest number of passengers per mile of any railway in the world. The railway was a success!

Soochow is a city of beautiful homes, pagodas, winding canals, and arched bridges. It is famous for its beautiful women and scholarly men, so in the proverb it is linked with Hangchow as the other part of "Heaven below." I attended a mission girls' school there which gave advanced studies in English and music. Here I studied hard at my lessons but closed my heart to Christianity and everything connected with it. When church time came, I made excuses for staying away—I had a headache or a backache and I threw out the medicine that they gave me. But these subterfuges did not work long, for the teachers saw through them. I was told that I must attend the services. This only increased my resistance, and I

Bridge at Soochow

made up my mind that I was not going to "eat" their Christianity, so I used to take a Chinese novel with me to chapel and read it as I knelt at the bench. I did not like the preaching. I thought it was very unpleasant and openly opposed it. Another girl, a Miss Wu, from a high-class family similar to my own, hated this teaching too, and we used to get together and give voice to our indignation. We even started to write a book denouncing all Christian teaching, insisting that Confucius and Buddha were our teachers and that we did not want Christ.

But again God used my love for English to draw me to Himself. A famous American preacher was to speak in English in our church; for a little while I let down the bars on my heart and listened intently. His subject was "Jesus, the Light of the World," and he used an illustration that stuck in my mind. He said, "If a piece of wood is kept in a dark place, all kinds of ugly insects will hide under it. But if we expose it to the light, the insects will run away, for they love darkness and hate the light. So it is with our hearts: if we do not have Jesus, the Light of the world, in our hearts, they will be dark too, and harbor all kinds of evil thoughts. The moment we receive Him and the light He brings, the evil thoughts will all be driven away."

From childhood I had especially feared all kinds of insects, so this illustration made a deep impression on me. One day while playing croquet in the yard, I saw a smooth white stone lying in the grass which reminded me of the illustration. I thrust my mallet under it and lifted it up. A big lizard, a centipede, and little bugs scurried away as the light shone in, and a voice inside me said, "You are just like this stone, smooth and white outside, and full of sin inside."

I now saw the hypocrisy of saying that I was following our Chinese traditions of love, righteousness, truth, and virtue, and I knew in my heart that I was a sinner, too. I dropped my mallet and hurried to my room, recalling that Miss Mary Leaman had often spoken of the importance of prayer. I took a quick look around to be sure nobody saw me, and knelt by my bed and prayed, "Lord, forgive my sin and help me to understand Thy Word." Then I got up quickly, my heart pounding and my face all red. At last I had found peace. The burden of sin and the pessimism of unbelief had gone from my soul! I had found Christ! From that time on, I opened my heart to the study of the Bible and found comfort in it.

I told Miss Wu of my experience, and how I had found peace when I found Christ. She was impressed, and after a while, accepted Him as her Saviour, and we had happy fellowship together. We did not tell our families, nor did we join the church at that time. Yet life was changed for us both: the old unrest was gone and all the world was a beautiful garden of the Lord to us. In my old home, Father used to have tiny fragrant jasmine flowers wired into pretty shapes for us girls to wear in our hair. I thought it was foolishness then, for I never saw any beauty in them. It had been the same way with music and poetry. Now there was a fountain of love in my heart and every bird, flower and blade of grass, every cloud and every star, sang a hymn of praise to God its Creator, and my heart sang with them.

Miss Wu was engaged to a young man whose sister was one of the students at our school. She wrote home that his fiancée was "eating Christianity." The Wu family soon heard this, and both families were furious. One day she was called from the classroom to find a relative waiting for her in the guest room. "Your parents sent me to take you home. Pack your things and be prepared to leave immediately. I have a houseboat waiting to take us up the canal," he said.

On the boat, he brought her a knife and a rope, saying, 'You have disgraced your family by eating this Christian religion. Didn't we warn you not to listen to it? Your family are very angry and do not want you as their daughter any more. If you do not promise to give up your Christianity now and return to our religion, you will have to choose between this rope to hang yourself, this knife to stab yourself, or the canal to drown yourself."

With a white face she answered, "I cannot give up Jesus. He died for my sins to open for me the way to Heaven. I belong to Him. You may take my life, but you cannot harm my soul." The relative was awed by her quiet determination, and did not force her to commit suicide. At home neither the angry accusations nor cruel punishment of the family could shake her, so finally they gave up the attempt. I saw her many times in later years and know she remained true to Christ, but the whole family have always opposed Christianity.

The Buddhists teach that the living children may help the deceased parent in the other world; my father had died, and my third sister wanted to send a gift to his spirit. She ordered a paper model made on a life-size scale, of our home at Nanking, completely furnished, even with servants, shoes, and chopsticks.

It is the superstitious belief that when this paper house is burned, it goes to the spirit world for the deceased to live in. To her it was an impressive display of filial affection; to the Buddhist monks it was a handsome source of income; to me as I see it now, it was a colossal exhibition of folly.

Each part was constructed in advance and assembled on the date named in a large, open place. She had already sent invitations to many friends and hired many Buddhist monks to say masses for the dead. Then she prevailed on me, as the only unmarried daughter in Soochow, who bore the name of Tsai, to be family representative and accompany the monks. I was just a young Christian at the time, and still wanted to honor my father; nevertheless, my conscience made me acutely unhappy all during the proceedings and for a long time after.

When the day came, I followed the chief monk, and a long line of monks followed me on a tour of this paper mansion. The chief monk first entered one chamber and while he chanted a long mass dedicating the room to my father's spirit, I knelt prostrate on the floor, the other monks around us, some beating drums, some clanging cymbals, some burning incense, and all chanting together. This procedure was repeated in each room and the whole ceremony took a day. At the end they made a great circle around the house, and chanted the masses again. I then handed a paper key to the head monk, who hung it on the door and set fire to the paper palace, while I remained prostrate on the ground till the last ember had turned to black ashes. After this, all the guests were invited to a feast.

You can imagine how my heart was torn by conflict: on the one hand trying to justify myself for doing my duty to Father and Sister, and on the other, unable to still the voice inside which said, "You're a Christian now, and should have no part with Buddhist monks. You have accepted Christ for your Lord—how can you still pray to Buddha?" The cloud of that spiritual defeat hung over me for a long time, until I learned that when "we confess our sins, Jesus is faithful and just to forgive us our sins, and to cleanse us from all unrighteousness." This experience also taught me never to compromise with heathenism.

Not long after this, I was baptized and joined the church, though I still lacked courage to tell my mother. But vacation time was drawing near when I had to go home, and I knew it would be better to tell them in advance. So, as the easier course, I wrote my sister-in-law and asked her to tell my mother what I had done. I soon had an angry letter from Mother telling me to come home immediately.

I remember entering the parlor of our home and seeing Mother chatting with my brothers; when she saw me she burst into tears. Sixth Brother's face flushed with anger. He said bitterly, "You have disgraced the whole family! We meant you to get an education, not to eat this foreign religion!" Then, seeing a Bible and hymn book in my hand, he snatched them away, tore them up and threw the pieces in my face. I was shocked at this savage behavior from a member of my own family, for we had always been polite to one another; but I said nothing and silently looked to God. Suddenly I saw a vision of Christ on the cross, a crown of thorns on His head and with nails in His hands, and I knew He had suffered for my sins; He had purchased my head with His crown, and my hands with His nails. Was there anything I couldn't bear for Him who had suffered so much for me? But to them I still said nothing.

Now they began talking together and sensibly decided that since there was nothing they could do to take this faith from my heart, they could only keep me at home as a kind of prisoner; but they found many ways of mocking me. When I bowed my head to say grace at the table, someone would remark, "If you have a headache you had better leave the table." At other times they commanded me to leave the table, saying, "If you do that, the devils will come out!" If one of my sisters found me praying beside my bed, she said, "She is sick. We must call the doctor." And when the time came to worship the ancestors, they dragged me along and threatened, "If you don't worship your ancestors, they will punish us." As I walked through the house, the servants stared at me and whispered together. Even the children were sternly charged to keep away from me. But I did not argue; I only prayed for wisdom, and God gave me grace.

One day, Eighth Brother, who was then more friendly than the others, approached me with a proposition. He had read Dickens' *A Tale of Two Cities* and liked the story. "Let's translate this book into Chinese together," he said. I was glad of the opportunity to talk to him as we worked over the translation. One day he said, "Tell me about Christianity and why you became a Christian." I told him about the stone with the insects underneath, and my conviction of sin; the prayer to God and the new peace and joy I had found. "That was a remarkable experience," he replied. "I have noticed that in spite of the way we treat you now, you seem much happier than you used to be. I think I would like to believe, too."

He even told Mother he was interested in Christianity, whereupon she burst into tears again and cried, "I can't bear it! I can't bear it! It is bad enough to have my daughter believing this religion. I will give her to anyone, send her to any kind of home to have her soon married and keep our name from disgrace! But you are my son! I depend on you to offer food and burn incense to me when I die. I forbid you to speak to her." After this she cried for seven days and seven nights.

One day she called me to her, saying, "Seventh Daughter, I want to betroth you. Here, let me show you the beautiful clothes and fine jewels I have set aside for your trousseau."

But as I gazed at the finery, I said, "Oh, Mother, Jesus is more to me than anything on earth! I cannot do this!"

She thought of another expedient and some days later spoke to me again, saying, "Seventh Daughter, I won't have you here in this house deluding your brothers with your Christian religion. You must return to Soochow and finish your schooling there." My family saw the futility of keeping me a prisoner at home, and to my great joy sent me back to Soochow.

Chapter 8

The Fruit of the Spirit

I WAS ONE of the first Chinese girls to graduate from a high school in China, an event so rare at that time that I was offered many positions. The principal of my school asked me to be vice-principal; another missionary asked me to be General Secretary of the Y.W.C.A.; and the mayor of Soochow asked me to tour the cities of the province and promote women's education. But I had an ambition dearer than these: to return home and lead my family to the Saviour, and have them enter into the same peace and joy that had driven away my dark pessimism. Various friends urged against this, saying I should work for all China and not stay in one place. But I felt clearly that I should go to Nanking, and refused the other offers. In Nanking I went to call on Miss Mary Leaman. "Would you like to have me help you in the evangelistic work?" I asked. She looked at me in astonishment, because such a thought had never occurred to her; but she was pleased and acccepted my offer, agreeing that I was to live at home and do my work from there.

My mother was the head of the family now. If she accepted Jesus, others would follow. I approached her but she would not listen to me, and coldly repelled all advances. Again and again I urged her, but she only said, "When I am dead and in my coffin, with the lid fastened down, then and then only will I believe in your Jesus."

Her love of music, however, was the entering wedge for Christ. One day when she heard me sing "He Leadeth Me," she remarked, "That's a pretty tune! Sing it over again to me." So I sang it again and then taught it to her, making no explanations.

Her love of stories was another. Since she could not read, she often would say, "Tell me a story." So I told her stories from the Bible without saying they were Christian, and she loved them.

Her opium-smoking habit proved the final wedge that opened the door to her heart. After Nanking had fallen to the revolutionaries and the Manchu Dynasty had been overthrown, the Republic of China was established; a new law was passed abolishing opium smoking and imposing punishment on opium users. Mother feared breaking the law and tried to stop the habit herself, but it was impossible. I told her of a Christian hospital for women in Nanking where doctors would help her, and finally persuaded her to go.

Breaking the opium habit was an agonizing experience, lasting for many weeks. When Miss Leaman brought her flowers and food that she could eat, she was grateful; and she appreciated the fact that we prayed for her every evening. One day she told me, "If your Jesus will take away this appetite, I will believe Him."

"Don't say 'If Jesus will take it away,' just believe that He will," I said.

That night she had a vision of Jesus standing before her and covering her with the light of His glory. That was the secret of victory for Mother; gradually she was relieved of the craving, and could take food freely.

She was a new woman the day she went home, bubbling over with joy. She showed her new allegiance in a forthright break with the past. She went to the family temple and addressed the idols, saying, "You have deceived me all these years, but I am not going to be deceived by you any longer." Then she picked up the idols one by one and threw them on the ground, stamping on them until they were in bits; but there was one idol she set aside-a gilded goddess of Mercy which originally had a pearl headdress and lungs and a gold heart. This idol had been worshiped by members of our family for over one hundred years. Later when Miss Leaman came to visit us, my mother gave the idol to her. "This is a keepsake for you. You have helped me to turn from idols and believe in Jesus. You shall have it to show that the Tsai family idols have all been destroyed."

When Eighth Brother heard of mother's conversion and deliverance from the opium habit, he and his wife came home from Shanghai where he was working, to make their confession of Christ. Then in the little chapel on Dye Factory Street, which Mr. Leaman had built, Mother, Eighth Brother and his wife, Second Brother and his wife, and two cousins were baptized together.

After this Mother and I became inseparable companions and fellow-workers. She started a family prayer group and invited her neighbors to attend. Such condescension was unheard of, and the neighbors came willingly, eager to see our house. I remember a Mrs. Lu who attended regularly. She and her husband, happily married for many years, kept a little variety shop. One day she came to us in tears. Her husband had brought a second wife into their home. To Mrs. Lu this was intolerable, and she wanted to kill herself.

Mother said, "Why don't you ask Jesus to help you?"

"How could Jesus help me?" she asked in astonishment.

"Ask Jesus to make the 'Little Wife' leave your husband. Come, we will pray about it together."

It was not long before Mrs. Lu came to the evening service again, her face beaming with joy and her heart bursting with good news. "What do you think has happened? The 'Little Wife' ran away yesterday, taking all my husband's money and clothes! He is furious and swore he would never see her again; but I know it was Jesus who answered our prayer."

After this Mr. Lu began to come to our church, became an earnest Christian and was later made a deacon.

Mother was about sixty at this time, and it grieved her that she could not read the Bible; so she called her little grandson Ever-Cheer to her and told him to bring his picture books and teach her to recognize Chinese characters. So the old lady and the child teacher studied together until she was able to read the New Testament.

Mother now enjoyed entertaining missionaries. Miss Leaman was the first one to be invited to our home, and I remember the day she arrived. She stepped out of her sedan chair, carrying an unusually large hen, which she presented to Mother. Mother was delighted with the hen for it laid a double-yolked egg every day! Another guest she enjoyed was Miss Ruth Paxson, who spoke her own Peking dialect and had fasted and prayed that she might be given power to break the opium habit. Among many other guests were Miss Alice Longdon, my loving piano teacher, who later married the Rev. Wesley Smith, and Miss Mary Culler White, my faithful friend, the humble but indefatigable evangelist who did a far-reaching work for the Chinese women in the area around Soochow. They were both a great help to me during my school days. Miss Mabel Lee often came with her guitar, and we sang hymns together. She called our home "The Church in the House." My brothers and the servants were especially glad when Mr. Drummond came, for he helped them with their spiritual problems. One of the early missionaries who came soon after Mr. Leaman, he stayed in Nanking through all the riots, wars, and political turnovers that had been our lot from the beginning of missionary work in Nanking.

My mother's gifts that in years gone by had been given to Buddhist temples, were now sent to those who served the Lord. One year the money that was to have been spent for her birthday was divided between the Mueller Orphan Homes in England, and the Jewish Mission work of Ruth Angel, in New York.

After mother's conversion, I was away from home much of the time, speaking and interpreting at various meetings and conferences.

The Holy Spirit was working in our home, not only among the family, but among the servants as well. One of the maids washing the clothes was suddenly convicted that her heart needed cleansing. She ran to Mother and knelt down, crying, "Lord Jesus, please wash my heart of all sin." A slave girl named Double-Joy had been indifferent to all appeals; but when an earthquake set the windows rattling, she fell on her face in terror, crying, "Jesus, save me!" My youngest sister's husband was a judge who had mocked us for believing; but one day, to Mother's complete surprise, he came and said to her, "I want to go to Tenghsien Theological Seminary and study to be a minister. Would Seventh Sister make arrangements for me to enter?" I did, and he went there to study.

One summer evening, I had just returned from a conference up north, and was sitting with the family eating a vegetable stew. They told me that one of our cousins had suddenly gone crazy. She had taken a bucket of water to our Ancestral Hall and started washing the tablets of our ancestors—to our non-Christian relatives' way of thinking, a terrible insult. For two weeks she had refused to eat anything they gave her, but went to the gutter and ate the worms she found there, so her brother had chained her in one of the rooms. Just at that moment there was a rattle of chains in the courtyard, and my family jumped up and ran out of the room. I gazed at my cousin's horrible, grimacing face, now thin and sallow, with long hair hanging about her shoulders. It was a hot summer night, but she wore a padded jacket and padded shoes.

"Seventh Sister's Jesus, save me!" she cried again and again. I had to think quickly, so I said, "If you ask Jesus, He will save you, but you must do what you are told. Sit down!" She sat down obediently enough, and I dished out a bowlful of stew and gave it to her. "Eat this," I said. She took it without a word and ate it. Then I gave her another bowlful, and she ate that, too. The rest of the family had returned by this time and were standing around looking at her. "In the name of Jesus, I command this evil spirit to leave you," I said. Immediately she slumped forward, her head drooping on the table. All the demon power which had enabled her to break the chain, was gone. We carried her to her room, and she was completely well from that day. Later, she went to Miss

Dresser's Bible school to study.

Sometime after this cousin had been cured, her brother was brought home from school, dying of typhoid fever. I, too, was down with a fever. As I lay on my bed reading the words of Jesus to the dying thief, "This day thou shalt be with me in Paradise," I seemed to hear a voice saying: "Why don't you go and speak to your cousin? This may be his last chance." I thought of many excuses for not going, but could not drive his image from my thoughts. Finally I got up and went over to his apartment. He was very ill indeed, but recognized me. "Cousin," I said, "don't you want to accept the Lord Jesus?" A smile lit up his face and he gasped, "That is just what I was thinking of. Won't you send for the minister and have me baptized?"

The minister came and baptized him, and was surprised that my cousin could answer all the questions. I now called Double-Joy, the slave girl, and told her to take care of the young master. While she was nursing him, he opened his eyes, exclaiming, "I see it! I see it! How beautiful it is! But the gate is shut, I can't go in! Oh, why is the gate shut? I want to go in!"

"Be patient," said Double-Joy, wisely. "Maybe the time has not come to open the gate."

"That's right," he replied; "I do have something more to do. Send for my family. I want to speak to them." So his brother and sister-in-law came in and stood beside him, while he fixed his eyes on them, saying, "I plead with you to accept Christ. Just a while ago, I saw the heavenly halls. They were so beautiful and I wanted to go in, but the gates were shut. Now I see them again and the gates are open at last." And with radiant face, he entered through those gates.

Such a testimony would have moved most people; but the Word tells us of times when seed falls on stony ground. To this day, so far as I know, the brother and sister-in-law are still hardened in their hearts to the call of Christ. But Double-Joy married a Christian man and they went to their village to live for Christ.

Chapter 9

Seed Sown in Good Ground

EVERY SUMMER we invited students from seven of the girls' schools to spend their vacation with us. Part of my work was teaching in a government normal school for girls, and I had about two hundred students in my classes. I used to talk to them in the intermissions about Christianity. Seventy-two of them accepted Jesus, and they came frequently to my home and to Bible classes in our church. One day two sisters, Spring-Hill and May-Hill, came to me sobbing, "Oh, Miss Seven, did you read the article in the newspaper reviling you?"

"No," I replied; "what did it say?"

"It said, 'The government normal school has employed a music teacher and gotten a Christian evangelist instead, who is teaching all the girls to cry, "God! God!" and making Christians of them. The parents are up in arms!'"

"Never mind," I said. "To be reviled for the Lord's sake is a great honor."

Three cousins named Long, from the normal school, came to our home frequently. They loved to sing "Heaven Is My Home." One afternoon three strange women appeared at our gate demanding to see me. They rushed into my sitting room without waiting to be announced. Each one took out a ball of opium about the size of a small nut and said, "We are the mothers of the three Long cousins. They are all we have in the world, and we sent them to school so they would be able to take care of us when we are old. You are teaching them to sing about 'Heaven! Heaven!' all day long. When we die, there will be nobody to send money and food to our spirits in the next world. Now unless you promise to keep them away from here, we will each swallow this opium and die in your house."

This was the worst threat a Chinese could make to his enemy. I tried to reason with them. "Suppose I kept a shoe shop. It would be right to try to sell shoes to anyone who came to my shop, wouldn't it? But if I went out on the street and dragged people in and made them buy my shoes, it would not be right, would it? Now you are the girls' mothers. It is your responsibility to forbid them to come here! But if they come of their own free will, it is my right and duty as a Christian to try to persuade them to become Christians, for that was Christ's commission to us."

"We have forbidden them to come, but they disobey us! Just now we had to lock them up in order to come here ourselves. No, you must forbid them coming here."

"I can't do that," I said.

"Well, if you don't, we'll just stay here with you."

"You are welcome to stay with me as long as you wish, if you don't mind our poor tea and tasteless rice," I replied. But they kept on arguing with me and would not leave till two in the morning.

The next day the three girls came to see me, and smilingly asked, "Do you know what our mothers said when they came home?"

"No, tell me."

"Well, they said, 'Fortunately for us, we three went together to see that Miss Tsai, and had one another for support and help. If one of us had gone alone, she would certainly have persuaded her to become a Christian.'"

Just at the time the article against me appeared in the newspaper, the normal school invited a Miss Plum, from Tientsin, to be their dean. She was small and pretty, energetic and discerning, but she was an atheist. While she was at home writing her letter of acceptance, her uncle came in to her study. He held a copy of the newspaper, and, pointing to the article about me, said, "Read this! You'd better not go to Nanking. I fear you too may be

The three cousins in the Tsai garden

inveigled into believing Christianity."

Miss Plum read the article; slamming her hand on the table, she exclaimed, "Don't worry, Uncle! The whole world may turn to Christianity" (and here she smote her breast) "but I will never believe."

As soon as she reached Nanking, she started to make it hard for those at the school who were Christians. Spring-Hill and her friend Joy-Bell, burst in on me one day with news. "A devil has come to our school! You know those leather-bound New Testaments you gave us students? Well, we heard Miss Plum was anti-Christian, so we hid them under our mattresses. She heard about them and searched our dormitories, seizing thirty-seven of them. Then she ordered a heap of straw piled in the yard and called us all to stand there before it. As the fire was lit she tore the Testaments and threw them into the leaping flames. Then she sternly told us, 'If any student is caught going to Miss Tsai's house again, she will be expelled.' Oh, Miss Seven! this woman will be either a devil indeed or a general for the Lord. We must pray for her, because we admire her ability, but we fear her power and want her to be saved." Those two students were very loving in trying to win her for the Lord.

When I went to the school, I met Miss Plum in the hall and stopped to speak to her. She hardened her face, turned her eyes away, and passed me by. The students in my domestic science class were giving an afternoon tea, and I asked the student assistant to invite Miss Plum and place me next to her at the table. When I sat down beside her, Miss Plum's face flushed with anger, for she saw through the plan. She turned away and would not speak to me. It looked as if we were up against a stone wall, but we put her name on our prayer list and prayed for her faithfully.

The missionaries at Four Flagstaffs were also interested in these normal school girls and invited them to a Christmas program at Ming Deh School. Miss Plum accompanied them as their chaperon, so this gave Miss Leaman a chance to meet her, and invite her to a dinner; but Miss Plum coldly refused all invitations. But prayers continued without ceasing. One day when the girls were having a prayer meeting at Miss Leaman's house and singing "For You I Am Praying," who should be announced but Miss Plum herself? She was very gracious and joined in the service, while they read the whole of Philippians together. Though she was still very reserved, some seed was undoubtedly sown that day and it began to take root in her heart.

Soon after this, there was a plague epidemic in Nanking and all schools were closed. It was Miss Plum's duty to accompany some of the students on a houseboat trip up the canal to their homes. As the boat was poled slowly out into the country, along green banks and fresh fields of wheat, the beauty of nature gripped her heart and a voice inside her said clearly, "Who made all this beauty? You are an atheist, but can you explain how all this came about? You know there could not be a wonderful world like this without a Creator!"

"A Creator," Miss Plum thought. "That is what the Christians say. Perhaps there is a God after all. I would like to read that book of Philippians, again. Just reading the Bible won't make me a Christian." So she began to read the Bible secretly, and her keen mind was no longer able to gainsay her hungry heart. One day she called on me in my home, saying in her direct way, "Do you have to keep the Lord's Day if you are a Christian?" I answered her in Jesus' words, "He that putteth his hand to the plough and looketh back is not fit for the kingdom of God." Her face fell and she turned abruptly away. Later she told me, "Your answer was like a bucket of cold water poured down my back, for it was my duty in the school to work on the Lord's Day."

I was called away to a conference at Peitaiho. One day while there, I had a letter from Joy-Bell which said, "Miss Plum has resigned from the normal school to become a Christian."

After this, the principal of Ming Deh School immediately invited her to be their dean, and Miss Plum, Joy-Bell and Spring-Hill worked with us for several happy years. Later they joined an indigenous group of Chinese Christians who have no paid workers, and who teach that it is the duty of every Christian to do his own missionary work. These three faithful women have been in charge of all their literary production and have served on the inner council. This group has had an extraordinary growth in the past years. It has spread over China and the islands of the Pacific.

We planned a crusade to reach all classes of people in the city. We visited Chinese government schools and invited the principals and teachers to attend a Bible class in one of our homes, and we invited the students to a class at our chapel on Dye Factory Street. We also enrolled in a half-day school one hundred and fifty girls who had never had a chance to go to school when they were young. How this school started is an interesting story of a small seed that grew into a great tree.

Miss Emma Strode, a friend in West Chester, Pennsylvania,

had sent us a gift of two big dolls that could shut their eyes and say "Mama," and the fame of these dolls spread like wildfire through our neighborhood. Children, girls, and people of all ages came to see them. One girl who had seen them the day before brought some friends and shyly asked, "Will you please show my friends the talking dolls? They want to see if they are real babies." When I brought them out, they stretched eager hands to hold the dolls.

"What beautiful clothes! But they aren't like our Chinese clothes."

"Look at the eyes! They open and shut."

"Look at the hair! It's real."

"Listen to the baby cry! Is it a real American baby?"

Soon another group appeared, and then another, till there seemed no end to the crowds asking to see the wonder dolls. While we were amused at the great stir caused by the dolls, we pondered how to turn their interest to more constructive ends. Suddenly the idea came: "Let's open a half-day school for these older girls who have never been to school. They can work at home in the mornings and study here in the afternoons."

This school met a great need; our chapel was soon filled with rows of smiling girls holding bundles of books tied up in colored handkerchiefs. We called it the "Gen Seng [Born Again] Half-Day School." The girls earnestly applied themselves to reading the Bible and reciting it page after page.

We invited the adults to church by advertising "Fishing Meetings." The girls were eager to bring their parents and relatives to these special services. Later the names of many of these parents and relatives appeared on the list of our church members. In a few years other churches followed, and many half-day schools were organized in Nanking and elsewhere. Some girls who had learned to read went on to higher schools, and some of them became evangelists. So the two "Mama Dolls" did a good missionary work, and who can tell how far their influence has gone?

I loved to do hospital visitation, and I found it was a good thing to take flowers, fruit, puffed rice, a comb, and postcards and pencils along; for I saw that many of the patients closed their eyes and turned their faces away when we approached, to show that they did not want us to talk to them about Christianity. If I saw a feverish patient, I'd say, "Would you like me to comb back your hair for you?" and the eyes would open in surprise and appreciation. The gifts removed the barriers. Sometimes I'd spot a country woman and ask if she wanted to send a letter to her family. Invariably she would be delighted. I sat by her side and wrote while she dictated, and then I read it over for her approval. The following week, perhaps, I often had the opportunity to read the answer she had received. In these ways, people were won for Christ.

Mrs. William Stewart, sister of Dr. W. W. White, founder of Biblical Seminary, New York, opened her home for a Bible class for wives of important government officials. Among the women who came was the wife of the governor. She was a northerner dressed in outlandish clothes, with an elaborate, but ugly, hair dress; among the other women she looked like an ugly duckling. She invited me to visit her home, and when I arrived, she called her servant to me and said, "Tell my amah how to dress my hair properly." When this was accomplished, she said, "Will you please lend me some of your clothes for my tailor to copy? I like the clothes you wear." When I agreed to this, her next request was, "I can't read, and have no education, but will you teach me to knit? And, oh, I want to learn to play the piano, too!" She was so eager to look and act right that I helped her all I could, and she was very proud of her accomplishments. I was pleased with my "ugly duckling" who had turned into "a swan." One day she invited twelve missionaries to a feast in her home. When the feast was over, she announced, "Now I am going to play the piano for you." She sat down and played "Jesus Loves Me" through three times, and turned around to face her guests, saying, "Jesus loves me, now I am going to love Jesus."

Miss Tsai taught at Jiangsu Girls' Normal School and led seventy-two students to Christ among more than two thousand students. During spare time, she often visited the sick in hospitals and held Half-Day Women Schools to teach women Chinese characters.

One Sunday afternoon before our women's service, an old lady of eighty years, Mrs. Summer, beckoned to me to sit down beside her. "I want to tell you something," she said. "You know my family have all gone to the West and left me alone to care for the house. I have very little to live on, but God has taken care of me. One day last year, I saw a nice green plant growing in one of my empty courtyards. I looked at it. It was like joo-hug-lao, my favorite vegetable, but I was not sure until I asked a neighbor, who recognized it. 'Where did it come from?' I asked myself. 'I didn't plant it and there never has been any here before. A bird must have dropped the seed here, so it grew in between the stones. I think God sent the bird to help me.' So I watered it and took away the stones, and cultivated the ground. It grew fast and spread. After a while I plucked off a small basketful of leaves and took them to a neighbor to see.

"'Where did you get those nice joo-hag-lao leaves?' she asked.

"'God planted the seed in my garden and I watered it,' I said

"'I'll give you twenty cents for them,' was her answer.

"I was very happy to get the money and went back to cultivate my plants again. They grew and spread till they filled the courtyard I had to work hard watering and hoeing every evening all summer. I have been able to sell all I grow, and how much money do you think I made this year?"

"I couldn't guess," I answered.

"Twenty dollars! Think of that! Now the Lord has given to me, I am going to give a tenth back to Him." She pulled out two dollars, as her contribution for the church work.

"So the seed fell on good ground, and did yield fruit that sprang up and increased; and brought forth, some thirty, and some sixty, and some a hundred."

Moon gates in Tsai home

Chapter 10

My Watchtower

IN MY HOME at Millstone Street, I had my own apartment with a bedroom and study opening to a high-walled garden. A winding incline led up to a glassed-in tower in a corner of the courtyard; there I could sit and look down on the treetops of my garden, and on the flowers and trees in the bigger garden on the other side. I also looked down on the grey-tiled roofs of the houses beyond, stretching as far as the city wall. Even in winter, there were blossoms; a yellow flowered plum tree bloomed even when there was snow, and filled the air with rich fragrance. We call it the Twelfth Month Plum, and we had many of these trees in our garden. During the warm weather, birds love our gardens. Our Chinese robin, black-coated and yellow-billed, was my steady songster. Sometimes in the beginning of summer, I'd awaken to a liquid musical call and look out to see a flash of bright yellow. Then I knew that the oriole had come to spend his vacation with me. At nights during the harvest season, I'd hear the Indian cuckoo flying overhead and warning the farmers, "The wheat is ripe, plant the rice." This tower, with its green panorama, became my prayer room, and here I spent many happy hours.

One morning while I was writing in my study, the maid brought me some letters. Among them was one from America. The envelope, the handwriting, and the postmark had become increasingly precious, for this correspondence started five years before while I was still in school at Soochow. I remember the day when I had been called into the office of Miss Martha Pyle, our principal. This American woman was my ideal teacher, and I was always thrilled to have her send for me. On this occasion my pastor was sitting there, too. Both smiled and motioned to me to sit down. The pastor laid a letter in my hand and asked me to read it. It was a proposal of marriage from a young professor in the men's university. I had seen him and knew who he was. Each time after appearing in public at a music recital I would receive many such letters, but had never answered one of them. I blushed as I read this letter and handed it back without a word. I did not know what to say.

"Miss Tsai," my pastor said, "your principal and I have consulted together and we feel this is an exceptional young man. He is an outstanding teacher and a Christian gentleman. We urge you to consider this proposal seriously."

"Yes, indeed, Christiana," my principal added. "I know the young man is the only Christian in his family, and he is considered the finest young man they have on the faculty. His principal has also sent me a letter asking me to be middleman for him. I don't know when such a request has given me greater pleasure, for I have such high regard for both of you, and feel this would be an ideal marriage. Please do consider it."

I had every reason to respect the young man, but since I was embarrassed I did not answer them, nor did I answer his letter. However, the young man was persistent in writing, and others got to know about it. Some of the teachers tried to persuade me, but I still paid no attention. When I returned to Nanking, he continued to send me so many letters that Brother, who handled most of the mail, soon came to recognize the handwriting and was curious.

"Who is this friend who sends you so many letters?" he asked one day while we were at dinner. Though I tried to appear unconcerned, I blushed. "Oh, ho! She blushes! I must look into this. It is a man's handwriting."

Mother now broke in. "You never told me about this person. Have you been answering his letters? Who is the man?"

I was in a corner and had to tell them of the young professor's proposal. "That sounds like a good young man. Twenty-one years old, did you say? I don't see how you could make a happier marriage. Why don't you answer him?" she asked.

"She's too embarrassed to write," Brother said, "so I will write for her." And so began a correspondence that changed my respect into admiration, and my admiration into love, and the university professor into my hero. We agreed that he should go to America to get his doctor's degree before we were married. So he went to America while I remained at home. In his last year at the American university, the spirit of his letters began to change. He had been an out-and-out Christian, but now the books he read made him skeptical. He wrote: "All these stories in the Bible about the virgin birth of Jesus, and the miracles He was supposed to have performed, could not possibly be true. They are no better than the Greek myths." Another time he scoffed at the Bible Institute students, saying, "They think they have only to take a tract in hand, and sit in a rocking chair, and, presto, they are saved." I was studying a Bible correspondence course at this time, and these remarks gave me deep pain. I wrote again and again, trying to show him that every page in the Bible is inspired by the Holy Spirit, and that "The secret things belong unto the Lord our God: but those things which are revealed belong unto us and to our children forever, that we may do all the words of this law" (Deut. 29:29). But my letters did not avail to change his mind, and I was unable to change my faith. Mother, who was pleased about the marriage, was now enthusiastically getting my trousseau ready. I could not tell her my grief which I kept locked in my heart.

Evening after evening, I paced up and down my garden, or knelt in the watchtower, praying for him and talking to my Lord. "He is a Christian. He has confessed that he is a child of God, and yet he does not believe in the deity of my Lord. How can we ever be happy if we cannot have fellowship in our faith? What shall I do? What shall I do?"

Then one day I looked at this letter with mixed feelings of

longing, hope and pain. Could it be that he had changed his mind about God's Word at last? But as I opened the letter and read it, my heart turned to stone. He told me of his graduation, of his doctor's degree, and how eager he was to come back to China and to me. But there was no mention of any change of mind concerning the things that mattered to me.

I took the letter in my hand and went up to the watchtower, but my feet were as heavy as lead. I spread the letter before the Lord, and a great battle began then and there. Should I follow my hero and deny my Lord, or should I follow my Lord and deny my hero? But I could not give up one or the other, and I went down with the battle still undecided. Day after day, night after night, the struggle went on.

Should I follow my hero and deny my Lord, or
Should I follow my Lord and deny my hero?
My Lord or my hero?
My hero or my Lord?

Then something happened. One day in the tower my eyes fell on a picture of Christ in Gethsemane, and I was transported in spirit. I understood His agony and He understood mine, so then and there I yielded myself and He satisfied me completely. Going down I was able to sing, but when I was seated at the typewriter, my fingers refused to move. How could I write that letter and break off the five years of happy fellowship, the many happy dreams we had shared together? But it had to be done, and I was given the strength to do it. I have never regretted the step. Since that day my Saviour's love has never failed me, and our fellowship has grown sweeter as the years have gone by.

My watchtower

Chapter 11

Out into the Highway

SOME APPARENTLY trivial incident often serves as the pivot upon which a man's destiny may turn; what seems mere chance may determine another's fatal choice; and a word spoken in jest may rouse the urge in someone which will work itself out in a lifetime career. But the Christian who looks back on his beginnings, finds that there was nothing accidental. There were no unfortunate incidents that marred his destiny; God, according to the good counsel of His will, had planned all his life, circumstance by circumstance, to prepare him for the work He intended him to do.

The incident which aroused my urge to learn English was trivial and amusing. While I was still a little girl, my older brothers were learning English. As boys will, they showed off their ability, and I, as a little sister, naturally wanted to learn. But try as I might, I could not pronounce the first words they tried to teach me, "breakfast, dinner and supper"; so they laughed at me. "Run away, little sister, you're hopeless! Your tongue is too blunt. You need a pointed tongue to speak English."

This stirred in me a wild ambition to excel them in English. This same urge led me to Ming Deh Girls' School and my first contact with Christianity, and later to listen to a preacher's sermon on the memorable day which led to my conversion. Now this love of English was to lead me all over China in the years 1914 to 1920.

An American millionaire, Milton Stewart, who was also a humble Christian, in one day distributed three million dollars for evangelistic work, and much of that money was used in China. Prominent Christian leaders from America were invited to hold hearings in many centers in China. In these evangelistic meetings I had the rare privilege of interpreting for Miss Ruth Paxson, Dr. Griffith Thomas, Dr. Charles Trumbull, and others. Since they spoke mostly to the Christians, I often had special services for the non-Christians as well. We spoke to Chinese Christian leaders at the seaside conference in Peitaiho in the north, and at Kuhng in the mountains of Central China. We also spoke to teachers and students of Chinese government schools, and the Christian missionary colleges and high schools in many of the large cities; to nurses in hospitals; and most of all, to the crowds in churches of various denominations. When there was no building large enough to hold the people, tents were erected. Milton Stewart did an inestimable amount of good for the world on that day when he gave a fortune for evangelistic work. The money gave preeminence to the gospel message, it helped link up scattered missionary effort, it trained the Christian Chinese leaders, it put good Christian literature in the hands of hundreds of thousands of people, and it scattered the Word far and wide.

China was enjoying a period of comparative peace while the rest of the world was at war. We could travel freely from one place to another, for many of the large centers were linked by modern transportation. We went from Nanking to Peking, and from Peking to Hankow in the west, by railway. We traveled by river steamers, entering the Yangtse from the world port of Shanghai. We sailed up its broad yellow waters, past low, marshy banks, overtaking many picturesque sailboats along the way, till we caught the first glimpse of blue hills. These lines of hills extending to the horizon, steadily increased in height as we sailed west. We stopped at the treaty ports of Chinkiang, Nanking, Wuhu, Anking, Kiukiang and Hankow. At Hankow we changed to the powerful steamers that took us through the rapids of the spectacular Yangtse Gorges, into West China. Another time we took a coast steamer from Tientsin, in the north, and stopped at the beautiful Chefoo and Tsingtao ports, before coming back

Islands off the South China coast

to Shanghai. At other times we went by coast steamers winding among the countless rocky islands that dot the South China coast, sometimes passing the yellow waters of a river-mouth, where sails of a fleet of fishing boats punctuated the water like exclamation points. Farther south the mountains became more rugged, the water a pure green, the style of junks changed, and we entered the lovely ports of Foochow, Amoy, Swatow, and Hong Kong.

In this way I had the opportunity of visiting eleven out of the eighteen provinces of China, and seeing the centers of Christian missions, and the wide scope of Christian activity. This was a transition era: the day of the pioneer missionary was passing and the Chinese church was growing up and beginning to call its own pastors and leaders. The children of the first generation Christian families were educated and ready for leadership, and the schools were pouring out an increasing stream of students. Who can estimate the results of missionary service in China? It made Christ known; it built churches, schools, orphanages and hospitals far and wide; it opened the door for women to enter the schools and have the same opportunities as men; it helped rouse the people to the evils of foot-binding for women and opium smoking; it healed the sick and brought comfort to the blind, the deaf, the dumb, and the lepers; it brought knowledge of sanitation, fed famine victims, and cared for the war sufferers; it helped prepare Chinese of the following generation to take over the missionaries' work, to carry on their own evangelistic campaigns, and build their own churches; it showed the infinite value of a human soul in God's eyes, and wherever the light of the gospel shone, it enlightened that society so that it soon outstripped other places in its progress toward modern culture.

As for me, my eyes and ears were opened not only to the need of mass education, but also to the problem of the many dialects in China. In the far north I heard the clear inflection of the Peking speech which has been chosen as China's national language. When I came to Shantung, I heard the nasal twang. The Nankinese had added high staccato tone, but lowered and flattened others. As we went down the Yangtse River to Shanghai, the sounds became more abbreviated and staccato, and the speech more rapid. As we visited Foochow, Amoy, Swatow and Hong Kong, there were many changes in both consonants and vowels, and the tones multiplied, so that in Canton we heard eleven tones to the Peking four. Not only so, even we Chinese were not able to understand one another, and in some places had to have an American missionary interpret for us. In the province of Fukien alone, there are so many dialects that the people on one side of a mountain are unable to understand those on the other side. But I was greatly impressed with the large percentage of Bible-reading Christians in districts where the missionaries had used Romanized (English letters used to spell Chinese sounds) translations of the Bible and taught the people to read. In Amoy, every old lady, it seemed, brought her Bible to church and was able to find the references herself; whereas in most interior places, only a sprinkling of the educated could read at all. The Romanized, while good, only gave the uneducated a chance to read their own dialect. China needed the wide use of the government's National Phonetic System by which all could eventually learn to speak a standard dialect, and the illiterates might learn to read and write for themselves.

In some of the student centers, I lived in the dormitories with the students and had opportunities of doing personal work with them. After speaking, sometimes three times a day, I would give the students a chance for personal interviews. Lines of girls waited patiently outside my door for a chance to speak to me alone. Often I was busy until one and two o'clock at night; and then, too tired to take off my clothes and go to bed, I would just stretch out on the hard floor to rest. In this way I learned the importance of personal work and the hunger of the young people for the Word of God.

In each city we went to, plans for our meetings and the places where we were to stay were arranged by an interdenominational committee. We were often appointed to stay at the homes of missionaries or Chinese Christians whom we had never met or even heard of before. A full program was always laid out for us, and we had to hurry from the boat or train to meetings. At Hankow I had to rush from the boat to the home of my hostess, and then go at once to a meeting in the church. In the hurry, the name and address of my hostess were mislaid. However, I remembered to give a tract to the ricksha man who took me to the church. When the meeting was over, I did not know how to go back. As I stood there in my dilemma, the same ricksha man came running. Showing the tract, he asked, "Do you want me to take you back again tonight?" The importance of tract distribution took on a new value to me that night!

In Hong Kong, I was impressed by the wealth of the Chinese, the expensive feasts they gave, and the fine homes and clothes they had. One day some girls invited me to their home on the peak of the island where only the very rich live. They showed me the view from their windows, and I looked down the steep mountain to the beautiful green waters of Hong Kong Bay, dotted with tiny junks and great steamers from all over the world, and across to the other side, to Kowloon City on the mainland.

The girls, wishing to give me a good time, kept passing around chocolates, saying "Miss Tsai, have a sweet."

Suddenly a thought came to me and I spoke up, "Girls, why don't you do something for the Lord with your money?"

One of them answered, "Oh, Miss Tsai, we'd like to, but we don't know how."

Another said, "I tell you. You be our missionary and we will support you."

But I answered, "Why don't you start a home missionary society and help evangelize China with Chinese missionaries?"

It was this unpremeditated conversation that acted like a lighted match dropped into a pile of straw. Some of these girls went to Kuling in 1918, where they helped organize the first Chinese

In 1918, Miss Tsai along with others established the Chinese Home Missionary Society that sent six evangelists to Yunnan and later expanded their horizon to Northeast China.

Home Missionary Society. Funds were raised, and a year later six Chinese missionaries were sent out to the far southwestern province of Yunnan.

So a jest stirred an ambition in me that bore fruit in leading me away from the high walls of my home to enter the wide fields of the Master's service. A resolve on the part of Mr. Milton released millions of dollars for world-wide evangelistic work. An unpremeditated conversation with some girls was a spark that started a fire of missionary zeal. Yet these were not chance happenings, but God moving "in a mysterious way His wonders to perform."

Chapter 12

Out into the Byways

THE MISSIONARIES entered the big city gates to build big churches and schools and hospitals and to form large communities like ours in Nanking. But they did more. A great pioneer work was done by Chinese and foreign missionaries going together in the countryside beyond, where modern ways had not penetrated and where life had gone unchanged for thousands of years.

I can see them riding the hardy Mongolian ponies over the desert wastes of China's great northwest, stopping at a caravansary to distribute tracts to the polyglot travelers from the remote corners of Central Asia. I see them seated in a springless cart, bumping along the dusty roads of the North, trying to reach a distant city by sunset. I can see them, legs doubled up, sitting astride patient donkeys that plod the steep hillsides to a hamlet four mountains and four valleys away. I see them propped up in a creaking wheelbarrow which is propelled along the rutty narrow path winding between flooded rice paddies; or getting off to relieve the wheelbarrow man and stretch their muscles, and talking to the blue coated farmers on their way to market

I can see them seated in a houseboat that is towed slowly along the banks of a canal, under high arched bridges where the village wives squat in a row, beating their clothes clean on the smooth stones. I can see them seated in a straw-roofed mud hut talking to the farmers' families while the dogs, cats, and chickens pick up scraps around their feet. I can see them in heavy padded Chinese clothes, resting for the night in some dirty inn while the curious natives stand around. I see them seated by a wayside teahouse at noon, munching a hot biscuit and surrounded by a crowd of curious children or followed by a hooting mob who yell "foreign devil" and cast stones. I can see them in a little Jesus Chapel, in a narrow street of an isolated town, teaching the unlettered country folk. And I see the plain, semi-Chinese house, at the rear of the chapel, where a missionary family lives, or where two single ladies may live together. Missionaries of the cross, sojourning by faith in a foreign land.

I remember particularly a trip Miss Mabel Lee and I took into the country. We had to take everything we needed, and our equipment was assembled and packed the night before: clothes, shoes, overshoes, toilet articles, a washbasin, and bedding were wrapped up in quilts and roped inside a piece of yellow oilcloth. A kerosene

Traveling by wheelbarrow in the country

stove, kitchen utensils, a dishpan, pails, tins of sugar, milk, bread, and tea were packed in a big basket with a net that kept things in place. We took small wooden boxes for tables and stools, two camp cots, a large roll of hymn sheets, packages of tracts, pictures, Bibles, and a guitar. We piled into the rickshas with all our baggage and were taken outside the city wall, where the houseboats were tied up along the banks of the canal. Bargaining was an important part of all business transactions, and it took knowledge of their ways and patience to find a fairly clean boat, and clinch the bargain for the day's trip.

The boatman and his family lived in the back of the boat, we took the front. The woman rowed at the back, and the man poled from the side, and soon they took us past the cluttered market stalls, under the bridges, and out into the country fields. It was spring and the winter wheat was beginning to beard. In some places the farmers were busy plowing with water buffaloes, and in others they were mending the mud-walled dikes that surrounded their little irregular fields, or fertilizing the soil with muck out of the ponds and canals.

In our part of China, as soon as the winter wheat was harvested, the fields were irrigated and planted for the summer rice crop. Along the narrow path that bordered the canal, the country people were bringing their products to the city. Donkeys laden with long sacks of grain jingled by, men carrying baskets of cabbage swung past, and wheelbarrows piled high with bundles of reeds for fuel creaked along. We passed white-washed brick houses with high walls, thatched mud huts, and red-walled wayside shrines. It was a long trip, but the air was bracing. We passed fields fragrant with yellow mustard, or sweet with the perfume of the bean flowers. Magpies and crows were building nests in the high trees, and the skylarks sung in the blue above our heads.

In the evening as we neared our destination, we passed great flocks of ducks swimming in our direction; the town we were going to is famous for them. It was already dark when we stepped off the gangplank at Chestnut Water, found carriers to take our baggage, and, heralded by a crowd of children, knocked at the door of the little street chapel. Elder East-Ear and his wife greeted us with delight. And while our things were set down in an empty room, Elder East-Ear lighted the little kerosene lamp, and we sat down together to exchange news while his wife took grass to fire the brick range and prepared us some noodle soup for supper.

Elder East-Ear, a tall man in rough country clothes, had a wrinkled face, scraggly whiskers and a nearly toothless smile; he was a hard worker, who loved the Lord and all His people. After we had eaten and had prayers, we went to bed.

The next morning we set up our own housekeeping with the things we had brought along, for there was no other furniture available. Neighbors began to drop in. The country women thought our box-stools and box-tables were wonderful, and one of them felt up Miss Lee's arm to see what she wore, and lifted up her dress to examine her underwear, exclaiming at everything and asking all kinds of questions. This was endured in a friendly way, for so it was meant. The Stones, a Christian family, who had a shop down the street, sent their eldest daughter with a gift of eggs. She brought two country girls with rosy cheeks and bangs hanging over their eyes with her, saying, "Here are two pupils for you."

I sat down on the bench near an old lady, and she launched into a long complicated story about her troubles, while I listened patiently. When she was finished, I said, "I've listened to you, now you listen to me." And I told her about Jesus. Only in this way could I win her attention. Elder and Mrs. East-Ear came in, saying, "We must go out and invite the people for the meeting this evening." Mr. East-Ear saddled his donkey and prepared to go to the farther places, while Mrs. East-Ear in a black headkerchief, accompanied us to the nearer homes. As we stopped at one home on the street nearby, we heard the click of the mah-jongg ivories, and suddenly the door was closed in our faces. "Why don't they want us to come in?" asked Miss Lee. Mrs. East-Ear smiled at me as I answered, "If we go in with our books while they are gambling, they think we will bring bad luck and cause them to lose." (The words "lose" and "books" are both pronounced "shoo" in our part of China.) At another place we could tell from the way they said, "We'll come, we'll come," that they didn't intend to do so at all. But at the third place the welcome was very sincere. The men of the family came in from the fields wiping their faces, and sat down to talk, while the children eyed us from a distance and the women served us poached eggs. They told us all that had happened during the past year.

We found other old friends. Mrs. Dai, a neat, intelligent woman, joined our party, and on the way told us a story: "Giving out tracts is certainly very good," she began. "Do you remember last year when we went to see Mrs. Wang who lives at Copper Well? You gave her some tracts and taught her 'I Pray Thee, Lord Jesus.' Well, this year I went over there again and called in her home, and there the tracts were pasted up on her walls; and she could read them, too. 'How did you learn to read?' I asked her. 'My son taught me. When he came from school, I'd ask him to read them to me. That is how I learned,' she said."

We arrived at a neat, white-washed thatched hut, and a middle-aged woman caught sight of us, dropped her broom, and rushed toward us. "O Miss Tsai, Miss Lee." She grasped our hands in both of hers and exclaimed. "God has certainly sent you. My water buffalo is sick. I think it will die. Won't you come in and pray for it?" We did not laugh at this request, for the water buffalo was almost sacred to this Chinese peasant. They called him their ancestor and he slept in the house with them at night. It represented a fortune to this poor woman, for without it her fields could not be plowed. So we went in and prayed for the water buffalo, and it recovered.

We were back in the chapel by evening, and the crowd began to gather. We sat beside the early comers and tried to teach them to read a little tract. I sat down beside a young mother with a suckling child in her arms, and a toddler who was tugging at her coat. Half of her attention was on her children and half on what I said, but she repeated the words as I pointed them out to her and nodded her head as I explained the meaning. Finally, the toddler nagged her so that she got up, and I went with her, continuing to teach her as I followed them around the chapel, "faint yet still pursuing"!

Miss Lee, who was very straightforward, caught sight of the women who had slammed the door in our faces, and said to them, "Unless you accept the Lord Jesus and ask Him to forgive your sins, He will shut the door of Heaven in your faces." She then brought out her guitar, hung up the large hymn sheets and we began to sing. Sing? No, not immediately. Each line had to be explained first and sung for them over and over again, while a few old hands joined in and helped us, each in her own tune and time. Though the harmony suffered, the good spirit made up for the musical defects and we knew it pleased the Lord.

I got up to give the message. I tried to use the words and experiences with which they were familiar, for they couldn't take in anything else. If I used a word outside their vocabulary, it was either lost entirely, or they gave it their own interpretation. For instance, once I used the Bible word for "porches," instead of their own word, and found, on questioning a woman, that she thought I said "wolves"! But the seed was sown and each year brought forth its own fruit, "first the seed, then the ear, then the full corn in the ear, for the Lord gives the increase."

From 1914 to 1930, China went through the suppression of Beiyang Army and the period of Northern Expedition. Miss Tsai managed to go to 11 provinces in China to evangelize and translate for famous American preachers. These photos show the then Chinese church architectures and the boat where she dined and slept while traveling on a canal.

Chapter 13

Through the Golden Gate

BETWEEN the eastern shores of my beloved land and the western coast of the beautiful continent of America, stretches the wide expanse of the Pacific Ocean. How I wish that the "Pacific" waters that break on the shores of each of these two great continents could preserve the peace that God meant to exist between us! Our two peoples have much in common, but only those who have crossed the ocean, or have known the people of both sides, can understand this and see that peace between America and China is one way to keep a bond of peace throughout the world. Our four hundred and fifty million people have been in political turmoil, as we have come out of our ages of seclusion and tried to adapt ourselves to the whirling modern world. Never, never could I have envisioned the conflict that is now going on between us! It would be useless to try to go over the political blunders that have brought this about. We can only say in the words of our Chinese people, "It is the will of Heaven"; for God has permitted it to come to pass that we may confess our evil ways, turn from them, and follow after His peace for all men everywhere, which is the peace of the cross.

Once a Chinese student in Shanghai asked me about America. "Why do you want to go to America?" I asked. "There isn't a student in Shanghai who doesn't want to go to America," he replied. This may be an exaggeration, but it certainly represents the spirit of my countrymen during the past fifty years, and it is partly a tribute to the missionaries who have come over, and partly a desire to see for themselves your fabulous material progress, or to have Ph. D. written after their names. I gladly welcomed the opportunity to accompany Miss Leaman on her furlough in 1921. While in Honolulu, we received a cable from some who were interested in missionary work, asking me to make a speaking tour of certain churches.

Our vessel passed the Golden Gate in the evening and the lights of San Francisco were my first glimpse of America. I noticed there was no confusion of shouting coolies on the dock as we tied up, and I was impressed by the orderly system of handling the baggage for custom's examination. In crowded China, there are generally a dozen people struggling for the same place; but here was room for all, and a strange Chinese girl named Christiana 'Tsai found true democracy and kindness wherever she went, whether from the taxi driver, the ticket agent, the Pullman conductor, or the cordial church members.

Miss Donaldina Cameron and Miss Tien-fu Wu, from the Presbyterian Mission for the Chinese in San Francisco, met us at the ship, just as they had met nearly every boat from China for many years. They took us to a nice apartment which had temporarily been lent to them for our use while the owner went to New York on a visit.

I would like to pay a tribute to these two women, now retired, for their great rescue work for hundreds of Chinese girls and little children caught in the snares of San Francisco's Chinatown. In her little room, Miss Cameron had a telephone by her bed, and at a call from the police, with whom she worked, she would rise from her bed at any hour of the night, go out and search for the person wanted, and then follow up the case in court, if necessary. While we were there, she received a call from the police asking her to find a Chinese girl who had been abducted to a house of prostitution. Miss Cameron went to the place, climbed up a fire escape, entered a room, took hold of the girl to lead her away, when suddenly, a sliding panel came between them and she was forced to loosen her hold and return empty-handed. But the case came up in court, and we went with Miss Cameron to the courthouse

In 1921, Miss Mary Leaman returned to the U.S. for furlough and was accompanied by Miss Tsai. They shared their testimonies in San Francisco, Detroit, Chicago, New York, Washington D.C., Massachusetts and other places.
It was also Miss Tsai's first time to Leaman Place in Paradise, PA where she resided for 35 years later in her life.
The photo above was taken at Leaman family's house in 1921, and the one below is the then Leaman Place ,
in front of which the road was not yet constructed into a highway.

for the trial. She stood before the judge with her face pure as an angel's, accusing the Chinese owners of the brothel, while the lawyer for the defense, like a snarling wolf, tried to prove that the girl was there on legitimate business.

Everyone calls Miss Cameron "Lo-Mo" (Mother) and Mji-Wu, "Auntie." A number of the girls said to us, "Lo-Mo and Auntie went down, as we Chinese say, to the depth of the sea, to the midst of the fiery furnace, into the dens of the lions, into the jaws of the wolves, to save us." Later, a large number of the girls married and were scattered to different states of America to witness for Christ.

On Sunday we went to the Chinese Church, where we met a zealous personal worker, "a hunting dog for the Lord." Miss Leaman mentioned by way of conversation that she regretted we hadn't had opportunity to speak to a certain Chinese family who had come over on the ship with us. After the service, we returned to our apartment, which, with all its modern conveniences, made us feel like babes lost in a mechanical woods. Miss Leaman had been away from the States for about twenty years, and I was a total stranger, so we had had no experience with modern conveniences. The first mechanical ogre we encountered was the self-service elevator. How were we to manipulate it? She tried to urge me, and I tried to persuade her to do it, but we both feared the terrible consequences of doing the wrong thing. So we climbed up and down the four flights of stairs! Our kind friends, Miss Cameron and Miss Wu, tried in every way to help us, but were not on hand and could not guess the extent of our ignorance. When the telephone rang, we were both frightened. "You answer it," I said. "No, you do," she said, for we were both sure we wouldn't be able to hear, and were too nervous to know what to say.

"There's no drinking water here," I said. "Do you think we can drink the tap water? Perhaps we had better boil some." So we boiled the water, as we had in China, not knowing the tap water was perfectly safe.

When mealtime came, and we were just sitting down to eat, there was a peremptory knocking at the door, making us jump. We found our zealous "hunting dog" friend at the door. "Here they are!" she cried. "I found them on the street and brought them up to see you. These are the Chinese you wanted to speak to on the ship, are they not?" Behind her was a bewildered Chinese family she had met and, with more zeal than tact, had taken in hand, hustling them up to call on us. Puzzled, they had followed, not knowing what it was all about. But they weren't the same people at all! We invited them in and they were pleased to find friends from China, though introduced in such a peculiar fashion. They proved to be from one of the leading Hong Kong families whom I had met previously, and were really very happy to hear our witness and to find Christian friends over here. So the faithful "hunting dog" did bring in her quarry for the Lord after all.

While we were in San Francisco, we heard many stories of the strange sects and cults that were so popular; but what distressed me most was to find that there was an American Buddhist temple in the city. We decided to see for ourselves what the place was like. Before we went in the door, we could smell the incense; stepping inside, we saw it was arranged like a Christian chapel, but up in front was a dais with a gilded Buddha on it; instead of a silk curtain, they had hung up over the idol a Chinese lady's embroidered skirt! A nun stood beside the dais, alternately striking the chimes and sounding the bell, while an American with shaven head, dressed in the orange robe of a Buddhist monk, was explaining to the audience that when Jesus was twelve years old, He hadn't gone to the temple at Jerusalem, but had gone to a Buddhist temple and received the teaching of Buddha. After the talk, they took up a collection, sang Buddhist prayers set to Christian hymn tunes, and at the close, the monk gave the benediction in the name of Buddha. This was sacrilegious to me. What a travesty to use Christian forms to worship an idol. I looked at the faces of the audience, and every one of them was sad.

We hurried away, deeply distressed. It was missionaries who had rescued me from Buddhism over in China, and now Buddhists were deceiving these gullible people over here! I had no words for my sorrow of heart. Outside on the bridge, I saw two women ahead of me, one short and dark and the other tall and thin. I recognized them as two from the audience, so I hurried up to the tall one and said, "Excuse me, please, but I am a Chinese girl who used to worship Buddha over in China, and I can tell you that you will never find peace that way. The only way to find peace is through the Lord Jesus Christ! I know, for that is how I found it."

The tall lady looked down at me and tears came to her eyes. "O little Chinese girl, please tell me where I can find peace! I am a relative of Robert Morrison. I have gone to all the churches over here, but I haven't found peace for my heart."

"Come to my house and we will talk about it," I said. "Here is my address." But as I took a pencil and paper out to write, the short lady turned on me in fury, and shoved me back, nearly knocking me down. "Don't you try to convert us, you little Chinese girl! You have been deluded yourself by these missionaries." And she jerked the tall lady away, pulling her by force down the street, while I stood stunned. Robert Morrison's relative in a Buddhist temple in San Francisco! Incredible! The first Protestant missionary to China, who did a masterly translation of the Bible into Chinese, and his relative unable to find peace in America! It was he who, when an officer on the ship jokingly said, "So you are going to try to convert the heathen," had answered, "I can't, but God will." And now somebody was trying to convert his relative to Buddhism. I never saw her again, but the experience made an indelible impression on my mind, and I have prayed that she will find peace in knowing Jesus Christ.

All the time I was in America I rode on the crest of the wave. I was thrilled at all I saw, and everyone except the Buddhist woman on the bridge was kind to me. I saw the democratic spirit in action in all classes of people, and the great scope of Christian work everywhere.

In Pasadena, Mr. and Mrs. Milton Stewart were the first to call upon us, and they invited us to stay in their unpretentious home and served us with their own hands.

In Detroit, when I was to speak before the Presbyterian General Assembly, I hardly ate anything for three days. But as I mounted the platform, instead of seeing rows of long, severe faces, I looked at an audience all wreathed in smiles, and my fear left me.

After I spoke at the Moody Bible Institute in Chicago, the whole student body rose up and sang "Crown Him, Lord of All," and to my dying day I will never forget the inspiration that gave me.

In New York, I spoke to the prisoners at Sing Sing, and it was deeply satisfying that all I met had been given Testaments and professed a faith in Jesus. They lined up after the service to shake hands with me, and tears fell on my hand. Many said, "I'll meet you in Heaven."

At Northfield, Massachusetts, when I spoke to a group of working girls in D. L. Moody's home, they each donated an extra hour's pay for husking corn to raise money to buy me a victrola for country work.

In Washington when I shook hands with President Harding, I gave him a box of ink which the Emperor of China had given my father, and he was so delighted he stopped to talk to me, and then ordered an attendant to show us around the White House.

At Leaman Place, in Pennsylvania, I remember with deep gratitude the helpful example of Miss Leaman's uncle, Dr. Henry Leaman, who for fifty-five years had been a practicing physician in Philadelphia. At six in the morning, without fail, he went to his room for prayer. Now he was blind, but still serene, and when I expressed my sympathy, he said, "The world is so full of evil, it is better not to see."

Several times when seated in a train or on a trolley car, someone

I did not know would slip a five-dollar bill into my hand, saying, "This is for your work in China."

At West Chester, Pennsylvania, and other places, I spoke to groups of children, and gave each child a Chinese brass coin with a hole in the center; I told them to fasten the coin to a window shade and remember that every evening when they pulled down the shade, it was morning in China, and to pray for the Chinese. Years later, during the Japanese war, some of those same children sent to a newspaper a letter suggesting that they tell the children of America whenever they pulled the shades down to remember to pray for the Chinese.

Pray for China when you pull down the shade.

Chapter 14

The Return of the Prodigal

NO ONE CAN RIDE the crest of the wave very long, as it is soon bound to topple and carry the swimmer down with it. It was not long before I passed through the deep waters. While I was still in America, Mother sold our house at Millstone Street, because it was too big and too difficult to keep in repair. She then moved to a smaller house at Fisherman's Wharf. This house was very gloomy and was quite a step down for us. She sent a cable which reached us in Japan, asking Miss Leaman to come and live with us, for she had given me to her for a goddaughter some years previously. Upon my return to Nanking I was very much shocked when the carriage deposited us at our new home, to find that our apartment was only a few rooms on the right of the main entrance. It seemed so public to one who had been used to living in the privacy of the inner courts, that I felt as if we were facing right out on the main street!

Mother looked especially well, and it was wonderful to see her and my family again. My own health had begun to fail, and many activities had to be given up. Then I received a great shock when my dear mother died suddenly the following year. I had gone to Kuling for a rest, leaving her well and happy; ten days later I received a telegram saying she had passed away. I hurried back for the funeral which I arranged to have carried out in accordance with her wishes, that is, with Christian dignity and simplicity, though some members of the family opposed this. She had told us that she did not want to be buried in Hangchow because she was now a Christian and wanted to be buried with the Christians. We buried her in a Christian hillside cemetery, in a plot adjoining that of Mr. Charles Leaman.

My Sixth Sister was a strict Buddhist, but she was impressed by the quiet, hopeful spirit of the ceremony. More than twenty-five years previously she had married into an immensely wealthy family in Nanking. Her father-in-law had held some of the same offices as my father, but he died soon and so did her husband, leaving her with three children, Enduring-Health, aged three, Bright-Cloud, aged two, and Enduring-Wealth, only six months. There were now three widows in this family, a grandmother, a mother and a daughter-in-law; so Enduring-Health was heir to a large part of the family fortune. With such a background, who could doubt the outcome? The three widows spoiled him when he was small, and could not control him when he grew older. Enduring-Health grew to be a vicious bully and a wild spendthrift. He sneered at their tears and protestations, and if they denied him money, rifled the family chests and made off with the valuables he found there. Thousands and thousands of dollars passed through his hands like water, all spent on wine, women, and gambling.

One night during an orgy of gambling, he lost heavily, so he went home in the early morning hours determined to bully his grandmother until she gave him the money. He stalked into her bedroom before she had arisen, demanding, "Give me the pearl necklace that belongs to me. I want it now!"

Startled out of her sleep, she gasped, "What pearl necklace?"

"The one you said you were going to give me when I married," he answered.

"That pearl necklace!" she cried. "That is worth a fortune and we are keeping it for your bride!"

"I want it now! You can give her something else when the time comes," he stormed. "Hand it over quickly."

Outraged at his arrogance, she replied, "No, you shall never have it."

He sprang forward and slapped her on both cheeks, crying, "Are you going to give it to me, or not?" She screamed and Sixth

Sister heard her and rushed in, but he savagely pushed her away. 'The cook, who was passing by, heard the screams and he rushed in, too, carrying a bucket in his hands. He saw what was wrong and threw the bucket and its contents at Enduring-Health who ducked just in time. The cook, now mad with rage, shouted, "I'll rid the family of this scoundrel!" and threw a big carved chair at him, but the young man ducked again and ran away.

He left Nanking and went to Wusih, where the family owned several big stores, and tried to bully the managers into giving him money. At the same time he wrote letters home, threatening to break his brother's legs and make him impotent for life, so he could not be the family heir. He even hired cutthroats to lie in wait and maim Enduring-Wealth as he went to school, but this plot was found out and his brother was hidden away. Sixth Sister wrote to the store managers in Wusih, telling them not to give Enduring-Health any money, and also to the police, asking them to arrest him; but he was too cunning for them all, and escaped once more. Eighth Brother tried to trick him by asking him to the house for a game of chess, and his mother notified the police to surround the house. Enduring-Health came in and sat down to play the game, but soon suspecting a plot, got away, and so outwitted them again.

Next he went to a store manager, and pointed a gun at him saying, "If you don't give me money, I'll shoot you." Some clerks set upon him and he had to flee. When poor Sixth Sister got this news, she was at her wit's end. There seemed to be only one course—have him arrested and put in jail, and she instructed the police accordingly. So Enduring-Health was finally arrested and imprisoned, and his mother put a notice in the paper publicly disowning him. This was a bitter day for her, and it was during this time that she brought Bright-Cloud and Enduring-Wealth to Fisherman's Wharf to live with us. Her Buddhist prayers and vegetarian vows had not helped her through this crisis, so she was more willing to listen as we told her how to find peace in Christ.

But it took many weeks of patient teaching and explanation before she accepted Christ, and then broke her vegetarian vows. Later, Bright-Cloud and Enduring-Wealth accepted Christ and all three were baptized. As the trials multiplied, her faith deepened, and she committed Enduring-Health to the Lord and prayed faithfully for him.

Enduring-Health wrote asking me to speak to his mother and have him released from prison. Miss Leaman had sent him a Bible, and he quoted verses from it to show how repentant he was. When I suggested to the family that he be released, they all objected, saying, "We will have nothing to do with him. If he is let loose, you will have to take the whole responsibility." However, I decided to give him a second chance, and wrote to him that I would be his guarantor, if he would come home and live with me and promise to obey me. He agreed, and I secured his release.

The family was gathered together for morning prayers, and we were reading in Acts how Peter was delivered from the prison, when there was a commotion outside, the door burst open, and Enduring-Health stood before us. I took one look at his thin face, his long hair, the glare in his eyes. I knew that he was unchanged, that hatred still burned in his heart, and my own heart sank. "He hasn't repented! He fooled me! What shall I do?" I asked myself. His mother spoke to him, but he ignored her completely, addressing himself only to me. I showed him a room in my apartment which he could use, and made it clear that he wasn't to leave the house without my permission, and then only in my private ricksha.

Sixth Sister, Second Sister-in-law, and others blamed me. "Don't you see he hasn't changed a bit? He fooled you. Now we have a tiger in the house and there is no telling what will happen to us."

In his room, he proceeded to post slogans on the walls, "Death to my mother!" "Death to the manager!" "Kill my brother!" And in his rage he kicked the door to pieces. I tried to talk to him but he made no response, sitting sullenly and staring at the floor. His

"Mother can you forgive me ?"

old amah said, "He is the worst scoundrel I ever saw. If this boy changes, all my village will believe in Jesus." I tried to find something for him to do, and asked him to copy some tracts for me. He did this but appeared to be just as stony as ever.

Then he started writing and composed some articles which he sent to a newspaper for publication. He had an excellent, witty style, and the paper paid him well for all he sent in. So he found an occupation which kept him busy for some time. After two years he took university entrance examinations and passed at the head of the list. A change had come over him. Where he had been extravagant before, he now became miserly; where he had been idle, he became diligent; and where he had been wild, he now became quiet. Throughout these years he had never once spoken to his mother, so we knew he was still bitter and had no conviction of sin; but his mother never gave up praying for him.

Sometime after graduation he went to Hangchow on a study of the different colleges in that part of China. There he contracted typhoid fever, and was brought home dangerously ill. For weeks he lay growing thinner and weaker, and hovering at death's door. In this great extremity, God answered his mother's prayers, and opened his eyes to see that it was he who had sinned against his mother and brother, not they who had sinned against him. Like the prodigal son, he came to himself at last, and was overwhelmed by the magnitude of his sin. He asked for his mother. As she bent over him, he looked into her face for the first time in years, saw the suffering he had caused, and wept. "Mother, you loved me and cared for me, but I was a vicious dog who bit the hand that fed me, and hurt the only one who loved me. Can you forgive me?"

"You are my son," she said brokenly. "Of course, I can forgive you, but you must ask Jesus to forgive you, too. Only Jesus can take away your sin, and cleanse your heart."

"Yes," he replied, "I do want to ask Jesus to forgive me and be my Saviour. Will you pray for me?" As she prayed, the tears coursed down his thin cheeks. From that time on he began to get well, and had almost recovered when the amah ignorantly gave him some contaminated food, and he had a relapse. One day he asked for the pastor to come and baptize him. In a few days, Enduring-Health closed his eyes on this world, only to open them again as he crossed Heaven's portal and looked in the face of his Lord.

Chapter 15

Queen of the Dark Chamber

THE YEARS WE SPENT at Fisherman's Wharf saw the death of Mother, Second Brother and his wife, a cousin, a nephew, Enduring-Health, and the breakup of our family. Since my own health was poor, Miss Leaman decided to move to a house which we had previously built back of our chapel on Dye Factory Street. We hadn't had money to finish it at the time, so the neighbors called it "a leopard skin coat above and bare feet below" because the upstairs was finished with windows all around, but the downstairs was patched up with an odd assortment of latticed doors.

The years 1930-1937 spent on Dye Factory Street saw Miss Leaman accomplish her greatest work, and saw me go through the deepest waters of suffering. Miss Leaman realized a dream of her father's, envisioned fifty years before when he was toiling over study of the Chinese language, first for himself, and then trying to teach others to read the Bible. He dreamed of a simplified system of writing Chinese.

To us Chinese, the written character embodies the best of our culture. It is not just a mechanical symbol, expressing a sound, as the letters of the English alphabet are; but each character is a pictorial composite of various elementary ideas to form a new thought, and its written structure and style expresses our deepest thoughts and artistic attainment. Learning to read and write Chinese is so engrossing it becomes an end in itself. But—and here is the fatal flaw—it takes so much time to master the mere fundamentals that only the leisured few can ever enjoy it, while the unlettered masses can only hope to learn to recognize a few characters at most. That means that even under a modern education system only two out of ten can learn to read and write.

But Western culture introduced a new concept, namely, that writing is an indispensable means of communication for the masses, not a luxury for the privileged few. China's new leaders saw that our greatest educational need was to wipe out mass illiteracy among the four hundred and fifty million people and unify the confusion of dialects that exists all over China. Without accomplishing these reforms, China could never take its place in the modern world.

Korea has had such a system for a thousand years, and Japan had already wiped out illiteracy by similar means.

So the Chinese National Government formed a five-year plan by which it hoped to introduce the Peking dialect as a standard all over China, and carry on a program of mass education. They evolved a phonetic system to simplify the process of reading and writing. By combining thirty-seven symbols into words of not more than three symbols each, a person could write anything that was spoken in the colloquial language and read what was thus written.

To enlarge the usefulness of the system, each phonetic word was combined with its corresponding character in a parallel column so that anyone who had learned the phonetic could now also teach himself the character.

The phonetic beside the character is not only an accurate indication of the correct pronunciation of each of the nearly five thousand characters found in the Bible; it gives the correct tone as well. A very complicated character with the phonetic beside it is no harder to pronounce than a very simple one. Thus could be accomplished in a few weeks of intensive study what would require at least ten years in the old way.

And as for the missionaries, trying to master the hardest language on earth, as Chinese is said to be, the study of the phonetic teaches them accurate speech and accurate tones, which they rarely acquire otherwise. There are many jokes on the new missionaries for the many ridiculous mistakes they make in pronunciation and tones; but it is no joke when they continue to speak in a faulty way.

Miss Leaman saw in this program the possibility of printing the Bible with character and phonetic in parallel columns, and putting it into the hands of the millions of the common people. "A Bible in the hands of every man, woman and child in China" was her aim. The Bible read by the masses could do more to spread the gospel than any other means, while the strength of the Christian church depends to a great extent on the number of members who can read the Bible.

One day, while at dinner we were talking with a friend about the possibility of cooperating with the government in this mass education program; the friend suddenly said, "I'll give you two thousand dollars to get it started."

It was a gift from Heaven, and Miss Leaman grasped it with both hands. At that time this sum in Chinese dollars was about six thousand, and would pay for the initial cost of launching the project. Miss Leaman obtained the services of an experienced printer and two apprentices, then secured a small office in Shanghai for them to use. All the work of finding the correct spelling and tones for the words, combining the character with the phonetic, designing the style of type, cutting the matrices, casting the type, typesetting, proofreading, and printing, had to be carried on by correspondence between Nanking and Shanghai. She undertook to do the proofreading, and they did the mechanical labor of casting, typesetting, and printing. The Bible Society agreed to do the publishing when it was done.

One lone woman with only two thousand dollars, undertook to have the whole Bible printed in character and phonetic for the people of China! It was a heroic task, but she was well qualified for it; she had a thorough knowledge of Chinese tones and common speech, an iron will, and a boundless faith in her task.

I was very much interested in this project, and prepared to

help, but little knew what was ahead of me. One very cold morning on a visit to the mayor about some business, I noticed he had two nice stoves in his office, and wished I had one like them. When I returned home, I found my big room had been changed to a nice cozy one for the winter. I was no more than settled when two men appeared carrying a stove exactly like the ones I had seen in the mayor's office. Someone had sent it to me. How I enjoyed my nice cozy room and bright fire before retiring!

But I did not see it again for more than a year. In the morning I woke up to find the house apparently whirling around me, while daggers of light stabbed my eyes, and my body stiffened like a corpse in rigor mortis. I could not tell anyone what was the matter. I could only grunt and move my hand. Miss Leaman and the servants understood and nursed me faithfully. They hung dark curtains all around the walls to keep out the light, and covered my eyes with a black band. A woman was constantly at my side, though I lay there more dead than alive, unable to eat, unable to move for seventeen days, unable to speak for eight months, and unable to open my eyes for a year and a half.

Dr. Daniels, of the Presbyterian Mission, visited me frequently and did much for me, but at the end of one year, after all kinds of specialists had been called in for consultation, they announced that the case was hopeless, and advised notifying my family. My brothers, sisters, and friends prepared the coffin and the grave clothes, but Miss Leaman, who never gave up hope then or afterward, sent cables abroad asking for prayer, and hired a tailor to work upstairs to prepare summer clothes for me, while the family prepared my grave clothes downstairs. My family insisted on calling a famous Chinese doctor to examine me. He took my hand and said, "Miss Tsai, we all respect your good name, but you must know that the oil is dry and the lamp is going out. You cannot live longer than three days."

I lay on my bed too near death to have any pains, and saw a vision of a beautiful crown being lifted toward Heaven. I heard wonderful singing, and I thought to myself, "What a welcome!" But I heard a voice, saying, "No, not a welcome, only practice."

And I awoke to hear Miss Leaman praying and sobbing at my bedside. I had sunk to the lowest depths, but now began to recover.

The next day, Dr. Daniels sent a note, saying, "We have diagnosed the case. It is pellegra and beri-beri. No medicine will help, only forced feeding." (However, after sixteen long years of suffering, it was discovered that the basic cause of my trouble is malignant malaria in the marrow of my bones.) It was agony for us all to try and force the food down, for I had been so nauseated. As I got more nourishment, feeling came back and fiery pains began. My head seemed to be burning with fire, so for two years I had to have ice bags placed around it, while the women frequently gave me an alcohol rub and fanned me. The malaria in my bones was so terrible that even on winter nights, though the windows were open and the snow blowing in, I could scarcely stand the thinnest clothing or bedding. Severe nausea made it difficult to eat and retain food. My mouth was sore, my hands black, and my knuckles cracked open to the bone. But I was able to take more food, and slowly God drew me up out of the depths and I returned to life again.

For a time, each step of progress was followed by a relapse. I'd get better, then the symptoms would return, and down I'd go again. But all through the darkness, the light of God's love never failed me. I could never tell all His great goodness to me, even if I had a thousand tongues, nor could I ever write of all His care and provision, even if, as the Chinese say, "The pen I hold could bloom," but I will tell of a few.

Across the Yangtse River about twenty miles away, was a little village. The farmers around there often heard the screaming and crying of an eighteen-year-old young woman, called Little-Beauty, who was beaten by her cruel husband and his family. One day after dark, Little-Beauty escaped from her home and hid somewhere in the fields. She trembled with fear as she heard the loud voices of her husband and her mother-in-law calling and cursing as they hunted for her. After midnight, everything was quiet and she started to run toward Nanking. Later she was brought to our home by a friend. She asked whether she might work in a hidden room, or just in the house, as she was afraid to go out, for fear her husband would find her. Thus she and I stayed together in the quiet of my curtained and darkened room.

She was a born nurse, and in her hours of rest she learned to read and write phonetic. A pile of books was filled with the nursing records she kept those days. She was most affectionate and thoughtful. I often felt her hot tears falling on my hand, and heard her say in a whispering voice, "O God of Heaven, when I am tired I can go out for a change, but when I come in, whether morning, noon, or at midnight, she is still lying here in the same position." For about eight months I was unable to talk much. I had to make my wishes known by a kind of grunt. She never had any difficulty in understanding me. Surely the Lord had put His love into her heart as day by day, month after month, and year after year, she nursed me with never a sign of murmuring or of complaint.

Since my room had to be kept quiet and dark, the rats started to have a good time. They played and danced around me. They liked to crawl up the curtain and jump to the head of my bed, then walk from my shoulder to my hand. For several mornings, before daybreak, I heard a tiny bell jingling outside my window. The little bell bothered me, and the women went down to see what it was. They found a beautiful pure white Persian cat, with a big, bushy tail and affectionate eyes, with a bell tied around its neck. Naturally, we did not want to keep anyone's pet. Miss Leaman tied a pink tract to the cat's neck and sent her off. In a little while she came back but the tract was gone. Miss Leaman tied another tract to her neck and sent her off again. Thus our pussy evangelist carried quite a number of tracts to different homes. Before long, she settled down and refused to leave us. You can imagine how rapidly the rats disappeared when White Queen walked around the house.

Outside my windows was a yard with a small peach tree and a mulberry tree. During the long summer days, the reflection from this open space was unusually hot. Two months after I was taken sick, a kind friend ordered three trees planted a few yards away from my windows, and before long, all around the yard, about thirty trees grew up in addition to the original three. If we had carefully planned where to plant them, we could not have selected such good places. They grew so quickly that three years later the once empty yard became a little forest. The tops of the branches and the beautiful leaves touched each other, and formed a big parasol covering the entire space. Friends often spoke of the view from my windows, the beautiful shade and the sunlight filtering through, and said, "It is a miracle."

Our old gateman, who had been with our family for forty years, never would answer me when I asked him to accept Jesus. He would only stand there without a word, neither refusing nor accepting. But on the day he heard the Chinese doctor say I had only three days to live, he ran over and sought the pastor, saying, "I want to go along with Miss Seven. I want to confess my sins and go with her." So at last in this my extremity he turned to the Lord. Now I can say from the depths of my heart, "My extremity has been God's opportunity."

During my illness a kind friend asked me whether I were lonely and tired spending my days in a darkened room. "Oh, no!" I answered, "the Lord is my constant Companion and real Friend. I am queen of this dark chamber and He is my King of Light!"

White Queen, the pussy evangelist

Chapter 16

The Light That Never Failed

DURING MY LONG ILLNESS, did Miss Leaman stop her work on the phonetic Bible to care for me? Oh, no! If you think that, you don't know my godmother, Mary Leaman. Difficulties to her were only evidence of the supreme importance of her task, and they were faced calmly but with immovable determination. As she helped me out of the valley of the shadow of death with her constant prayers, her loving care, and her iron will, so she went ahead with her self-imposed task of translation with equal dedication. Perhaps many imagine her as a strong, active, healthy woman. She suffered from a spinal injury which left her in constant pain and weakness, so she rarely could go out. In her spare time, after taking care of my many needs, she would sit in a reclining chair, with a typewriter beside her and a reading table on her knees, and work into the early hours of the morning. In this way, she carried on her wide correspondence and the endless, exacting labor of proofreading. She also trained many students and teachers to help with the proofreading, and enlisted the services of anyone she could interest in the labor. She taught the servants to read and used them for demonstration purposes. Miss Helen Struthers spent two years helping with publishing and promotion.

There was a Mission Phonetic Promotion Committee in Shanghai who also backed her, and numerous missionaries who had the vision and made the effort to teach the common people to read by this method. Curiously enough, neither the illiterate masses, nor the literates, nor the missionaries as a whole, welcomed the opportunity or believed in this method. They were too wedded to using the character, too doubtful of the possibilities of

Miss Mary Leaman at work

adapting the Peking spellings to the local dialects, and too easily discouraged by the difficulties of launching a new system. Many started full of enthusiasm, and stopped quickly when they met the apathetic response of the people; for illiterates will take great pride in knowing a few characters, but will resist any new ideas, especially what seems like a foreign language to them.

What seemed so easy to a Westerner, used to a phonetic system of spelling, was extremely difficult to the mind-set of my people. The Chinese were used to learning to recognize each character by memory alone; and though they spoke in tones, they never recognized them as tones, thinking of them only as different words. With their minds directed toward the recognition of the character more than understanding of the subject, they often missed the meaning entirely unless it was put in extremely simple form. In fact, the difficulties of this program were so many that without the government to enforce it, individuals could do very little. But when a dull, stupid woman was coaxed over the hurdles of spelling, and the light of the meaning from some tract or Bible verse illuminated her mind, it so stimulated her emotions and awakened her dormant reasoning power that she was transformed. When she realized that she was reading Chinese (not English as they ignorantly supposed at first), that she could write her own letters; and when the wonders of God's Word dawned on her mind, she became entranced with the Bible and glowed with a new-found intelligence. An old lady corrected a preacher for mispronouncing a word, saying, "In my Bible [the Phonetic] that word is pronounced this way." And sure enough, she was right and he was wrong!

The Book of Jonah was the first to be finished and printed, and it was followed by others. So we had several textbooks for a group of country children who came in to study in our chapel. The country people are very busy most of the year, but in the winter, after the China New Year, they have time to study, and that is when we have to work the hardest. Children learn much more quickly than adults, and these children learned to spell and read and write very well in six weeks, so we sent them home with their books and told them to continue with their reading and try to teach others. When they got home, they were proud of their new-found education and often sent us postcards written in phonetic. Later, a farmer from their part of the country came in to see us, his face full of smiles, bringing a "thank you" gift of eggs and puffed rice, and a story to tell.

"This phonetic," he began, "is a living treasure. My daughter, Precious Pearl, was in your short-term school this year. When she came home, she amazed us all by reading the Bible to us and keeping our accounts as well! So our neighbors used to drop in and ask to hear her read.

"'This is nothing short of a miracle,' one said. 'This child did not know one character before. Now she can read the Bible. Who ever heard anything like that?' Another said, 'Maybe she isn't reading correctly. Let's call in one of the big boys who has been to school to test her.' So they called in one of the boys and gave him a Bible to look at and asked her to read from hers. She read every word correctly. That boy had studied five years and couldn't read as well as she did. Now when our people find some new and difficult character, they come to her, and if there is phonetic beside it, she can tell what it is. So they all call her 'Little Dictionary.'"

The story of the painter and the carpenter is another interesting case. We had hired a man to paint our house. This man was an earnest Christian, a diligent worker, but an illiterate. He was greatly impressed the first day on attending our morning prayers, to see the cook, the washwoman, and the coolie each with a New Testament in hand, take turns reading the lesson. Afterward, they urged him to learn the phonetic, too; he stood there, face red, ears burning, unable to say a word. He was a stutterer! But he wanted to learn. So it was wonderful to see him in his spare time, seated on a stone, a page grasped in both hands, spelling, 'b-b-b-b-ah bbah, p-p-p-ah ppah, m-m-m-ah mah, d-d-d-ah dah." Even standing on the ladder busily painting, he kept on repeating, "Bah, pah, mah, dah," and while he was working, he would stop, lay down his brush, take up his book, and hunt up some new word.

One day he told us that the wood in some of the doors and windows was rotten, and we should get a carpenter to fix them before painting. The carpenter arrived, but had hardly begun work when the painter came over and persuaded him to study phonetic. When the carpenter opened his mouth to pronounce the sounds, they both guffawed. Everybody came around to see what the joke was. "He is a stutterer, too," said the painter. But the stuttering teacher and the stuttering student were encouraged, rather than discouraged, by their mutual handicap. They were often seen under the trees on a big stone, each with his book, drinking tea together, and reading with great gusto.

Even Mrs. Wu, the cleaning lady, could read.

The government plan for the phonetic was now in full swing. All primary school textbooks contained it, and many public notices as well. The mayor of one city ordered the people to attend public classes to learn the phonetic, but few enrolled. "We are too busy," they said. So the mayor stationed teachers at the city gates to examine all the people entering the city in the phonetic, and to allow only those who could read to enter. This solved the problem, and the classes were well attended, because the country people all needed to come into the city to do business.

In Nanking, in June, 1937, the Board of Education called a conference of one hundred delegates from all over China for a month's training in methods of teaching phonetic to the people. The head of the Department of Mass Education knew of Miss Leaman's work, and asked her to send some phonetic pupils to demonstrate to the delegates. She got in contact with a Miss Garden, an old Chinese friend of ours, who had started evangelistic work in the country about twenty miles south of Nanking. This woman had contributed her own savings to build a little chapel and she personally helped the masons and carpenters. She was teaching a

Three servants reading the Bible in phonetic

class of boys and girls to read phonetic. They worked all day, carrying vegetables, digging edible wild plants on the hills, pulling rickshas, keeping buffaloes, or gathering fuel, and came every evening for a half-hour class in phonetic. Miss Garden now hired two carriages and told her pupils they were going on a trip into the city with her. They squeezed into the carriages just as they were, the boys carrying books in their hands, and the girls, heads tied up in black kerchiefs, with their books in baskets. The children thought the trip was a great lark, and stared wide-eyed at the wonders of the capital. Miss Leaman met them and they drove in through the imposing gates of the Department of Education.

But their eyes opened wider as they were taken into the great assembly hall, and up to the platform in front, where they saw the great company of educators. But they were too simple to be frightened, and they went through all the tests with flying colors. The delegates were invited to test the children, so one of them came forward, picked up one of their books, opened it at random, and asked a child to read. He did so, successfully. Then another delegate came forward with a book of his own containing phonetic, and gave it to one of the boys to read. Though he had never seen that book before, he was able to read the words. When a third educator pointed to an inscription on the wall, and asked one of the girls to read it, she was able to do so. This demonstration made a great impression on the educators. They awarded Miss Leaman a set of phonetic records prepared by Dr. Y. R. Chao, an authority on phonetic, and asked us to prepare a message on the value of the phonetic, to be broadcast over the Central Broadcasting Station. I was just well enough then to dictate the message, and later dictated for publication several booklets on the importance of the phonetic.

Miss Leaman and Tsai worked on the Chinese Phonetic Bible from 1930 to 1941.

Chapter 17

Wanderings in the Wilderness

NANKING was the capital of China from 1927 to 1937, and during those years the population mushroomed from two hundred thousand to a million. Wide streets were cut through the city and country; bus service was started; numerous government buildings sprang up; and the city was thronged with strangers from all over China and all over the world. The government was working feverishly to unify China, reform its laws and educational system, and modernize its army, all of which were colossal tasks.

But there were enemies without as well as within. A great nation on the other shore of the Yellow Sea knew the strategic importance of China to her own ambitions, and had plans to conquer it. While the Chinese government was trying to reform the national economy, the Japanese were encroaching in the North, biting it off piece by piece. Could China in these short years become strong enough to defend herself? Because it looked as if she might, the Japanese decided not to take the chance.

In the summer of 1937, Japan struck first north of Peking, and then at Shanghai on the central coast. There was nothing to do but hold them off at Shanghai while the government was evacuated to the mountain vastness of West China, and then draw them in until they bogged down in the primitive maze of the interior. So, as the Japanese army advanced from the coast, the people fled to the west. All government personnel and their dependents were ordered to leave, and with them went the young, the rich, the patriotic, and the intelligentsia; behind stayed the poor,

Mountains of West China

the old, and women and children. Higher educational institutions moved en masse across those thousands of miles. Modern factories were dismantled and carried piece by piece overland. Nanking was a bottleneck through which millions of frantic refugees tried to pour, for they were forced to make a choice between staying to suffer the terrors of a Japanese occupation, or fleeing across the jigsaw paths of the interior. The few railroads, bus lines, and steamships could accommodate only one out of a hundred of those who wanted to go. I cannot describe that great exodus but I will tell you a little of God's wondrous care for His children in those days, both for those who went and those who stayed.

Miss Arrow and Miss Willow, two Chinese evangelists, had decided to go by train to the country south of Nanking. When they got to the railroad station, it was crowded with thousands of struggling people, trying to get on an already packed train. They discovered that some baggage had been left behind, and Miss Arrow went back to get it. She did not find it, and before she returned, the train had gone, taking Miss Willow, the money, and the rest of the baggage. Miss Arrow stood there in the seething crowd, five dollars in one hand, and a small handbag containing a change of clothing in the other. Another train was going south, but it was already jammed and people were climbing through the windows to the coach tops. There seemed no hope at all of getting even standing room. As she stood there, a stranger asked her, "Do you want a seat on that train?"

"Certainly," she said, "can you get me one?"

"Come with me," he replied, and took her to a coach which had been reserved for the families of government officials. She was thrilled to get a seat, but later dismayed to find that the train did not stop at the appointed place, but went on far beyond it to a strange town where everybody got off. Here, too, the Lord provided! One of the families on the train hired a house boat and invited her to join them for the next stretch of the journey. When they parted at the second town, she found a Christian chapel where she

Flocks of refugees fleeing

stayed and then joined another Christian group who were going farther on. Thus step by step she went west, where she found a home and work to do.

Miss Garden's wanderings were similar but even more prolonged. She went from town to town throughout inland China, carrying her little satchel and a few dollars. Everywhere she went she found little Christian chapels and mission stations where she was entertained, and that were directed by devoted Christians who were mostly members of the China Inland Mission. She slept on straw on the floor, washed at the well, ate the simple food they provided, preached at the evangelistic services, taught Bible classes, and joined new groups of refugees who went west as the news came that the Japanese were approaching. They traveled by houseboat, wheelbarrow, donkey, or on foot all through the picturesque hill country of central and southwest China. The Christians of the interior welcomed her and asked her to preach to the crowds that passed along, so the opportunities for witnessing were unlimited. For eight years, from the beginning of the war in 1937, she wandered through ten provinces, preaching, teaching and witnessing with no other means of support than what she received as she went along; she did not return to Nanking till the war was over in 1945. She told us that until then she had no idea of the far-flung work of the China Inland Mission and their sacrificial service and hospitality to the people of China in those days.

There was old Mrs. Wang who left with her family to hide in the country not far from Nanking. They had rented the middle house in a row of three in a little hamlet. The young women in the party hid under the boards of the floor all day to escape the bestial lust of the roving Japanese soldiers. One day they saw a Japanese soldier approach, and the girls hid while the older ones watched and prayed. The soldier entered the first house and came out, but just as he started to enter the middle house, a dog sprang at him and he turned to chase it away, so that he skipped the middle house and went to the third.

Old Mrs. Chen and her family were too poor to hire rickshas to get out of the city, so they remained at home. Some Japanese soldiers entered their house, saw the men standing in the courtyard and fired, killing them all, and left. She and her daughter-in-law, the only ones left, witnessed the shooting and were frantic. What could two helpless women do all alone? In their terror they jumped into the well. While they were struggling in the water, another Japanese soldier entered, heard the noise, and looked down the well at them. He smiled at them and indicated that they were not to fear. Then he let down a rope, drew them out, got them some dry clothes and gave them money. When they tried to express their gratitude, he said simply, "I am a Christian."

An American woman missionary with sublime courage, walked out on the streets time and again when the atrocities were at their worst, and gathered up screaming women who knelt and implored her help. She brought them to Ginling Women's College where she and a band of heroic friends turned the beautiful buildings into a huge refugee camp, using the protection of the American flag. For five months they fed and protected the women against outrage. During those months tens of thousands of refugees were housed in several other such refugee camps, operated by missionaries. The women of Nanking used to say, "It was that American missionary who saved us Nanking people. We thought she was Christ Himself."

As for Miss Leaman and me, who had lived in the shadow of Japan's aggressive designs for many years, and had seen the tiger appeased again and again, we never knew just when it would spring. We went on with our lives just as usual, hoping for the best. Miss Leaman was trying to finish the printing of the Bible and at the same time shield me from worry. I did not know what was happening until a Chinese friend came into my room one day to tell me of the mass exodus and to urge us to go to the foreign concession in Shanghai, which the Japanese had not attacked at that time.

We decided to pack and leave at the earliest opportunity. Mr. Wang, our printer, spent three days at the railroad station before he succeeded in getting us a first-class compartment. Later, the conductor kindly allowed our three women servants to stay in the room with us instead of putting them in third class. Had they gone third class, they would have had to wait for the next train, and would surely have been lost in the mélée. They were simple country people who had never been on a train before, and one of them, whom we called Little-King, kept moaning all night long, "O my mother! O my mother! What is going to happen to us? How can we all live in this little room?"

Suddenly, for the first time, a terrible thought occurred to me, and I said, "Miss Leaman, where are we going to live in Shanghai?"

"I don't know, dear," she answered. "The Lord will provide." The train was on time when we arrived in Shanghai, and Miss Leaman, looking out of the window, cried, "There is Joy-Bell to meet us!" There she stood among the thronging masses, and a nurse with a wheel chair was with her. We were expecting Joy-Bell for we had sent a telegram asking her to meet us. What we did not know was that she had not received the wire, but in her morning devotional watch, she had been guided to go down and meet that train. And now our car door stopped at the very spot where she was standing. As we pushed through the frantic crowds, another miracle appeared—two empty taxis waiting at the curb.

"There are mountains and oceans of people, all trying to find a place to live here in Shanghai," Joy-Bell told us. "There is no use trying to hunt for a place today. You had better get a room in a hospital for the present." But a hospital room was small for us five, and the price was too high, so we telephoned Eighth Brother to find us a place.

"There isn't a square foot of empty space in Shanghai!" he exclaimed.

"Try your best," we urged. So he sent his son Ever-Cheer and daughter-in-law Bright-Cloud to find us a room. They walked the streets all morning but found nothing. By noon they were hot and tired, and they sat down to eat in a little Russian restaurant on the Street of the Coiled-Dragon. Just across the street was a row of brick houses. While they were eating, a Russian woman appeared and pasted a tiny square of paper, the size of a calling card, on the door of one house.

"Let's see what it is," said Bright-Cloud. "It might be a room." They ran across the street and found it was notice of a room to rent! They had seen it in the nick of time, for other room hunters were prowling the streets! The woman was still outside when they appeared at the door, and she took them upstairs to see the room which had a bath adjoining. It was ideal for our purposes! So Bright-Cloud stayed in the room to hold it from room-hunters who followed them, while Ever-Cheer went to telephone us.

Three refugees in a pedicab in Shanghai

"We've found a room for you, but if we leave the house now, we'll lose it," he said. "Just come over to this address as quickly as you can."

Joyfully we entered our new home in exile and unpacked our things, just seven hours after our arrival. "Get Miss Leaman some fresh clothes out of her trunk," I told Little-King.

When she opened the trunk, she cried out, "It's full of phonetic books. There isn't a piece of clothing here."

"What!" I cried, "didn't you pack her clothes?"

"She said to pack these phonetic books because she needed them," was the answer.

"Well, Little-King, you will have to lend her a suit of your own clothes till we make some new ones," I said.

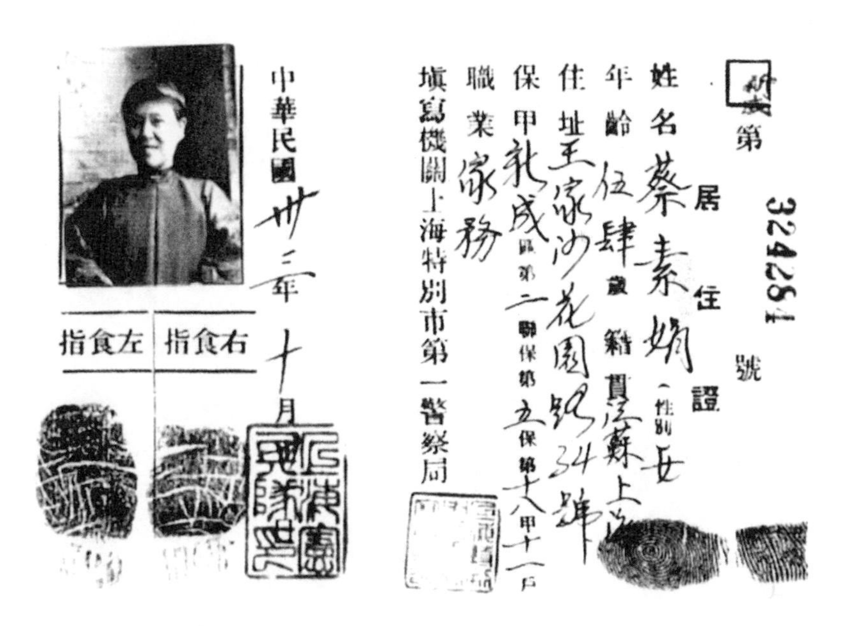

第 324284 號

居住證

姓名 蔡素娟（性別 女）

年齡 伍肆歲 籍貫 江蘇上海

住址 王家沙花園路34號

保甲 新成區第二聯保第五保第十八甲十一戶

職業 家務

填寫機關 上海特別市第一警察局

中華民國卅二年十月

右食指 左食指

Miss Tsai moved to Shanghai French Concession in 1937.
This is the residence permit in Shanghai where Miss Tsai's fingerprints were inked.

Chapter 18

Three More Sheep

THE FOREIGN CONCESSIONS in Shanghai were sandwiched between the old and new Chinese cities. Here Shanghai had its British and American quarter, French quarter, Japanese quarter, Russian quarter, and later its Jewish quarter. The aliens were only a sprinkling in the Chinese population that now overflowed every corner and swelled the city to three times its normal number because of incoming refugees. Though Shanghai's foreign concessions were a thorn in the flesh of the patriotic student class who resented China's lack of sovereignty, they were a haven of refuge to the wealthy people who found security in their international control. During the first part of the war, from 1937 to 1941, Shanghai became a vast refugee camp.

We lived in the French concession, but there were very few French living there. The largest foreign element around us were the white Russians who had fled here after the Russian Revolution and it had become the Russian quarter. Around the corner was Avenue Joffre which was then commonly known as "Little Moscow Boulevard" because of the Russian shops that lined the street and the many Russian people who strolled on its sidewalks.

Scarcely a week after we moved there, the Japanese siege of Shanghai began, and though no bombs fell in the concessions, the Japanese and Chinese fired at each other across this area. The screaming of the shells and the roaring of the artillery never ceased until Shanghai fell to Japan three months later.

Miss Leaman went on with the proofreading of the phonetic Bible. Some time before she had all the printing apparatus moved from Shanghai to Nanking; when we left Nanking it had to be moved up the river to the buildings of the Religious Tract Society, in Hankow, where it remained intact for the duration. Had it been left in the original Shanghai office, which was in the Japanese quarter, or in Nanking, it would have been destroyed and Miss Leaman's labor and capital lost.

Our landlady Olga was a white Russian as were most of the other occupants of the house. The afternoon we arrived she was away playing mah-jongg, and the Chinese servant known as "Boy" showed us the room. In the evening Olga clattered upstairs in her high-heeled shoes and came to visit us. She was an attractive young woman, dressed very stylishly and she spoke in broken English, "You are the new guests, Miss Leaman and Miss Tsai, "yes, see I bring you a sheet and some plates. Please you use them."

"Thank you very much. You are our landlady, I suppose. What is your name?"

"Please, my name is Olga. You like to play mah-jongg with me?"

"No, we don't play mah-jongg. We are Christians."

"Not play mah-jongg! Why not?" and she turned away and click-clacked down the stairs.

In a few days she came back. "Please you pay me rent now?"

"But we paid you rent when we took the room."

"No, no, not this month. Next month. I play mah-jongg and lose very much money. Please you pay me now."

So whenever Olga came to see us, it was either to ask us to play mah-jongg or to borrow money. The rest of the time, though we could not see her, we heard her yelling downstairs, "Bo-o-oy! Come here!" or "Mimi, [her dog] where are you?" When she lost at mah-jongg, the glasses, plates, forks, and spoons would begin to crash, and the dog would yelp, as Olga beat her and chased her into the hall. She quarreled with all the roomers except us. I could often hear doors slamming and angry voices and screams, for they often came to blows. Nearly every day the police came to the house to investigate the quarreling and fighting. Olga had been living with a Swedish man named Nils for seven years, though they were not married. He worked as a guard in the municipal jail during the day. When she got mad at him, the plates and glass and silver crashed. Often they went out for dances and returned in the early hours of the morning, singing noisily, too drunk to go to their own room. Our servants going down in the morning would stumble over them sleeping on the stairs.

The boy, who had a speech difficulty, used to come upstairs and pour out his woes to me because I was a Chinese. "Missy throw her shoes and stockings on the floor and tell me to pick them up. She has plenty dresses, but she no like them. She roll them up and throw them in the closet."

Olga's mother, sister, nephew, and niece came down from Port Arthur, and they all slept in one room under mine. Olga often fought with them, grabbing her screaming niece by the hair; the mother and nephew jumped on Olga, and down went the table, chairs, Olga, niece, and nephew together.

One day one of the tenants had a birthday and invited Olga to play mah-jongg with her. They played continuously for forty-eight hours, and Olga lost two hundred dollars. To pay the debt she sublet her own room, and tried to move a heavy trunk. In so doing she injured herself severely. For months she was so weak she could hardly drag herself around. One day she came upstairs to see us and sat down groaning on the chair to tell us the doctor said she must have an expensive operation. Miss Leaman had often talked to her about Jesus and now urged her to pray for herself. So Olga went to her room, got on her knees, and prayed, "Dear God, I am a naughty, naughty girl. Please, You make me well and I promise You I will never, never play mah-jongg again. And I won't drink, or dance, or quarrel any more." Immediately she felt well inside. Nils came home that night saying he had made arrangements for her to go to the hospital.

"No, no, Nils. I tell you good news. I am not sick any more."

"Nonsense! The doctor said you could not get well without

an operation."

"Please, Nils. I don't need an operation. Jesus made me well." And she refused to go, for she really was well again. As soon as she could, she hurried up to our room, and though we were entertaining company, she could not wait to tell us the news of the miracle.

Olga kept her promise, for she was a changed woman after that. The house became quiet at last. She would often come upstairs to pray and read the Bible. She prayed in a simple childlike way, "Father, You know I may fall down. Please You pick me up." One day while reading Proverbs her conscience smote her and she told us, "The Bible tell me, 'You lazy little thing! Go look at that ant. It works all summer to get ready for the winter.'" So she pulled her discarded dresses out of the closet and started to learn to sew for herself.

She went to pay her gambling debts, too. As she stood in the doorway of the gambling room, she feared to go in lest she be tempted again; but when she looked at the greedy faces and trembling hands of the gamblers, a surge of relief went through her that she was delivered from that old slavery, and she praised God for the new life she had found.

Now she wanted to help her boy, and asked Miss Leaman to teach him. "Please you teach him. I have a new heart and I want him to have a new one, too. The Bible has many lovely things and I want him to read them."

But this new way of life did not please Nils, who said, "You say don't dance, don't smoke, don't drink! I work in jail all day and now you make my home a jail too."

However, Olga had learned to go to God in prayer, so she prayed, "Please, Father, I love Nils. I want him to go the same road with me. But if You wish him to leave me, all right. Please You put Your wishes in our hearts." And God answered her prayer, for one day Nils had a holiday, took her to a church, and they were married.

Our house was full of noises of all kinds. An educated Chinese woman rented one of the rooms downstairs. Her husband had cast her off and she tried to find comfort in Buddhism. Every morning at daybreak, she would raise her voice and loudly chant her prayers. Most of the other roomers caroused at night, and they complained that she disturbed their rest in the morning. We spoke to her often of the comfort of Christianity, but she showed no interest. Finally, one day she told us that she had decided to go to the West and find her husband, so we gave her a Bible as a parting gift. Some months later we received the following letter from her:

> Miss Tsai and Miss Leaman:
>
> I have not seen you for a long time, but I often think of you. After I left Shanghai and went to find my husband, I was arrested at Hankow for a spy and put in jail, where I will have to stay six months. Here I had nothing to do so I read the Bible you gave to me, and it has brought the true peace into my heart. The more I read the more wonderful it becomes, and I like to tell the other prisoners about it, too. The jailers allow me to read the Bible to these people. Thank you so much for this wonderful gift.

Her next letter told us that she had been released from jail and found her husband, and that they were reunited.

Another tenant was a Jewish woman, a refugee from Europe, whom we heard crying much of the time. Her terrible experiences and sorrows had undermined her health and left her mentally unbalanced, and her husband's scolding made her worse. She was sent to a hospital and put in a strait jacket. After a while she returned, only to break down again. She refused to listen to any words about Christ, and when she visited us during the Passover Week, she even refused to drink a glass of water in our room.

However, after a while she began to read a Bible we had given her. These Words of Life brought comfort to her heart, and she found peace and quiet at last. Some time afterward she had an opportunity to go to America, and she took her Bible with her, writing us that she was continuing to read it every day and find comfort in it.

Three lost sheep! A refugee Russian, a refugee Chinese, and a refugee Jewess! But the Good Shepherd found them all, and brought them safely into His fold.

Chapter 19

Clouds and Sunshine

CLOUDS MAY GATHER over our home in times of sickness or bereavement; but the influence of a sweet Christian character shines through the clouds with a golden radiance, bringing a lasting blessing to those who remain. The story of my sister-in-law, Class-Leader, demonstrates this.

Living in Shanghai, we frequently saw Eighth Brother and his family. His eldest son, Ever-Cheer, was married to Bright-Cloud; his daughter, Ever-Wise was a nurse, and his younger son, Ever-Famous, a student in college. As for his wife, Class-Leader, she was as bright and cheerful as a ray of sunshine, and we all loved her.

One afternoon in autumn she came over to have a brief chat with me and then left with a cheery good-by, walking away through the evening shadows. Neither of us dreamed that this would be our last visit together. A few days later she was taken sick and was sent to the hospital.

On Thanksgiving Day, Eighth Brother came to see me; although he tried to hide it, I knew he realized Class-Leader would soon leave us. All day long, my heart was fixed in prayer that Class-Leader's home going might prove a blessing to the ones she left behind. That afternoon at the hospital, the north wind rattling the window panes of the little room was the only sound as her loved ones gathered round her bedside, intently watching her every move. About sunset Class-Leader opened her eyes for the first time in her illness and taking hold of Bright-Cloud's hand pointed upward exclaiming, "What a wonderful place! What a beautiful sight! Can you see it?"

In a little while she left us and went to that beautiful place to be greeted by her heavenly Father. It was all joy for her, but my brother had lost his best companion and her children had lost their sympathetic mother. They missed her at every turn. Ever-Wise told me, "When I woke next morning, I saw nothing but my white (the color for mourning in China) mourning shoes and my white mourning dress before me!"

Yet Class-Leader's voice was not still. She continued to speak to her family, this time through her will: her last request being that she be buried wearing her golden cross and with her Bible by her side. This impressed Ever-Famous, who now decided to read his Bible every day, and often came and read at my bedside. But when Christmas time came around, the emptiness in his house seemed unbearable. There could be no party this year for there was no mother to entertain his non-Christian friends, no one to tell them the Christmas story, serve them tea and cakes, and give them gifts. But here Ever-Famous, who was more than economical, thought of a very fitting way to celebrate instead. He took his carefully hoarded savings and bought twenty Bibles to give his non-Christian friends in memory of his mother. Then he wrote the name of each friend on the flyleaf and took the Bibles to their homes.

One friend, Hidden-Treasure, became especially interested, and they used to spend hours in Bible study and prayer together. Afterward she became a Christian, and in a short time they became engaged and now they are happily married. So the sweet faith of Class-Leader continued to be a blessing to her son, leading him to a Christian wife and home.

Nor was this the only blessing her last words bequeathed, for on my birthday, Ever-Famous burst into my room, his face all aglow with good news. "Auntie Seven, what do you think our old servant, Old-High, said to us today?"

"I can't guess. Tell me."

"She said, 'I can never forget the smile on my tal-tal's (Mistress) face before she died and her words, "What a beautiful place! What a wonderful sight! Can you see it?" ring in my ears day and night. She used to urge me to believe, but my heart was hard and sinful, and I made her sad by refusing. Now I want to see that beautiful place, too. For twenty years I have refused Jesus, but now I believe and want to be baptized.' "

After Ever-Famous had left, Little-King, who was in the room at the time, said to me, "Miss Seven, I've been with you seven years and I have believed in my heart for a long time. Now I want to confess Jesus before others. May I be baptized with Old-High?"

Little-Field, our washwoman, soon heard the news and she too, came to me eagerly, saying, "You know, I believe Jesus and I want to be baptized too."

So one afternoon the three women servants gathered around my bed for three hours of instruction and prayer for the coming service. I was thrilled by the marvelous change in the three women. They were full of joy and had many experiences to relate, especially Old-High. She told how she had forgotten to ask God's blessing before eating her rice, so she had asked the Lord to forgive her and help her remember each time. "And now, He always reminds me," she said.

Another time she declared, "Now I am going to write a letter to my old man ("Venerable One," her husband) back home and tell him how happy I am and urge him to believe, too." A third time she described how she had already been talking to a neighbor's servant and teaching her. This servant in turn told her mistress that she wanted to believe Jesus, but the mistress had scornfully replied, "What do you know? You can't read."

"No," was the answer, "but knowing how to read is not necessary, for the Bible says, 'If you believe in your heart, you will be saved.'"

"And I told her," Old-High continued, "'Don't listen to what people say; just listen to what God says. It doesn't matter if they laugh at you; it only matters if God is pleased. You see, we can pray at any time and God always hears, even when we are cooking or washing or sweeping the floor.' "

The clouds in our refugee corner, too, have been cleared away, and darkness has turned to light. The servants are so eager to read the Bible they get up at daybreak and call us to prayer. They can read their phonetic Bibles; when they come across some wonderful new thought, their faces light up and they catch their breath with joy. Each morning they meet Old-High at the market place, and talk about the Lord to those they meet.

But even this was not the end of Class-Leader's parting bequest. She, being dead, continued to speak: Shining-Virtue, an elder widowed cousin who had been living with Eighth Brother for many years, and who had also refused to believe all the while, had been deeply impressed by these events. Since she was educated, she now began reading the Bible at last, and in so doing found the Lord and sought to be baptized.

Easter came and among the crowd of war-refugees that filled the makeshift chapel (the beautiful church had been bombed) were Shining-Virtue and these three women servants to be baptized; Ever-Famous and Ever-Wise received communion, and Ever-Cheer and Bright-Cloud's two little daughters were dedicated to the Lord.

So, likewise with me, it has not been easy to be called away from active work and to lie sick in a darkened room for over twenty years; but I always try to remember that even when I cannot see the light, behind the dark clouds the bright sun still shines.

Chapter 20

Shades of the Prison House

PROOFREADING for the phonetic required endless hours of eye-taxing concentration; promotion required patient, persistent work as well. Since she could not go out, Miss Leaman had to use every opportunity to interest those who came to see her; the ever-increasing number of callers indicated the appreciation people had for her work. No matter how tired she was, her rule was that no caller be slighted or hurried. In many ways she is more Chinese than the Chinese, in her correct tones and idiomatic language, in her Chinese clothes, and in her Chinese ways. When guests came at mealtime, meals were postponed, or they were invited to share her simple Chinese food. Sometimes when Old-Salt, our cook, put down covered dishes of food in the center of the table, and a bowl of rice before each person, Miss Leaman was too engrossed in her discussion of the phonetic to notice the food or take off the covers, until the poor guest was halfway through the dry rice. Old-Salt, though she worried inwardly, did not make such a breach of etiquette as to suggest to her mistress that the covers come off.

Early in 1941, just before the last chapters of Revelation were finished, Miss Leaman's sight gave out, and it was not easy to do the proofreading of the last sheets. Furthermore, it was not till later that she finally persuaded the Bible Societies to bind the separate books together, and sell the Phonetic Bible as a whole. Only when this was done did she feel her work was accomplished, and then it was too late to take the last evacuation ship to America. Soon after the Phonetic Bible was completed, came Pearl Harbor, and the Japanese took over the Shanghai concessions. For a year, however, the "belligerent aliens" (as the Japanese called those whose countries were at war with Japan) were given partial freedom to go around the city, but they could not return to America with those from the interior of China, who were sent on the first exchange ship in June, 1942.

In 1943, concentration camps were set up in a number of places, and the "belligerent aliens" were herded into these camps, but the aged and the sick were given another year of grace. So Miss Leaman did not receive the summons to go into camp until June, 1944. Though we tried to keep this fact from being known, so we could have opportunity in the allotted five days to make preparations, all of our friends heard about it; in the last few days while I tried desperately to have all the things packed which she needed, the guests poured in, forty and fifty a day, to express their sympathy. Miss Leaman never once suggested to anyone that she was too tired or too busy to talk to them.

The night before she left, it was one o'clock when the last guest departed, and she came into my room to have prayer. Little-Field, our servant, who was incredibly stupid but devoted to her, broke the key in the lock of my room, and another hour was spent trying to open the door.

Early the next morning guests began to arrive again, and her room was soon crowded. Late in the morning a relative and friend of mine, Mrs. Ling, came to call on me. She was a granddaughter of the Magistrate Ling who burned the British cargo of opium at Canton, in 1830, and so precipitated the Opium War. I had known her from childhood when we studied Buddhism together, and now she was a high-ranking Buddhist. While I often urged her to become a Christian, she tried to persuade me to return to Buddhism. She had a quilt over which hundreds of famous monks had read thousands of prayers, and which she kept to cover her in her coffin when she died, believing it would be efficacious for her in the next incarnation. She had several rosaries, all highly polished, that represented hundreds of thousands of her own prayers as well, so in Buddhist circles her virtue was supreme. When she entered my room, she noticed all the callers thronging Miss Leaman's room, so she said to me in surprise, "What is all this about?" I told her that Miss Leaman had to go to concentration camp that very noon, and she was shocked.

The day was unusually hot, and at noontime about fifty friends had gathered at the gate to say good-by to Miss Leaman She came smilingly to my room, and after prayer she said good-bye to me. After the noisy sounds of the rickshas and bicycles had ceased, Mrs. Ling kept on exclaiming, "Not to cry! Not to faint! Just a smile and a prayer! And she's going to prison! I never saw anything like it!" Then she stood up and turned to a Chinese friend from her native city of Foochow, a Miss Lake, who was with us and said, "What religion is this that gives such power to Miss Leaman and Miss Tsai, to enable them to smile under such conditions? Is it possible for me to believe Jesus just in my heart?"

Miss Lake answered, "You ask Miss Tsai about it."

I explained Romans 10: 9-10 to her: "If thou shalt confess with thy mouth the Lord Jesus, and believe in thine heart that God raised him from the dead, thou shalt be saved." Mrs. Ling said nothing at the time, but she seemed to be thinking it over. A couple of hours later other friends returned saying they had seen Miss Leaman enter a truck that was waiting to take the prisoners to camp. Hardly had these friends seated themselves when Mrs. Ling rose from her chair, and said: "Friends, if Jesus gives such power, I am going to give up Buddhism and accept Jesus as my Saviour." We hardly knew whether to take this announcement as a real confession or not, so said little in answer.

For a month I did not hear further from her, and in the meantime I had moved to another place, so I asked Miss Lake to call on Mrs. Ling and find out what she meant by her statement that day. Mrs. Ling said, "I have been trying all month to get the chief monk here in Shanghai to take my name off the Buddhist membership register, but he refuses to do so. We have been arguing back and forth all this time. As soon as this is done I am going to join the Christian Church."

Five months after Miss Leaman went to camp, Mrs. Ling was baptized, joined the church, and became a regular attendant. One day she fell and broke her leg, but instead of complaining, she said sweetly, "Maybe the Lord doesn't want so much activity, and would rather I spent the time in bed reading my Bible."

The Lincoln Road Concentration Camp where the Japanese imprisoned about two hundred and fifty of the sick and aged for fourteen months, was the last word in cruelty and deceit. The authorities had promised that there would be full medical care, but when the internees entered the gates of the compound, there was nothing but an empty yard, empty houses, and cruel soldiers. Some of the internees came on stretchers, some on crutches, some with open sores, some blind, some tottering on canes, some bowed with pain and suffering. They were assigned to dormitories without discrimination, the crippled to take care of the helpless, and the aged to take care of the bedridden, with only the bed and belongings they themselves had brought along. No medicine, no nurses, and no doctors! After three days three prisoners had died, and many more died later. In fact, they would all have died but for fifty able-bodied young people from the other camps, who volunteered to do the hard work and care for these pitiful cases. Different nationalities and religions, hardened sinners and gamblers, the profane and worldly, missionaries and scoffers, rich and poor, senile and children, were all herded together, and in the face of stark reality all masks were off. The selfish became more selfish, the unselfish literally killed themselves serving the others, the complainers complained, the profane swore, the gamblers gambled. But they pooled their strength for the common tasks they were required to do, and shared their medicines; doctors and nurses among them cared for the extreme cases. A diet of poor fish and rice sweepings from the floors of the warehouses started many cases of dysentery, and the swarming mosquitoes brought

The concentration camp

malaria. Miss Leaman, who had gamblers at her side playing cards much of the time, sat in her bed and peeled potatoes or cleaned the dirty rice. Of course, she shared some of the food I sent her and did what she could to help others, but she was taken sick with dysentery and malaria and lost forty pounds in fourteen months; her spinal curvature got so much worse she lost five inches in height.

As for me, I had almost no money, and our servants were all gone. Old-Salt died, Little-King went home to her only son who was dying, and Little-Field went to her mother-in-law. I rented an attic room in an old house in Brown-Family-Gardens. This I kept dark, since I could not bear the light, and as I could not walk, I learned to crawl on the floor whenever I had to move around. A Christian teacher next door got me a warm meal once a day when she came home at night, and the rest of the time I lived on hard biscuits and salted vegetables.

Many a time I said to the Lord, "The way is too narrow, I cannot pass through"; but He always answered, "Hide in Me and I will take you through." A friend saw my straits and found a unique way to help me. Some Buddhist nuns were also in great need, and one of them, a Mrs. Temple, agreed to make a Buddhist bargain with me. She promised to help me in this life, if I promised to help her in the next life. She faithfully carried out her part, helping me cook and keeping me company, and we became good friends. She and I sat in the dark room together, she counting her beads and I at my devotions. But she was willing to learn to sing hymns and read the Bible and pray with me. At the end of the year she and her daughter accepted Christ and He made them His children for eternity. So I was able to carry out my part of the bargain.

Some foreign friends had agreed to send Miss Leaman a package each month, but they soon came over and said they had no money to do it. I had only two small cans of fruit and some charcoal to send her that month. Nourishing food that would not spoil was almost unprocurable in Shanghai. As bank accounts were frozen, I sold everything I had and then borrowed money at exorbitant rates to get her wheat biscuits, dates, peanut butter, and other things. As for milk, it had to be bought at the black market and carried out of the shop one little tin at a time, carefully hidden in the clothing. It was Miss Lake and others who searched the shops to find things for me.

There was a general report going around that the Japanese were trying to starve the internees, and one morning I prayed for a five-pound tin of powdered milk to send Miss Leaman. A couple of hours later, our friend Spring-Hill sent me a telephone message saying, "Brother Willow, a rich merchant, had hoarded three five-pound tins of powdered milk, but when he went to church on Sunday the preacher said anyone who doesn't give his tenth or help God's needy children is stealing from the Lord. So Brother Willow asked me to take one of the tins over to you to send to Miss Leaman."

You can imagine how my burden was lifted and how my faith was strengthened! It was a Godsend, because I couldn't have gotten it otherwise at any price. These packages saved her life and those of others as well, but they and other expenses put me in debt three thousand U.S. dollars.

V-J day came at last, and Chinese friends flocked to the concentration camps with food and gifts. One man had hidden some coffee and canned milk, and now he opened a stall offering the internees all the coffee they could drink, free of charge. A woman brought roast chicken and baked potatoes for them. The Generalissimo and Madam Chiang gave each one a gift of money, and others found different ways to help them. Since I could not ride alone, a woman doctor went with me in a ricksha to see Miss Leaman. I was shocked to see how thin and short she had become. She told me she had been forbidden by the American authorities to leave the camp for one month and that she had to return to America as the doctors had examined her spine and told her she must avoid any lifting or jolting, for fear her spine would break.

When I returned home, I had a long string of callers who kept me up till two o'clock in the morning, and the next day there were many more. The result was that I woke on the morning of the third day shaking violently all over. The nun held me in her arms, but could not stop the trembling. I finally fell back on the bed unconscious and I remained in that state for four months. Miss Leaman heard of my illness, and happily a way was opened for her to come to see me. One of the American authorities took her to the city in his car, and she went to the American headquarters and asked permission to leave the camp, saying she could not stand going back to camp and that she had a bed and room near at hand. At the end of the day after much pleading the doctor gave her permission to stay for three weeks, and she walked slowly all the way to where I lived, a distance of about a mile. I did not recognize her when she came in, and called her "Big Brother." So here she was with a nearly broken spine, and I unconscious and burning with fever. War, inflation and prison camps had wrought havoc with people's money. She was penniless and I was three thousand dollars in debt. But another miracle happened. A friend whom I had met only twice, came in and asked for me. Miss Leaman explained my condition, so he threw a packet on her lap, saying, "I do not need this now. You use it and repay it when convenient."

"What is your name?" Miss Leaman asked. "Don't you want a receipt?"

"Miss Tsai knows me, and I trust her. She is a Christian." Saying this he left. Miss Leaman opened the package, and it contained three thousand one hundred dollars in U.S. money. Food, medicine, and servants could be procured once more, the debts gradually repaid. Where there was life there was hope!

Chapter 21

Just a Hunting Dog

MISS LEAMAN sent for our old servants, Little-King and Little-Field, and obtained for me all the medical care that was available. But for a year and a half I lingered on, unconscious much of the time, for the fever in my bones could not be stopped. Doctors now diagnosed the trouble as a combination of pellagra, dysentery and malignant malaria. The reason why malaria had not been discovered earlier was that the parasites were in the bones and in the brain cells, not in the blood stream. Dysentery and malaria are of many varieties and I had several kinds of them. Only one medicine of the many new remedies was able to stop the fever, and that was Aralen. The story of how we got it was another miracle.

One day Dr. Mandel came and examined me. He told Miss Leaman, "If it were anyone else but Miss Tsai I would say that within three days she would die. But I can't be sure, and our only hope is to find some way of stopping the fever." Miss Leaman told him that a Chinese friend, Mr. Grass-Head, was interested in my case. He had seen a bottle of a new medicine for malaria which had just been brought over from America, and had told the owner not to sell it until we had a chance to buy it. However, she did not know Mr. Grass-Head's address and had no way of finding him.

After the doctor left, it suddenly came to her that before she went into the concentration camp, Mr. Grass-Head had given her his address to take with her, in case she was repatriated; for safety's sake, lest the Japanese get hold of it, she had written it scattered through the leaves of her Bible. When she found it, she called him up and asked him to get the medicine right away and take it to Dr. Mandel. Then she called Dr. Mandel and asked him to stay at home till Mr. Grass-Head arrived. While Dr. Mandel was waiting, his wife showed him an article in a magazine describing a new remedy for malaria. As he was reading it, Mr. Grass-Head arrived and this proved to be the same medicine, Aralen, described in the article. As far as we know, it was the only bottle to be found in Shanghai. The Aralen soon brought down my fever; the crisis passed, I regained consciousness, and once more emerged out of the valley of the shadow of death. Though I improved, I have never been able to walk alone, or to bear the light. Until God performs another miracle, these chronic diseases can only be alleviated; there is no human cure as yet.

How Miss Leaman carried on during this time is another epic of faith and will power, for she had to spend most of the time in bed. Her attic room next to mine was furnished with only a bed, a table, and a few straight chairs, while reconstructed packing-cases and makeshift shelves lined the walls. Half of the room was curtained off for the servants and the stores of food. We had a second white Persian cat which invariably stayed beside her. On one side of the bed was a packing-case table on which were a telephone, bottles of medicine, and an electric hot plate; a typewriter, Phonetic Bible, address book, and other things were on the bed, or underneath, so she could reach them without getting up.

From morning until late at night she was busy. Our electric fixtures were invariably breaking down, and the electrician had to be coaxed every day to send his apprentice to tinker with them. The manservant would come in with the marketing and Miss Leaman had to check accounts with him, plan the meals, and dole out the supplies of rice and oil. Mr. Season, a refugee pastor and amateur carpenter, was often there hammering new shelves and packing-case furniture. The tenants downstairs and neighbors next door spent hours every day airing their problems with her. The hypos had to be sterilized, the doctor assisted, and medicines administered, and everyone fed at different times. The busy

This evangelistic Persian cat was called "White Queen." Miss Leaman often tied gospel tracts on her neck and shared the good news with those who encountered White Queen.

servants had to be caught one by one and encouraged to read the Bible and pray. Students of the phonetic were often working with her in the room. Besides, she had to answer the telephone, which was the only one in the house, and send for the person wanted.

All the while these other things were going on, there was a steady stream of callers coming and going; or they sat around, singly or in groups, waiting their turn. Each of these had to be entertained for a few minutes, or a few hours, as they chose; before they left she always prayed with them. Her guests included businessmen, refugees, missionaries from the interior, old Chinese friends, neighbors in trouble, newcomers to Shanghai, and teachers and students from all over China. She welcomed all and with every opportunity she explained the importance of the phonetic. At night when she had to do her writing, often the telephone would ring. Some lonely foreigner in Shanghai, who wanted a friendly chat, had mistaken her number in the telephone book. She faithfully told them God's way to satisfy lonely hearts and influenced several to go to church.

During my illness Sixth Brother came to see me frequently. All these years he and his family had persistently refused to accept the Lord, but now he was moved at my suffering. One day, unknown to me and on his own initiative, he called the members of our family together. They gathered, wondering what he had to say; but he soon told them. "I have an announcement to make to you," he said. "I have been to see Seventh Sister many times and wondered how she could endure all this suffering. Now I can see that she has been given some sustaining power and can only explain it as coming from God. So I have decided there must be a God after all. I have read the Bible and realize that I am a sinner. So here and now I want to tell you that I have accepted Christ as my Saviour, asked Him to forgive my sins, and promised to follow Him."

So the brother who tore up my Bible and persecuted me in the early days, at last confessed my Lord. In all, fifty-five of my relatives, adults and children, have become God's children and expressed their faith in Jesus. I have never been to college, or theological seminary, and I am not a Bible teacher; I have only been God's "hunting dog." I simply followed at the heels of my Master, and brought to His feet the quarry He sent me after.

Chapter 22

From Shanghai to Paradise

DURING 1947 and 1948 two Chinese doctors, Dr. and Mrs. Martial, lived near us at Brown-Family-Gardens, and they gave me injections and medical treatment. They were a young couple, both atheists, but they were skillful and kind, and I owe them a great deal. I am thankful to say that after two years, on Christmas Eve, the wife openly confessed the Lord Jesus, and her husband was later influenced to follow. They and many other friends urged us to leave Shanghai, because they said I could never get well in that malarial climate.

You can imagine how questions thundered in my mind like the rolling waves of the sea. How could we ever climb up and down that steep gangway to the steamer? How could we invalids travel halfway around the world? How could I ever stand the light and sounds again after being in a quiet, darkened room so long? Who was going to hand me the many things I needed during the day? How could I ever manage to enter into entirely different surroundings after being shut in for eighteen years with my loyal but ignorant country women who cared for me so patiently day after day and night after night, like a mother would care for a sick child? How could I suddenly leave my loved ones, friends, doctors, servants and also our phonetic work for the millions of illiterates of China? There seemed no end to such questions.

One day we thought we had better go to Hong Kong; the next we planned to go to Manila; the third day we decided to stay in Shanghai; and the fourth, fifth and sixth days we had other ideas! Early one morning, the words of Mrs. George Fitch, a missionary of great influence in Shanghai in the early years, brought rest to my soul:

"Say then to thy troubled soul, 'Rest thyself in His control, not just the part, but rest the whole.'"

Three nights in succession the Lord said to me, "Daughter, thy faith hath saved thee; go in peace." At last, about daybreak, I took up my telephone and told Miss Leaman that the Lord had told me to go to the United States, and that I was ready to go.

She answered, "I have applied for reservations, but there is no space on the ships. I have been told that there are three hundred on the waiting list." However, three or four hours after this, the morning mail brought a letter from the President Lines telling us they had a room for us, and that the "President Wilson" was to sail in a week! Dr. Martial left his other work for the day to take us to the ship, and two other friends, Dr. Thorngate and his son, carried me the whole length of the dock. Five more friends, and three weeping servants, accompanied us. All of them pushed and pulled and half carried us up the steep gangway, and took us to our quiet little cabin. So, on January 18, 1949, the "President Wilson" took us across the Pacific Ocean away from our dear old China. The Lord's provision all along the journey was wonderful. The stewardess and the room boy could not have been better. When the time came to go on deck, I did not dare lean on Miss Leaman, for fear of hurting her back; the Lord provided a friend just at the right moment.

On the third of February, long before sunrise, our boat moved slowly through the Golden Gate into the Bay of San Francisco. We were met by Miss Lorna Logan and Miss Tien-fu-Wu, and received many telegrams and airmail letters of welcome. There was a taxi strike on in San Francisco when we landed, but two private cars were loaned for our use. The next day Miss Logan and Miss Wu drove us across the lovely Bay bridge to Oakland, where a red cap with a wheel chair awaited us and took us to a little compartment on the transcontinental express to New York. Here the porter proved very kind and thoughtful. Because of unusually heavy snows, our train was delayed, and we spent four days and nights in our compartment. The delay disrupted our schedule and sister Lucy's as well, so the porter suggested that we telegraph for wheel chairs to meet us at Lancaster, Pennsylvania, our destination. Though it was four-thirty on a cold, dark winter morning when our train made a special stop at Lancaster, we found two men with wheel chairs waiting for us on the platform!

Our hearts beat fast as we drew near home. Nothing was ever more beautiful than the lights of home, and nothing warmer than the welcome that awaited us. The whole house was lighted, and sister Lucy and cousin Mary were standing at the door looking for us. It seemed as if I were transported to Heaven. I thought of the last Home-going, the wonderful lights up there, and the Father waiting for us with His welcome smiles, and my heart was thrilled. All I can now say is, "The Lord led us all the way from faraway Shanghai to Paradise (the name of the town where the Leaman home is located), to the beautiful old home belonging to

Leaman family's old house with more than two hundred years history brought people new life.

my godmother, Mary Leaman, her sister Lucy, and cousin Mary. I am deeply grateful that they have given me such a happy shelter and quiet security." And now from my home in Paradise I want to add a few lines to this story.

When we went away from Shanghai, we had to leave behind all the matrices, type, and paper-mache shells needed for reprinting the Phonetic Bible, and though various efforts have been made to have them shipped out, all have been futile. But for a providential encounter and a bit of foresight on Miss Leaman's part, there would now be no chance to restock the already depleted supply of Phonetic Bibles. But God, who sees the end from the beginning, provided for that emergency.

A short time before Pearl Harbor, the work of preparing the Phonetic Bible was completed, and the printer who had successfully bid for the job unexpectedly came to tell Miss Leaman that the presses were ready to begin printing. Of course she was delighted, but foresaw a disastrous eventuality. What if America should be drawn into war with Japan? Such a possibility could spell the ruin of this great task.

"Before you print the Bible," she said, "I think it would be a good idea to buy the best white paper you can procure in Shanghai, and run off ten sets using only one side of each sheet. We can keep those sets for lithographic reprints if we should lose our matrices and paper-mache shells."

"Oh, Miss Leaman," the printer exclaimed, "good paper is too expensive under these war conditions. We can't afford it. You couldn't get that done for less than three hundred American dollars!"

"God will provide the money," she said; "you do it."

So it came to pass that he brought her ten sets on fine white paper as soon as he could, and she cached them in different places—one in the Swiss Consulate, one in the Hong Kong and Shanghai Bank, one in the loft in a German friend's home. Soon after this came Pearl Harbor, so it was not till after the war was over and

On Oct. 8, 1949, Mary Leaman along with her sister Lucy, cousin Mary and Miss Tsai celebrated Mary Leaman's seventieth birthday in the Leaman house's backyard.
Lucy and Mary Leaman's cousin
Mary were both missionaries once to China.

she was released from concentration camp, that she could send for her cached Bibles. Only three sets were intact, and these sets we brought with us when we came to the United States.

Now there is a need for a new edition to teach the standard Pekinese to the many thousand overseas Chinese who speak Amoy or Cantonese and whose children know no Chinese at all. The American Bible Society wrote us that they have requests for the Phonetic Bible, but have none in stock; they asked if there is any way to make a reprint. You can imagine our joy and thankfulness to tell them of these sets and to urge them to print a new edition.

We have received encouraging news of the work of the Phonetic being carried on in Formosa as well. I quote from a letter written by Mrs. Twinem:

> My dear friends C.T. and M.L.,
>
> I am enclosing a book to show you that no prayers and no letters of entreaty are needed now for pushing the work of the phonetic on this island. It is used universally on street signs, newspapers, etc.
>
> Lovingly,
> M.F.T.

There is a laymen's movement going on among the Chinese over there called the Gospel Jacket Crusade. It started some years ago with a stuttering Christian who was burning with zeal for the Saviour. He wanted to witness for Christ, but he had difficulty. Determined not to be silenced, he found two pieces of cardboard on which he wrote in large characters, "Good works will not save you," and "Believe on the Lord Jesus and be saved." These he hung, one in front and one behind like a sandwich man and walked slowly from one street to another. First one person and then another came up to read the words and he was soon accompanied by a crowd of men, women, and children.

The interest aroused was so inspiring that soon other would-be witnesses followed his example, but they wrote verses on squares of white cloth which they sewed to their clothes. From city to city and town to town the movement spread; the white cloth squares were replaced by white sleeveless jackets, and the Christians started going together in bands, blowing trumpets and singing hymns. When they had collected a good crowd in some open space, they stopped and one of the number started to preach. As a result of this spontaneous Gospel Jacket Crusade, many Christians have found they can witness, and thousands of listeners have confessed their sins and accepted Christ.

Just as I thought my story was closed, I received a letter from my niece, Bright-Cloud, which brought me both grief and comfort. It told news of my nephew, Ping-Ping. As I read this I recalled the last time I had seen him. I was sick in Shanghai, and the doctor had said I might die at any time, and Ping-Ping had brought his bride to my bedside. He held my hand, and could only say in a choked voice, "Seventh Auntie." I was touched by his affection, and answered in a whisper, "Ping-Ping, whatever happens, trust in Jesus. He will comfort you and give you peace." The servants who accompanied them out later told me what they said as they left.

"Do you know Jesus?" Ping-Ping asked his bride.

"No," she answered; "this is the first time I ever heard the name. But Seventh Auntie must know Him very well since in her illness she could say, 'Whatever happens trust in Jesus. He will comfort you and give you peace'!" So the words in Bright-Cloud's letter that brought me comfort and grief were these:

> Ping-Ping has been killed, leaving his wife and little daughter. But his wife has found comfort and peace in Jesus and has joined the church.

I have indeed found peace out of pain, joy in suffering, light in darkness; after over twenty-years in bed, I can say it is worth while to pass through the valley of the shadow of death for the joy of knowing the Lord Jesus Christ.

I want to finish this testimony by quoting from a poem. This poem sums up the past, present, and future in words that express my own thankfulness and trust.

> O fathomless mercy! O infinite grace!
> With humble thanksgiving the road I retrace.
> Thou never hast failed me, my Strength and my Stay!
> To whom should I turn for the rest of the way?
> Through dangers, through darkness,
>   by day and by night,
> Thou ever hast guided and guided aright:
> In Thee have I trusted and peacefully lay
> My hand in Thy hand for the rest of the way.
> Thy cross all my refuge, Thy blood all my plea,
> None other I need, blessed Jesus but Thee!
> Fear not the shadows at close of life's day,
> For Thou wilt go with me the rest of the way.

CHRISTIANA TSAI

II

蔡蘇娟

Trapped by illness in a darkened bedroom, Christiana Tsai, the "Queen of the Dark Chamber" has an incredible impact worldwide.

"To Christiana Tsai He entrusted the ministry of serving Him with a bed for a pulpit, a darkened room for a 'workshop.'"

—RUTH BELL GRAHAM in the Foreword

Contents

Foreword

This is one of the most fascinating and challenging autobiographies I have ever read. It is the life story of a Chinese lady of distinction, a devout Buddist whose father was governor general during the late Manchu dynasty of the province of Kiang-su, where my parents later served as medical missionaries and where I was born and raised.

Christiana Tsai tells how she came to trust, love, and serve the living God through His Son, and how she was used, despite a lifetime of incredible suffering, to win thousands to Him.

I had the privilege of reading *The Queen of the Dark Chamber* and later meeting this living legend in her dark room, aware of an unseen Presence with us there.

It is that Presence—the Lord Jesus Himself—that this book is all about; how He in His wisdom and love selects some He can trust with an unusual ministry.

To Christiana Tsai He entrusted the ministry of serving Him with a bed for a pulpit, a darkened room for a workshop, years of incredible suffering as her constant companion, and hundreds of people won to the Lord Jesus as her reward.

Read it and worship Him!

RUTH BELL GRAHAM

THE GROWING DARKNESS CLOSES IN

Ruth Bell Graham

The growing darkness closes in
like some thick fog,
engulfing me—
a creeping horror—
'till I learned,
"The darkness hideth not from Thee."

"The earth was without form
and void."
Upon the deep
such darkness lay:
O Light, Who first created light,
do Thou the same
today!

As in a darkened room
one knows—
knows without sight—
another there,
so, in the darkness,
sure I knew
Thy presence
and the cold despair,
formless and chaotic, merged
to a soft glory;
As a child,

terrified by dark,
lies quiet
within his mother's arms,
no wild
fears shall torment
my weakness now,
The dark—the dark—
surrounds me still.
But so dost Thou!

The future is a blank without a view.
That which I wanted most, You have denied;
I cannot understand (and I have tried);
There's nothing I can do but wait on You.

Earth offered much, and I had lingered long
outside her lighted windows, wistful grown—
till at my side I heard a voice—Your own.
Lord, how could I resist a love so strong?

Take all away. I am content to know
such love is mine—for life is all too brief
to grieve for pleasures bringing only grief;
give me but You; it is enough just so.

Enough—and more! Such love in You keeps growing—
in You I find my deepest joy complete,
all longing satisfied, and pain made sweet;
in You my cup is filled to overflowing.

Preface

When I wrote my first book, *Queen of the Dark Chamber*, published in 1953, I was able to spend a year in comparative quiet concentrating on nothing else. I weighed and prayed over every line. After the book was published, a flood of visitors poured into our home: military officers from Taiwan, Chinese seamen, students, internationals, American women's missionary societies, church groups, and Sunday school children.

Jesus Christ, my Saviour and Lord, has continued to be the light of my dark chamber, the dimly lit bedroom in which I have spent more than forty-seven years. What has happened since I arrived in America in 1949 has been a continuing drama directed by the Lord. The reasons I am bedridden in a dark room and what has happened there and beyond is my story.

May God receive all the glory for what He has done in my dark chamber. My unceasing prayer is that He will always keep me humble. If the day ever comes when I am more interested in exalting myself than in exalting my adorable Lord Jesus Christ, God will surely put me aside. He has said, "My glory will I not give to another" (Isaiah 42:8).

It has been my privilege through the years to have met many friends in the Lord. They have contributed most helpful thoughts and advice to enable me to finish this sequel. It would not be fair to acknowledge one and omit others, so I want to express deep thanks and appreciation to all those who had a share.

Christiana Tsai

Acknowledgements

I praise the Lord for Christian friends who have helped me write this book, which is truly a cooperative effort. Initially, I was helped by Ellen L. Drummond, an old friend from China, who helped me to write *Queen of the Dark Chamber*.

Later, I received the able assistance of Leona Choy, who spent many hours piecing together material out of my various speeches to visiting groups, as well as information growing out of our discussions, into a unified manuscript.

I am also grateful for the help of Jerry Jenkins, managing editor of *Moody Monthly*, who prepared the final draft.

Finally, I would like to recognize the generous help of my three co-workers, Susanna Eshleman, Grace Ng, and Frances Stoltzfus, who have been with me more than twenty years.

Introduction

My job was simply to shape up an existing manuscript, and edit and rewrite as necessary. It probably could have been done without my meeting the queen, Christiana, but what a privilege missed!

Moody Press thought it would give me added insight and a feel for the woman and her dark chamber. I wasn't quite sure what to expect. How bizarre, to think of a tiny Chinese woman, born into wealth in 1890, only to become a Christian at a girls' mission school, strike a lifelong friendship with the principal, serve the cause of Christ with her friend until they were forty and fifty years old, respectively, traveling throughout China and the United States, speaking, and writing.

And when a ravaging, mysterious illness (which took sixteen years to diagnose) relegated Christiana to bed in a dark room in 1931, it affected neither her nor her friend China Mary's ministries, nor their friendship, which lasted until Mary's death in 1972.

So here was a woman who had fled China for the United States in 1949, the year I was born. She was sixty then and had already been bedridden for nearly two decades. Four years later her book, *Queen of the Dark Chamber*, would be printed for the first of thirty-six times by Moody Press, enjoying a worldwide readership in dozens of languages.

Did the queen truly have material for another book, or would there be too little to write about after being in bed so long? Could the last twenty-four or so years be as exciting and interesting as growing up in China, converting from Buddhism, and enjoying a fruitful, mobile ministry?

As it turns out, of course, the story of a woman who continues to engage in outreach, even from her darkened chamber in Pennsylvania, is a mind-boggler. From this little room in the huge old house emanates prayer, letter writing, and personal witnessing unparalleled by most who can walk.

The old Leaman home, left to Christiana by her lifelong friend, Mary (the last of the Leaman sisters), is a gigantic structure in Paradise, Pennsylvania. Christiana's small room is on one end of the house, right off the dining room. As you enter, you see a Chinese light fixture which brightly illuminates one end of the room. A black kerchief blocks the light from Christiana's view. The shades are pulled. Two other small lamps are similarly draped to allow light on one end of the chamber, keeping the other end almost totally dark.

The little woman in the bed sits regally with back straight, shoulders square. Even in her dark chamber she wears the blackest sunglasses, old-fashioned with perfectly round lenses. The colorful Chinese lamp is a stark contrast to the dark bedspread, Christiana's black jacket, and the dim light. Her face is almost always brightened by a smile, and when she lifts her glasses to read with a magnifying glass, her smooth, full face evidences a soft beauty she has always called "plain."

She claims to be nervous about meeting yet another guest, though she has entertained hundreds and hundreds. And she works hard at breaking down the barrier caused by the strange scene of the Chinese queen in the big bed in the dark room in the big house.

To a stranger who knew nothing about this saint, the entire atmosphere could be frightening. It's a trip into the past. The rest of the house is filled with antiques, many of them much more than two hundred years old. The food is prepared from recipes that are either early Chinese or very early American. A guest is treated like a weary traveler and is made the center of attention—from a bowl and a pitcher of water (along with fruit and a box of crackers) waiting in his room, to Susanna and Grace (two helpers Christiana calls her co-workers) bustling in the kitchen and making sure he eats all he wants and takes more than he can eat.

Susanna is a quiet, matronly, at-ease American woman who calmly and quickly goes about her chores. Grace is a delightful Chinese woman who is constantly checking to make sure everything is just right.

Nothing in the house is new. It seems as if the world whizzes by outside this old home, and you leave not caring if you ever catch up with it again.

And the memory of the queen and the dark chamber is not of the darkness but of the queen and her Lord.

JERRY JENKINS

Chapter 1

Bird of Paradise

The news spread like a prairie fire throughout the Pennsylvania countryside. "Miss Leaman brought back a Chinese to live with her!"

Indeed, when I came from the great, flowery kingdom of China to live in Paradise, Pennsylvania, I felt as if I were on display like the turkey I had bought in Shanghai many years before. Turkeys were rare in China. I heard that for some strange reason Americans were fond of eating them when they celebrated their Thanksgiving festival. I went to great lengths to purchase one as a special gift for my dear missionary friends, the Leaman family. I dragged my precious cargo in a cage on the train to Nanking. Fellow passengers nearly overwhelmed me to see and touch the strange bird. "What does it eat?" I was embarrassed to admit that I had no idea. Unfortunately, someone fed it malted milk, and it died before it could be properly prepared for the Leamans' extravagant dinner!

I became the strange bird of Paradise in my comfortable bedroom in the ancestral Leaman home. It was through the kindness and generosity of my lifelong friend and missionary co-laborer, Miss Mary Leaman, that I had arrived. Having been bedridden for nineteen years already, I could not escape. I learned how my American missionary friends must have felt when we had gone together on evangelistic trips to the China countryside. People were inquisitive about their white skin, blue eyes, and golden hair. Because I was often the only Chinese accompanying them, village women would unceremoniously push aside my dress to examine my skin to see if it were really the same color as their own. "Are you pure Chinese?" they would ask.

I dearly loved my new friends in America, but we had a lot to learn about each other and from each other. They would shyly file into my room to see the "Chinese girl," who was already nearly sixty years old! They were often ill at ease and at a loss to start a conversation. Finally came the inevitable question: "What do Chinese eat?"

I tried to be both polite and accurate. My childhood had been luxurious, with dozens of servants bowing and waiting on us to attend to our every wish. "In my province in the morning we had steaming bowls of soft rice porridge, biscuits, cold fish, and several vegetables. At noon we had soup, three vegetables, three meats, and rice. At 4 p.m. we always had tea and fancy cakes. Between meals we had many kinds of fruit and nuts. For dinner—"

Before I could add a detailed description of our main meal with its countless varieties and delicacies from far and near, eyes were wide in astonishment. "Oh! We thought Chinese were poor, ate only rice, lived in huts, had long fingernails, queues, and bound feet!"

Yes, America was to be a far different life than the one to which I was born behind the imperial walls of a wealthy home in China during the last days of the Manchu Dynasty. In His mercy, God did not permit me to see from the beginning that I would spend more than half of my lifetime as if in a goldfish bowl, continually on exhibition and seldom alone. I was to be helpless to the extent that others would have to attend to all my needs. From my childhood, such exposure and lack of privacy had been my worst dislike and deepest fear.

During my youth in China, the favorite sport of my many brothers was to tease their "plain" sister. They laughed at me because I was so different from my twenty-three other brothers and sisters. Most of them favored either the handsomeness of my father or the beauty of my mother, who was so charming that her relatives all called her the "Peking Beauty." "You are not our sister!" they taunted me. "You must have been born in a hut!"

This made me unbearably shy and sensitive. I would run to my nursemaid and sob, "Why didn't I get just a little of my mother's beauty?" I became afraid of strangers. I was such an introvert that in the excitement and bustling crowds of public occasions like the dragon festival, I would hide behind my nurse's apron and peek out at people. My throat seemed locked when I had to eat in front of people.

I would hide behind my nurse's apron and peek out at people.

Chinese daughters of the wealthy studied within the family courtyards under the same tutors as their brothers until the age of ten. Then they were separated with lady tutors for the feminine arts. This gave me some relief from my brothers' harassment, but it resumed each time we gathered for New Year celebrations at the big pavilion in our garden.

There, out of earshot of our parents, we all did what we chose. Our father, understandably, disliked having his solitude disturbed by the boisterous ways of his two dozen children. We were allowed eighteen wonderful days to celebrate the new year, act out our own dramas, feast to our hearts' content, consume all manner of Chinese New Year goodies, gamble, and play our musical instruments. My brothers would run around me, clanging cymbals in my face and jeering, "See, see, your face is flat and shiny like the cymbals !" They pointed at a pan of water. "Round as a basin, too!"

I fussed and lamented before my mirror, trying to create a hair style to cover more of my face. I became obsessed with the desire to be alone.

As I grew older, I majored in classic Chinese. I loved to write Chinese characters. With brush in hand, I forgot all else. I devoured every book I could lay my hands on. "Books are much better friends than people!" I rationalized. They opened the doors of the outside world to me,

I had just three desires. Surely, I thought, they were not too much to ask of life. When I dreamed of the future, my wishes focused on a quiet life-style.

First, I felt I would be content if I had a fine study with an elegant desk, a comfortable chair, a good light, and solitude for open-ended reading and writing. But more than half of my life has been spent lying and sitting in a bed, unable to take care of my simplest needs. My blankets are my desk. Because my illness impaired my vision, I must use a magnifying glass, and I can read very little and with difficulty. The lamps and windows are covered with dark cloth to shield my light-sensitive eyes. For nearly fifty years I have been the "Queen of the Dark Chamber."

The second of my life desires was to have a handsome piano, not for performance but for expressing the melodies that surged in my heart since my conversion from Buddhism to Christianity. Jesus Christ brought joy and harmony to my life. I became proficient in playing the seven-stringed Chinese instrument, Tsih-Hsien-Ching, and studied piano under Western teachers. But for nearly a half century my infirmity has prevented me from touching any instrument or hearing loud noises. Sounds that others scarcely hear pierce my eardrums like a thousand gongs. The unceasing roar of heavy trucks on the highway outside my bedroom window thunders like a waterfall. When I first came to America, many a night I awoke taut with pain to find my fingers wedged inside my ears, thinking fretfully, *If they have to drive so fast, why can't they do it quietly and in the daytime?* When I am weak with my recurring malaria attacks, I seem to hear hundreds of spinning wheels whirring in my head.

My third desire was to possess a fine library of books and files, neatly organized and available for my every taste and convenience. My dearly treasured Chinese classics and Western favorites were lost as a result of my escape from China and much traveling. My few remaining important books, letters, and files are tied with identifying ribbons under my bed and stuffed in cheap cardboard boxes. Properly brought up and fastidious, I would never have allowed anything to be stored under my bed in my early years! Now I must bend over and search under my bed for what I want, or forever trouble others to do so.

I had other simple desires—to stroll in cool forests, run in fields, wade in sparkling streams, climb mountains, and explore countries I had read about while behind my courtyard walls. When I first became ill, before my fortieth year and in the prime of my active life and service for the Lord, my doctor had warned, "You might even be in bed as long as three weeks!" I had sobbed uncontrollably.

"How can I endure such a long illness? Nearly a month!" It now has been nearly half a century.

Is God cruel because He has withheld almost all my early desires? No! "No good thing will He withhold from them that walk uprightly" (Psalm 84:11). Do I call the Lord unjust? No! "Shall the clay say to him that fashioneth it, What makest thou?" (Isaiah 45:9). Throughout my many years of illness, I have never, never, never dared to ask God why He allowed me to suffer for so long. I only ask Him what He wants me to do. With the apostle Paul, I testify, "For I have learned, in whatsoever state I am, therewith to be content" (Philippians 4:11). I believe that all that has happened to me was God's best choice for me. It has been far more satisfying than my three desires. I have no disappointment in His appointment.

When I finished *Queen of the Dark Chamber* in 1953, I thought certainly that my life's story was completed. Surely the next page would contain the longed-for words, "The End." Then I would be lifted out of my dark chamber to triumphantly greet my King of light, Jesus Christ, face to face in heaven. The poem that I quoted on the last page of my book was "The Rest of the Way," because I doubted that there was really much left for me.

My Lord planned otherwise. There was a sequel about to take place with a new setting: Paradise, Pennsylvania.

Often in my weakness I do not even know what lines to speak to meet the deep spiritual needs of those whom God has brought from all over the world to this out-of-the-way place. But over and over again, the Holy Spirit has been the never-failing Prompter who supplies the lines and speaks through this weak channel. Jesus Christ, the light of my dark chamber and the light of the world, continues to shine brilliantly into the hearts of men and women as they have come to my bedside through the years. All the glory belongs to Him.

Chapter 2

Raised in Luxury

To awaken to a chorus of birds outside the latticework of my window in Nanking, China, was a childhood delight. Our nurses would prop up the youngest group of my twenty-three brothers and sisters like a row of hungry swallows. They tucked our gaily colored silken quilts around us and brought in boxes of delicious English cookies. Some were shaped like fans, others like vases and butterflies; they had been given to Father by British businessmen who sought his political or economic favor.

We did not fully realize how noted Father was until gradually we observed the homage and respect paid him. He came from an old Confucian family that for generations had produced scholars who took China's ancient civil service examinations. Father held a number of important offices under the Manchu Dynasty, among them the governorship of Kiangsu Province. We children were born in the lap of luxury, prosperity, and fame. But within we were spiritually dark.

We were more impressed with the gifts lavished upon Father by business associates than with his position. He received cases of imported soda pop, a rare and expensive product in those days. But no one dared drink this foreign potion—who knew but that one might turn into a foreign devil? Our servants were instructed to pour the contents down the gutters and reuse the bottles for soy sauce and sesame oil. Far more elaborate gifts, which I now wish we had appreciated, were beautiful, shiny coal-burning stoves, complete with pipes and connections. Literally dozens of these expensive items were given to us, and the servants just stored them in a corner of our garden. We played our imaginative games around them while they became weatherbeaten and rusted.

We certainly did not enjoy any pal relationship as children do with their "daddies" in the Western world. We stood in awe of Father, bowing to him in reverence: We were allowed to eat with him only at New Year's.

One of our favorite events was the dragon procession with its many floats. All the officials sat on a big reviewing stand. Father would be dressed in a splendid gown. (Particular costumes were worn only at certain celebrations each year and then carefully put away.) For this event, trays heaped with silver medals were stacked before him on the platform. As governor, he awarded the performers.

Our excitement mounted as the sound of drums, cymbals, and many other instuments approached from a distance. A long silk dragon, maneuvered from the inside by soldiers, would writhe and wind and leap around, eventually dividing and forming four Chinese characters: *Tien Hsia Tai Ping*, meaning "world peace." Skyrockets and fireworks, which we watched from the garden at night, were set off for the occasion. I was always afraid of such commotion and hung close to my nurse.

Father was not a Christian but was friendly to the foreigners. As acting governor when the antiforeign Boxer Rebellion broke out in 1900, he received the Empress Dowager's edict ordering him to kill all foreigners. At the risk of his own life, he altered the documents to read "protect" instead of "kill" all foreigners, saving the lives of Westerners in our province. As things turned out, the empress never learned of this change, for she herself soon had to flee from an allied army that marched on Peking to release foreigners, inside the besieged city.

As children, we were not much aware of the world beyond our high walls. We lived in spacious separate apartments. When my brothers married, they and their brides moved into their own apartments with us. Eventually there were about one hundred people within our walls. We would not have dreamed of mingling with those of lower rank.

But isolation did not insulate us from sin. We knew the difference between right and wrong. We often deliberately did wrong. I remember as a child sneaking nuts, lichees, and sweets right off the supposedly sacred altars of our ancestors at Chinese New Year. We children took turns being on watch while the transgressions went on.

I was closer to my nurse than to my mother, and sometimes while Mother was occupied gambling, I would steal candles from her apartment and give them to my nurse, who sent them to her home in the country. Piled in a certain cupboard were strings of one hundred Chinese coins. Time and again I stole a string of cash for my nurse.

Most of my family were addicted to opium smoking. It began when Western powers seeking to trade with China insisted on paying for fragrant Chinese tea with Indian opium. The Chinese government justifiably resisted such immoral enslavement of its people, but Chinese merchants were not so conscientious.

Each member of our family was given his or her own beautiful silver-engraved pipe, which the servants kept clean and polished for his drug habit. When opium is smoked, pain goes, strength decreases, and a lazy, withdrawn feeling sets in. Appetite is diminished. (I often heard the warning that China would surely be overrun and divided by her enemies because opium smokers would not have the motivation to resist.)

Seeing the rest of my family indulge, and being aware of the negative results, I resisted opium even before I became a Christian. I often had stomach pains, but I determined that I would not smoke opium to get relief. Once when the pain was particularly bad, I was persuaded to take just a little ball of it. The relief was so instant and pleasurable that it scared me. I was strongly tempted to continue, but when the pain came back, I refused to become a servant to any drug. I would rather die.

I diligently practiced the prayers, burning of incense, and

reading of Buddhist classics. Often one of my sisters-in-law and I went to worship in the Ling-yin Buddhist temple on a hill in Hangchow. A long flight of steps led to the top, and we tried to bow on every third step. I took Buddhism seriously, even having prepared to enter a convent. And I was very zealous to fulfill all religious requirements, but my physical endurance was small. We young girls, not seeing anyone around to check on us, waited until we nearly reached the top before we started our bowing!

Monks often came to our home to do sorcery. All our family believed in their powers. It was this belief in fortunetellers that changed the course of my life regarding marriage.

When I was only a child, the year, month, day, and hour of my birth were matched with those of a boy child whose family was seeking a favorable arranged marriage for their son when we would both come of age. My statistics were interpreted as being either extremely good or extremely bad. His family decided not to take the risk! In His marvelous plan for the ages and for each of our lives, our heavenly Father watches over even the superstitious actions of men, guarding us from misfortune until we come into His fold.

By the time I was sixteen, my spirit longed to fly away and learn new things in new places. I had long since exhausted the books and scrolls my tutors considered proper for females to study. A school for girls had been opened nearby by some missionaries named Leaman, and I gave my father no peace until he allowed me to study there. My nickname was "Too Many," based on the comment of my father at my birth. (His house was already overflowing with children!)

Even so, I was a faithful daughter and beloved of my par-ents. But my father did not consider his fondness for me reason enough to transgress the ancient tradition against advanced education for girl children. I continued to plead with him. Finally relenting, he warned, "But beware not to eat Christianity!"

"I promise, Father!" I cried happily.

Chapter 3

"Eating" Christianity

It was in part the vision of American missionary Charles Leaman's wife, Lucy, that brought the Ming Deh Girls' School in Nanking into being. She realized the strategic potential of a Christian girls' school when as a young woman she served on the faculty of True Light Girls' School in south China. Girls in China rarely learned to read, nor were they interested in doing so. Mrs. Leaman advertised for months, with all manner of enticements to obtain pupils, but none responded. The first pupil had to be paid to study!

No one would have dared to dream that during the lifetime of the Leaman daughters the school would have an enrollment of sixteen hundred students. Ming Deh was the pioneer girls' school and forerunner of dozens of such schools right in Nanking.

You can imagine the commotion when I arrived at the school in 1906 in my fashionable clothes and sedan chair. "I want to register so I can learn to speak English and play the piano," I announced. I had an air of authority befitting my station in life, but it was so out of place in that peaceful mission compound.

That was when I met Miss Leaman, the daughter of Charles and Lucy Leaman. She was tall and thin, dressed in simple Chinese clothes. I was a sixteen-year-old girl. She was the twenty-six-year-old principal. Her quiet manner and voice conveyed to me the inner beauty, peace, and strength that I had sought but missed all my young life. In the mysterious plan of God, Miss Leaman and I were destined to live and work together for the Lord for fifty-eight years.

Upon learning who I was, Miss Leaman dared not accept me

as a boarder to share the "coarse food and household chores." I was to be a day student, but only if my mother would come in person to give permission for me to enroll. Although such action was beneath Mother's station and dignity, she reluctantly agreed and I was accepted.

Mingling with common girls in a classroom was a new lifestyle to me, but I was eager to break through to the outside world. I questioned my classmates during my first exposure to chapel service. I was bewildered. "You say we are worshiping, but I do not see any idols or gods. There is just a plain platform with a man speaking from it." I did not understand the strange theological vocabulary. My mind wandered. I started to chatter with the other girls, distracting them. Lucy Leaman quietly cornered me and explained that we were worshiping a God that we could not see. Often bored, I would slip a detective novel into my pocket to read during the sermon.

But that thirst for knowledge was the gateway to my salvation. Despite my lifelong training and the rash promise to my father, I began to attend a Bible class with the other girls, merely as another opportunity to improve my English. "I can quit anytime I want to," I reasoned.

Then one day in chapel I heard the famous American preacher S.D. Gordon speak about "Jesus, the light of the world." My spiritually blind, rebellious eyes were opened. I saw my sinful condition before the Lord and His provision for my salvation through the cross of Christ. I fled to my room and yielded my heart to Him. Peace and joy and light flooded my soul.

Though my father had already passed away, the rest of my Buddhist family threatened me, mocked me, and made me a prisoner in my own home. But my Lord never failed me. Eventually He answered my prayers to melt their hard hearts.

One day while strolling in my private garden, I thought of how peaceful and pleasant life was in the security of our palatial home. I was walking slowly up the steps to my private tower when my attention was drawn to the window. Was that smoke billowing up over the horizon of Nanking in the distance? My Bible lay open to Psalm 91:2: "He is my refuge and my fortress: my God; in him will I trust."

I had just committed this psalm to memory, but now its almost staggering promises seemed to leap out of the pages. Was God preparing me for something? My eyes followed the suspicious line of rapidly spreading smoke. It had turned from gray to an ominous black. Red flashes leaped into the sky behind it. My heart began to pound. Would Nanking be next in the unceasing fight between the warlords of China?

Many, including some members of our family, had already fled to the Shanghai Concession for safety. But several of my brothers and their families didn't want to leave our comfortable, luxurious mansion. My mother and I had also stayed, taking our chances, hoping that the worst would not happen. I looked over the treetops of my garden. A heavy, strange stillness hung in the air.

The bombardment of guns in the distance shook my glassed-in tower. My servant girl pounded on my door. "Seventh mistress, hurry! Soldiers are coming! The South City has fallen to the bad ones, and bullets are flying everywhere!" She fell to her knees. "They are looting *our* street!"

I could hear the crack of rifle fire from the streets and nearby houses. A manservant ran up my stairs and his words tumbled out: "They are searching for the master and mistress of each house! They hang them and beat them, doing terrible things until they give them everything. You must flee!"

A third servant joined them, sobbing, "They are coming toward our house now! They are shooting at our iron gates!"

My brothers and the rest of the family raced to a secret door of escape. What did it matter now how beautiful, ornate, or valuable our possessions were? Children screamed, women wailed, and the men tried to keep them quiet so the soldiers would not discover us.

Soldiers are coming!

Chapter 4

Brush with Death

I pulled my mother from her quarters as she struggled along on bound feet. She was not used to walking rapidly nor far, and in her panic she twisted her ankle. "Daughter, I can't go on—I'm hurt! I will only slow everyone down, and then all will be caught and murdered. Go on without me. I am old and useless—go!"

"No, Mother. I love you. You are precious to me—and to God!" I prayed under my breath, "O dear Lord, I claim all those promises I have just been reading. Protect us all. You promised that 'it shall not come nigh thee'(Psalm 91:7b). Dear Jesus! Save us from this destruction!"

The rest of the family had escaped over the wall, and I was left alone with Mother in my arms. She cringed with pain, and our dog, Proper, followed us, whimpering and barking. I commanded, "Proper, stay!" and he obeyed. Had he followed us, he might have revealed our hiding place. The rifle fire was getting closer. I heard swords clang against our iron gate and feet kicking the massive doors.

The Lord gave me sudden wisdom and unusual strength. Though slightly built, I hoisted Mother to my back and staggered toward the rear entrance to the servants' quarters. By now bullets were flying over our heads. Mother was in a near faint and like a dead weight. I could hear the soldiers laughing and ranting while the servants tried to appease them with our best food and wine.

I kicked open the servants' quarters back door and frantically looked for a dark place under the stairway. I tried to quiet my mother's sobbing so that we would not be discovered. I, who had always been so fastidious, unable to stand the least dirt or discomfort, found myself crouched beneath the stairs in wet muck. Years of accumulated spider webs hung from the musty beams, and spiders of all descriptions brushed against my hair and cheeks. I clapped my hand over my own mouth to keep from crying out. The moldy odor filled our lungs with the chill of a tomb. I sat in the mud and held my mother on my lap. "Mother, Mother," I whispered. "Jesus will help us. He promised!"

Though a new Christian, I realized that the Lord had placed me in a very responsible position as His witness. He would not forsake me. My teeth chattered as I prayed, "Lord, help me to be a good testimony for You. I am no use dead!"

Having had their fill of wine, the soldiers grew bolder in their search for the rest of the family and their treasures. They demanded that the servants reveal the hiding places. Several staggered across to the servants' quarters in the very courtyard where we hid. Mercifully, my mother had fallen into a dazed stupor and was not aware of our brush with death. As the heavy footsteps came within inches of us, I held my breath and prayed more desperately, again pleading the promises from the precious psalm which God had given me that morning:

"For he shall give his angels charge over thee, to keep thee in all thy ways" (Psalm 91:11).

The heavy boots moved on. Although we were under the stairway for only a few hours, it seemed like an eternity.

When a siren pierced the air, my mother roused and cried out, not remembering where she was, and clinging to me with such fierceness that her fingernails dug into my arm. The soldiers cursed and stamped their feet, calling to one another gruffly that it was time to return to their barracks.

Before long, the noise of the firing faded into the distance, and silence settled over the whole courtyard. We remained huddled under the stairway until the servants resumed their normal work and tried to straighten out the chaos left by the soldiers.

Finally, I stretched my legs, numb from the dampness and

cramped position. Mother's ankle was swollen to nearly twice its normal size, and she cried out as I tried to drag her into the light. I hoisted her to my back again, trembling with weakness. My legs felt like rubber as I staggered back over the winding paths to the main house.

My brothers and sisters also had crawled out of their hiding places after the siren had drawn away the soldiers. They were grief-stricken, supposing the worst, expecting to see Mother hanging mutilated by the soldiers. When they caught sight of me with her on my back, they ran crying and throwing themselves on the ground before us with relief and joy.

"It is God who has saved us," I whispered faintly. "Hurry and wipe the cobwebs from Mother's face, change her clothes, and soak her foot."

As I sat huddled in blankets with my servant trying to rub circulation back into my feet, my brothers came to question me further about my saying the Lord had delivered us. I sensed their embarrassment and said, "Brothers, it is the only true, living God who can deliver us in trouble. Idols and incense are no use in the face of disaster. They cannot save us. They cannot give us peace." I saw an unusual gentleness and the first flicker of faith in their eyes. I knew it would not be long before the Good Shepherd would bring more of my family into His fold.

Because of the continued danger and looting, we were advised to flee Nanking and go to Shanghai. "We will keep house for you," promised one faithful old servant and his wife. What to take and what to leave behind? Every refugee faces such painful decisions—that is, if he has enough time before his flight. He never knows whether he will ever return. Because my own treasure was in heaven, I did not face the heartbreaking decisions my family had to make.

As we began to leave, my brothers said, "Sister, you look too much like a wealthy person. You will be robbed and beaten for your valuables, whether you are carrying any or not. Why don't you disguise yourself?"

I borrowed my servant's rough jacket, padded trousers, and simple cloth shoes. "Oh, mistress, your face is too light and your hair too stylish," said my servant girl. While I fastened back my hair into a bun, she ran out for a pan of water in which she had soaked walnut shells. "Here, rub this solution on your face. It will make you look darker."

As we stepped outside our gates, it was as if we had fallen into a roaring sea of people who swept us along. Shouting, crying, pushing one another, we were all on an equal level. We were just part of a human mob desperately fighting to escape for our lives. Servants accompanied us, some struggling under heavy bundles of our valuables, others pushing wheelbarrows of provisions.

I said to one of my brothers, "You are strong; you go ahead of us and push. I will carry Mother again."

Arriving at the train platform, we pushed ourselves through the narrow door with hundreds of other frantic people. People were jammed together on the train with scarcely breathing space between them. Baggage filled the aisles, and the odor of human sweat hung heavy in the air.

"Please," I begged two women already squeezed into a single seat, "let my injured mother have a little corner of your seat. She can't stand up." In kindness and pity, they huddled still closer together, and I dropped my mother into a safe corner. Mother still had her bad opium habit and was in such pain that I was forced to give her pills at intervals.

Although I was disguised as a poor servant so that even my mother was startled, in my heart I was still rejoicing that I was the "child of a King"—Jesus was my Lord. It must have shown through. A gentleman came over to me, staring curiously. "Do you believe in Jesus?" he asked.

"Yes, I do!" I replied without hesitation. Mother looked at me, questioning, "Tell me, daughter, what kind of a sign did you make that a stranger would know that you belong to Jesus?" I just smiled.

Chapter 5

Miss Mary Leaman

Joy and relief overwhelmed us when we finally pulled to a jerking halt in the Shanghai station. "Hurry, hire rickshaws," ordered my brothers, and within minutes we were on our way to my fifth sister's house. Mother was still on my lap, and the servants were still piled high with baggage. It was nearly midnight when our servants knocked at the gate. We had had no way to notify my sister of our coming.

We had caught a glimpse of a newspaper when we alighted from the train. It declared in bold headlines that the city we had just left was burned to ashes, and all the people had been killed. Now from inside we could hear wailing and cries of mourning. The odor of incense floated to our nostrils on the damp night air. Then it dawned on us—it was probably for us they were mourning! They were burning paper money and other paper replicas so that we might have provisions for our journey into death!

The servant who came to open the gate turned white when she saw us. She ran away without opening the gate, and we were left shivering in the night, knocking.

My fifth sister was astonished when she saw us. She could not contain herself for joy! I committed Mother into her care; but because of their already crowded quarters, the rest of us had to search for a hotel where we could have a room. When I finally entered a room in the wee hours of the morning, I collapsed on the floor.

Much later I was awakened by one of our family who had heard peddlers outside and bought me a bowl of dumpling soup. I ate it eagerly and fell back to sleep. In my semiconscious state,

I could hear my family whispering.

"Wherever did Seventh Sister get such strength, wisdom, and courage to carry Mother like that?"

"It must have been her Jesus helping her."

I believe it was this incident that really planted the seed in Mother's heart, causing her to realize the love and power of Christ.

After we had returned home to Nanking, Mother tried to break her opium habit in a Quaker hospital. Miss Mary Leaman fasted and prayed for God's deliverance. At the end of two weeks of struggle, Mother suddenly seemed to be aware of a glow of unusual love as she gazed on Miss Leaman's face. She broke out with heavy perspiration, and at that moment the opium habit left her.

Miss Mary Leaman was the most influential person to Miss Tsai. They had a multiple-dimension relationship of teacher to student, friend to friend, and mother to daughter. Miss Leaman loved China for her whole life and was called "China Mary" Her Chinese name was Meilin Li.

After she returned from the hospital, Mother announced to her children, "It was Jesus who answered the prayers of Miss Leaman and healed me." She urged, "My wish is that all my children and I will serve the living God." One of my brothers had believed secretly before her conversion, and through the years, fifty-five of my relatives accepted Christ. At this time I chose my English name, Christiana, after I was so moved by reading John Bunyan's book *Pilgrim's Progress*.

Mother was baptized at the church Charles Leaman had built, and seven of our family joined her. Mother was an intelligent but illiterate woman after the custom of women in China. She was taught by her grandson Woodrow to read from a picture book of the New Testament with big characters. In the summer, even neighbors joined us for prayers. They marveled that Mother, who had been far from talkative before her conversion, now began to witness to them with great liberty.

One day Miss Leaman and I were in my prayer tower studying the Bible when Mother called to her. "Miss Leaman, I don't know how to express my gratitude to you for leading our family to find the true God through Jesus Christ. Would you accept my seventh daughter to be your daughter in the Lord?" From that time on, we accepted this beautiful spiritual relationship together and I called her Godmother.

Miss Leaman often bore much pain and suffering patiently and silently. As a result of a fall and injury to her spine when she was three years old, she found it hard to stand in the pulpit and address a crowd. Moreover, her gift from the Lord was a deep and quiet one. She was behind the scenes, in prayer, doing personal work and spiritual creative thinking. When traveling from place to place for meetings in China, she had to lie flat while being carried. So when we joined together to serve the Lord, He used her to prepare me for a public ministry which I had always shunned. She pushed me to the front and pulled me out of myself to allow the Lord to use me. "But Godmother, I don't want to," I often complained.

"Suppose you had a pen that refused to write. Would you stop writing?" she prodded me. "Of course not. You would change to another one. You can't change God's plan by refusing to do as He asks. He will change to another instrument, and you will lose your opportunity!"

When I was asked to speak at my commencement exercises, I was literally sick with fear. But the audience applauded every sentence, to my embarrassment. When it was over, they applauded so much, asking me to come out and bow again and again, I thought

I would faint. A teacher had to prepare a special drink to revive me!

The mayor invited me to tea, and I was further embarrassed as he bowed to me, just a schoolgirl. He offered to arrange for me to speak to large audiences in cities throughout China on the importance of women's education. But I declined, saying that I was there to study.

When I graduated, many positions were offered me: to become vice-principal of my school, general secretary of the YWCA, and traveling lecturer to promote women's education. It was not that I was so much better than others, but that I was one of the first and very few Chinese girls to obtain a Western education. A Chinese proverb sums it up: "Where there are no big trees on the mountain, even the blades of grass are honored."

But the new King of my life had not called me to any of these honored positions, but to witness for Him. I traveled through most of the provinces of China, speaking and interpreting at various meetings and conferences. Many times it was in the company of such notables as Miss Ruth Paxson, Dr. Griffith Thomas, Dr. Charles Trumbull, and others.

It was a special joy for me to be a friend of the well-known speaker and writer Miss Paxson. I must have interpreted for her about three hundred times. She was known for speaking so rapidly in English that others could not keep up with her. But God gave us a oneness so that we seemed to think unitedly and deliver the messages with one spirit. I translated into Chinese her famous book, *Rivers of Living Water*, and also a compilation of her prayers and exhortations,

Thus God had begun to work through me.

After graduation, Miss Tsai returned home and led her mother and whole family of 55 people to Christ. This is the church built by Charles Leaman where Mrs. Tsai and her family were baptized.

Chapter 6

Stricken

How I marvel at my naiveté as a high-born, daintily raised girl! At Laura Haygood School every subject was taught in English by resident American teachers and by the wives of professors from a university. Miss Mary Culler White, a missionary-evangelist much used by the Lord in China, took some of us who were "more refined" girls along to conduct meetings on her houseboat. We knew little about taking care of ourselves, as we had always been waited on by servants. So we were totally ignorant of common daily chores. We just sat around with folded hands, while she, a missionary, cooked, cleaned, washed the dishes, and cleaned the commodes. She even ate from our plates like a servant after we had finished!

Often I prayed and worked with this dear missionary until after midnight, translating her messages into Chinese. I have always had the deepest respect for the missionaries who left their comfortable lands and homes for the sake of the gospel. Many sacrificed their very lives for Him and for my own countrymen.

Later, I accepted a position as a music teacher in a Chinese government girls' school. Seventy-two of the two hundred students accepted Christ through opportunities I had to talk with them during intermissions. They often came to my home and to Bible classes in our church. The newspapers reviled me, calling me "the music teacher who is an evangelist, teaching the students to cry 'God, God!' and bringing anger from their parents." Indeed, many of my students did suffer persecution for their new faith in Christ and were faithful through great trials.

Because the missionaries with whom I traveled spoke mostly

to Christians, I often held special services for non-Christians. We spoke to teachers and students of government schools in China, to mission colleges and high schools in many large cities, to nurses in hospitals, and to crowds of various sizes. When there was no building large enough to contain the crowds, tents were erected. In some of the student centers, I lived in the dormitories in order to be close to the students.

After speaking sometimes three times a day, I was busy until late at night with personal interviews. Besides the ministry in the cities, we traveled to the countryside and remote villages, living in primitive conditions. We traveled by railway, riverboats, coastal steamers, sedan chairs, wheelbarrows, houseboats, and rickshaws. We encountered many oppositions and trials, but the Lord was our vanguard to prepare the hearts of countless people in all walks of life to receive Him.

Rather than accepting other honored positions, I finally joined in serving the Lord with my dearest companion and co-worker, Miss Mary Leaman. God gave us deep love and harmony in this ministry together. I was able to continue living in my own home. If I had not, it would have been impossible for any Christian to enter our house, because the class distinction was so strong.

I teased Miss Leaman in later years that she had never actually invited me to join her. And when I did offer myself, all she quietly commented was, "May the Lord Jesus guide you." Time and again when I asked what she thought of my doing this or that, she did not commit herself but used this same reply. I must confess, it almost irritated me as a young believer. I said to myself, "Why doesn't she have that sentence printed? Every time she writes me she could just enclose a copy!"

But how right she was. In life's decisions we should get our directions straight from God. We may ask counsel from fellow believers and those with spiritual insight, but in the final analysis God must speak to our own hearts.

We lived and worked together, caring for one another through illnesses, civil wars, crises of life, and seemingly insurmountable problems. After I started working with Miss Leaman in Nanking, a storm of questions arose. The principal of Soochow school, Miss Ruth Paxson, and many other missionaries came, one by one, all with good intentions, to ask her why she kept me from working for the Lord nationwide. "Nanking is just one place," they argued.

But she certainly had not "kept me"! It was the Lord who intertwined our lives and destinies. But it showed again the wisdom she had in the way she always answered me—leaving the decision up to me.

Beginning in 1930 and continuing for seven years, Miss Leaman was to accomplish her greatest work. Her conviction was that the illiterate masses of China must have the Chinese Bible in some more simplified form than the complicated ancient Chinese written characters. This launched her into a monumental work. She transcribed and printed the Chinese Bible, putting the phonetic simplified characters in parallel columns beside the standard characters. The Chinese Nationalist government had already endorsed this phonetic system.

Miss Leaman was both completely unqualified and superbly qualified for this task. She operated on a shoestring budget, had a cubbyhole for an office, used volunteer proofreaders, and had only one expert printer-mechanic who cast the type matrices by hand. Already retired from her mission for physical disability, she was in constant pain and weakness, and her goal seemed impossible. She faced opposition and lack of sympathy even from unexpected sources. But she had a thorough knowledge of Chinese, an iron will, and a boundless faith that this was the job to which the Lord had called her. The phonetic Bible would not be off the press for more than thirty years.

One winter morning in 1931, I awakened with unbearable pain piercing my eyes, the room whirling, my head burning with fever, and my body stiffening. I lay more dead than alive, unable to eat, unable to move, for seventeen days. I couldn't speak more than a grunt for eight months and could not open my eyes for a year and a half. As I became more desperately sick, Miss Leaman had to lay aside her translation work and devote most of her daylight hours to nursing me. That left only her tired-out night hours for her proofreading.

Six doctors of different nationalities were called in for consultations. They all pronounced my case hopeless. A most famous Chinese doctor was asked to come and see me, and a large sum of money had to be paid in case he was kidnapped between his home and ours. He held my hand, saying, "You are like a lamp without oil. The longest you can live is three more days." My family prepared the coffin and grave clothes.

But Miss Leaman's prayers, faith, and courage kept me alive by God's power through this valley of the shadow of death, and through many more such valleys in the years to come.

In 1937, just as Miss Leaman had begun to make headway on her translating, the Japanese invaded China. But that did not stop her. After the Japanese attack on Pearl Harbor in 1941, she refused repatriation with other missionaries in order that she might complete her job. Because of that, she was imprisoned for two years in a Japanese concentration camp with other sick and crippled foreigners. I continued on my sickbed with malignant malaria of the bone marrow for the whole time she was in the camp.

On Christmas Eve of that year, much to everyone's amazement, I was still alive. One doctor publicly told her large atheistic family, "I have watched Miss Tsai's case so long that now I know there must be a God. My son and I have decided to believe in Jesus as our personal Saviour!" God wonderfully saved my old gateman, the head of those who guarded the main entrance, courtyards, and gardens of our home during the thirty-five years of my father's life as a government official. When he heard of my hopeless condition, he went to the pastor and said, "I want to go where my 'Miss Seven' goes." Thus, he was instructed in the faith and believed and was baptized a few months before he went to be with the Lord.

Once when I was near death, I saw a vision of heaven and heard wonderful singing. I thought, *My time has come. What a welcome!*

But I seemed to hear a voice saying, "No, not a welcome, only a rehearsal!" My illness was not correctly diagnosed for sixteen long years of suffering, and by then it was too late for a cure. The malaria, with many related afflictions, laid me permanently aside from the physically active ministry I had before. My ear canals, that give balance, are all disconnected, so my equilibrium is destroyed. I cannot walk without reeling back and forth like a crab and falling if not supported. My eyes cannot bear direct light. I stay in a dark room with shades pulled, lights covered, and wear sunglasses.

One day in America an ear, nose, and throat specialist walked into my room and announced, "Miss Tsai, I know you are a refugee in this country. I am a specialist. You cannot afford to pay me. I want to give you a good examination to see why you cannot walk, just for curiosity."

He made the room dark and turned me in all kinds of directions. I was most thankful when he stopped. Then he said, pointing up to heaven, "Miss Tsai, only *that* Doctor can make you walk again. You will never walk in your life. You know, of course, that each ear has three canals that give balance. The canals in both your ears are all disconnected." He didn't know what had caused this. I begged him to operate, but he just said with a smile, "I repeat, only the Doctor in heaven can make you walk again."

Chapter 7

Timekeeper

When we fled Shanghai one steaming day in August, we were trying to find some clothes for Miss Leaman to change into. "Why, there's nothing here but phonetic Bible materials!" I exclaimed as we rummaged through every one of Miss Leaman's suitcases. It was just like her—putting God's work before her comfort. She had ordered that none of her personal effects or clothes be packed, giving priority to the Bible materials she wanted to be kept safe. Our old servant, Pooh, loaned her something to wear.

In fact, we had not packed at all in the rush of leaving. Pooh had packed. And for some unknown reason, she had also packed a secondhand clock bought by Miss Leaman's father in Nanking years before. It was beautiful, kept good time, and had always been in the Leaman home. The servants just loved it, so they sneaked it along. The clock refused to tell time after its long, bumpy trip, but it did remind me that when Miss Leaman went into the concentration camp and I moved to my attic room, among our joint possessions was that broken clock.

One day a friend asked me to pray for a Chinese school teacher, his wife, and three children. They had barely enough to eat. "He repairs watches and clocks so he can buy food for his family," he said, asking me if there was any way we could help by letting people know about the availability of a repairer of clocks.

I told him that if the man would come to my home, I would give him our broken clock to repair. The friend said that the clock repairer was not able to come and get clocks, but I maintained that if he wanted the work, he would have to come and see me. Meanwhile, I spoke to some of my friends about his need and accumulated considerable work for him. I even offered to pay his rickshaw fare to my place.

Finally he came, with a very long face. Inviting him to sit down, I talked to him about salvation in Christ. He never answered one word. He wanted the job but was not eager to hear about Jesus. I kept back some of my friends' watches and did not give them to him all at once so that I could keep him coming. He took the Leaman clock to his home first.

Early one hot summer morning as I was being visited by a missionary, Mrs. Allison, who was waiting to go back to America, I heard bitter crying outside my screen door. I asked someone to go and see what the trouble was. A beautiful lady, as lovely as cherry blossoms after the rain, came shyly in.

"Miss Tsai, I am the clock man's wife," she said. "He is dying of tuberculosis. The blood just flows out, and there is no way to stop it. We have a tiny room with one bed for five of us. I have no money." When Mrs. Allison heard the story, she gave the equivalent of one or two American dollars to the lady. "I will tell my husband to go to see your husband," she promised.

When Mr. Allison called on the clock man and mentioned the name of Jesus, the sick man turned his face to the wall. Mr. Allison explained to him fully the way of salvation, but he seemed to pay no attention. Day after day, that missionary went to that tiny room full of germs, hot as an oven, trying to tell the dying man the wonderful story of Jesus Christ.

I sent word to Dr. Mary Stone, a very dear Chinese physician friend of mine, who immediately asked her co-worker to take the money she had set aside to buy watermelons and other fruit for herself, and share it with him. Other Christians also wanted to help this dying man. A great deal of prayer went up on his behalf.

The faithful Mr. Allison sat by his bed day after day, telling him about Jesus. Suddenly one day, the man turned to him and said, "Is it possible for me to enter that beautiful heaven that you describe?"

"Yes! The Bible says in John 3:16 that whosoever believes may be saved," Mr. Allison said.

"I have been listening with my back to you day after day, ignoring you," the sick man said, "but you never gave up on me. Jesus took pity upon me and opened my heart. I am accepting Him now. I don't want to wear that blue funeral gown hanging on the door. I want to enter heaven in a white gown, because I am cleansed by the blood of Christ now." Praise the Lord, even though Charles Leaman was in heaven by then, his clock still spoke and brought people to the Lord.

Chapter 8

God Is Able

The day after Miss Leaman entered prison, word came that three old people had already died—there was no mention of names. Rumors were everywhere. I moved to an attic, dependent on others to care for me in my continuing illness until Miss Leaman would return.

Prisoners depended largely on what could be sent to them by those outside. I didn't have anything to send her except two tins of jam which she had seldom touched anyway. What was I to do? If she didn't receive anything when other prisoners received their packages, what would she think? A Swedish missionary advised, "You have to send it to the Red Cross through someone like me who is neutral. They forward it to the prisoners." I had a little empty box in which I put the jam and packed some leftover charcoal around it, marking it for "Prisoner Mary Leaman." That was the first package I had ever sent anyone!

Chinese money devaluated fast. Even an empty tin cost six hundred dollars. Meanwhile, the China Inland Mission headquarters had to be closed, and many items were being auctioned. A friend bought me twelve dozen beautiful quart jars and a German food grinder. These were a great help. Every month it was my greatest joy to get a package ready for Miss Leaman. I sold everything I could, and the Lord wonderfully provided.

Friends were able to purchase big, fat Peking dates for me. I steamed them, cooled them, and packed them tight in the jars. Then I got peanuts, fried them, shelled them, and got a friend to help me grind them on my new grinder into peanut butter. Miss Leaman didn't care for sweet things, so I put a little salt in it. I prepared food that would not require cooking or even hot water. There was a fifty-pound limit.

Many of my friends could not understand why I sent such a quantity each month when Miss Leaman could not eat much. But I knew that she wanted to help other prisoners who might not get anything. After the prisoners were released, many wrote of how much they appreciated the things I had sent to Miss Leaman. Several said that their husbands were diabetic and could eat no regular Japanese prepared food. They depended on what I sent her. She always shared her best foods with the sick.

Daily the prisoners had to pick out the rice from floor sweepings that were full of dirt and mold. They then put potato peelings and carrot skins with the moldy rice and cooked it in a big pot. They had to line up and hold out their buckets to receive the food.

Every morning at roll call, the prisoners had to stand straight, arms down. If anyone moved a finger or a foot, they were beaten. It was very cruel because those old and sick folks could not stand straight. It was especially hard for Miss Leaman, then sixty, with her spinal condition and crippled body. But she trained herself and prayed that she could stand motionless during the roll call. Later, I learned that every prisoner except Miss Leaman was beaten.

Two difficult years somehow passed. One quiet afternoon a pastor's wife told me, "I have heard Miss Leaman's voice!"

"What do you mean?" I cried.

"The Japanese have surrendered, and the prisoners are free! She called me to notify you that she is free."

I was so stunned I forgot where I was and who I was. I had waited and waited for her for so long that this surprise was too much of a shock to my system. It took me a long time to recover. All the kind Chinese friends who had come to see her off to prison now were able to go into the prison to visit her. From morning until night a stream of sympathetic friends came to tell me that

Miss Leaman was free and to report to me whatever news they could about her. That taxed my strength to the uttermost as I lay sick in bed. Every day I was so exhausted, yet I had such a longing that she would now be back any moment.

But day after day, she still did not come back. Why? I waited and waited. Friends came and went, and I begged them to tell me why she did not come home yet. They didn't know. "Are there other prisoners still there?" I asked anxiously.

"No, just one or two are left. All the others are free and gone."

"Well, why can't she come home?" No one could tell me.

After more than a month of anxiety, I was frantic. Her little room had been ready for so long. At eleven o'clock one night a friend brought a big, beautiful basket of fresh flowers and said, "Congratulations, Miss Tsai. Miss Leaman will return!" That false hope aggravated my delicate condition so that my exhaustion began to turn into a feeling of greater illness.

Before dawn I started to have a chill and shook for about an hour and a half. A former Buddhist nun, who had been converted by my bedside, heard my trouble, rushed to me, and held me in her arms. "Don't be afraid, Miss Tsai, the Lord is with you!" she said. I still shook. Then I dropped into unconsciousness.

Seeing my critical condition, a friend rushed to the prison to tell Miss Leaman my situation. The prison was in the suburbs, a long way from the city of Shanghai. Another friend happened to be driving back to the city, so Miss Leaman, picking up only her Bible, left the prison with him. She lay in the back of his car and asked that he drive her to the American consulate.

Now the mystery was being solved. The American prisoners, by regulations, were all examined by American doctors before being allowed to leave the prison. When Miss Leaman was examined, her back was so bad that the doctor ordered her to be flown at once to America.

At the consulate she asked permission to have her return to America waived to allow her to stay with me for a while. "My adopted daughter is very sick," she said.

"No!" declared the consul. "You are ordered to fly back to America immediately. There are no exceptions. It is for your own good, because you need medical care and recovery. I will not allow you to stay here!"

She said she would not leave me because she was the only relative I had. He did not relent. In her extreme weakness, she sat on the hard bench at the consulate all day and waited and waited. Finally, the time came for the consul to leave. The door had to be closed. She still stubbornly sat there. What a pitiful sight she must have been—so weak, thin, sick, and tired. What a love from the Lord she must have had in her heart for me! The consul was finally so frustrated with her that he disgustedly gave her permission to stay for only three months longer.

She thanked him, got up, and walked a mile to where I was living, an unbelievable feat in her condition! When she came to my bedside at last after two years, I was so delirious with fever that I called her "Big Brother." Somehow I had enough presence of mind to hand her a bag with all the records of how much money I borrowed from friends, amounting to about $3,000 U.S. currency. When the rumor spread that I was dying, friends came by to be sure Miss Leaman knew how much money I had borrowed from them.

One day a missionary who didn't identify himself came to see me. I was unconscious, so he gave Miss Leaman a package. She asked him if he wanted a receipt, but he refused. "No, no, I know she is a Christian," he said. The package contained exactly $3,100 U.S. currency! How marvelously God provided! With $400 she bought a refrigerator, which really saved our lives. After being in prison, Miss Leaman was very hungry but couldn't eat much at a time. That refrigerator was a great help to us both.

Now she had money to consult many doctors about me. No one could diagnose my illness. My fever went up to 106 degrees Fahrenheit. One doctor told Miss Leaman, "Please do not trouble to call me again. Miss Tsai is beyond help. Even if you called all the doctors in Shanghai, they could not save her! There is only one last doctor for you to try, a brilliant young man who, when he arrived in Shanghai, got polio. He has had both legs amputated. Since he cannot practice, he has devoted his time to laboratory work, specializing in malaria research."

Miss Leaman was desperate, since I was again at the point of death. She called this young doctor, and he came with his father and two nurses. "I want to give Miss Tsai a sternal puncture," he told her. "It might be about five inches long, about as thick as a baby's finger." He gave me an injection near my collar bone to deaden the pain. The doctor held my arm, the nurses tried to count my pulse, and he drilled an instrument into my bone. When he pulled it out, the blood was as black as ink. The nurses took turns stopping up the wound from which the blood oozed. It took another half hour to stop it.

The doctor told Miss Leaman, "There is no hope at all; the blood is black. I don't even need to go to the lab. It is full of malaria germs." He turned to me and said, "I'm sorry, Miss Tsai, you will die in this room."

I could only whisper, "God is able."

He said, "Miss Leaman, don't bother any more doctors. Giving her any more medicine would be just like pouring a cup of water on a burning house. It is absolutely no use." Later he sent the lab report anyway. There are thirty-six kinds of malaria germs. I had three of the most severe kinds, male and female, with generations already multiplying. The red corpuscles were being destroyed so the blood had become black.

The war had just ended. Many GIs had contracted malaria; row on row of them were lying helpless in hospitals without relief. It was then that some doctors in America finally discovered an effective medicine. They didn't dare publish its name, but only referred to it by a number. A doctor telephoned Miss Leaman, informing her that if she could find out where to get that medicine, it might be tried as a last resort. He gave her its number, but no name, for fear the Japanese would get it.

Miss Leaman suddenly remembered that when she was entering prison, a Chinese gentleman had given her his name, address, and telephone number. He had asked her to write him if she got to America, because he wanted to go, too. Not daring to keep all the address on one piece of paper, she tore it up and hid the pieces among the pages of her Bible. The Lord helped her to retrieve the pieces and put them together. When she tried phoning him, sure enough, he answered the phone himself! She asked if he knew anywhere she could find the medicine.

"It just so happens that a friend of mine returned from America only yesterday," he said. "America won't allow anyone to bring cash to China, but you may bring things like medicine, watches, et cetera. My friend brought back all kinds of medicine and things for resale. I'll go to see him. If he has brought something like that, I'll phone you…", He phoned later, saying, "Yes, my friend got one bottle of this medicine, numbered such and such. It is marked one thousand pills. The prescription says that it takes only ten pills for a cure, but my friend insists that he has to sell the whole bottle at once. The price is $350 U.S. currency. Take it or leave it!"

Miss Leaman prayed, "Dear Lord, please provide." She bought the whole bottle and immediately called the doctor. He took ten pills and ground them into powder to force down my throat. I had not been able to swallow, but somehow I managed to get this down. In a day or so, the fever went down to 104 degrees. The doctor came back to consult Miss Leaman. "Ten pills was supposed to be a cure; but since her case is so critical, shall we force another ten pills?" he asked. They agreed, and on the fifth day they tried to get me to open my mouth to take it again. By this time I had recovered a little of my understanding, but I still could not swallow at will. They had to force it down again.

After a few days the fever went down to 102 degrees. By then

I was conscious and finally knew what was going on. You can imagine how I looked by that time. My face was broken out all over and my body was emaciated and in a terrible condition. I could not move a finger for six months. The doctor said he had never seen a case as severe as mine, so he decided, "Give her three pills a day and see what happens." This continued until all one thousand pills went down! This was an unbelievable dose for any human body to absorb, let alone my tiny, frail one! Even then my fever still lingered between 100 and 101 degrees.

A lady Dr. Woo, who lived near us, was a medical doctor, and her husband was a surgeon. She kindly came twice a day to give me intravenous feedings because I could not eat. Though she had been an atheist, at Christmastime she announced to her family that she had become a Christian from watching how God had brought me back from the grave. Once she asked me, "Did you know that your family had been summoned to your deathbed and cried over you?" I said I had no such recollection. She told me that the only sign of life was that my shoulder moved a little. "In such a condition you were, and you are still here! I told my atheist family that my son and I had decided to follow the living God."

Then she asked me a favor. "Instead of my coming to give you an injection, will you let my husband come? Let him also see what a living God there is. I want him to believe in the Lord Jesus, too."

"No," I begged, "in my weakened condition I would rather have you." She continued to ask me, and the inner voice of the Spirit impressed me that I should let him come in spite of my own inconvenience. The tenderhearted Dr. Woo, her husband, although an unbeliever, was a wonderful man. Every day he continued to give me injections. When my head was clearer, I shared with him about the Lord.

One day he suggested a new method of medication that might lead to a cure. He asked me if I would be willing to try it. I said that I would do anything that might help me. So every day he gave me three kinds of antimalaria medicine in three injections. Then he changed off and gave me injections for leprosy, syphillis, and snake poison.

"Doctor, I don't have all that trouble!" I complained.

He explained that he had to use poison to counteract poison, and that I had a body full of poison. The Lord helped me to again survive all those injections in my frail body. Finally I grew so sick that I couldn't eat. Struggling day after day, I became as weak as a rag. Oh, how I longed to get well! Then I started to get reactions and vomited morning to evening as if my insides had become a fountain. Kind Dr. Woo sat beside me, holding a cracker. "Just take a half piece," he urged, "even though you may vomit, some will stay down." I couldn't even talk any longer, the vomiting continued so hard.

Outside the rain was pouring. "Well, Miss Tsai," he said, "on the way to your house I learned a lesson. I saw a building that had been halfway erected, but the rain had interrupted construction. The builders had to wait until the rain stopped. I suppose we have to follow the example of that building and stop injections until you get a little better. Then we'll start again." What a relief! Little by little, oh, so slowly, I began to improve, and by and by I could eat a bit. Eventually the fever disappeared and my skin turned a sickly yellow. It was many, many months before I was once more just out of danger—temporarily!

For sixteen years my condition had scarcely changed, and there was little hope for me to be much better. Then the Lord wonderfully caused a change to take place. Miss Leaman wrote about it to her family in America in August of 1947:

> I can hardly believe it is true, but day by day we watch Christiana coming back to life and strength! We bow our heads in wonder and thanksgiving for all that God has done. As the terrible pain and indescribable suffering have lessened and flesh has come on her bones once again, and her movements become free, we realize that the Lord

has wonderfully preserved her in body, mind, and spirit through so many years. These terrible malaria germs in her bones which bound her in weakness are diminishing and, as they decrease, she gains. The Lord in His great loving kindness and mercy seems to be restoring to her "the years that the locust hath eaten," (Joel 2:25).

As she lies there she does not look older than she did before this illness came upon her! Let us pray and ask many to pray that this restored life may be used just as the Lord sees best. It is a great trust not only for her but also for us who have prayed with her through these long years of pain. May each day and each moment be used in the Lord's service just exactly as He desires.

Chapter 9

Flight

The war closed in around us in Shanghai, and conditions grew worse. We were forced to consider fleeing China for the United States. Fear gripped the hearts of Chinese and foreigners alike. The Japanese had been a terrible threat from outside of China, but now there was an even more dangerous threat from within. It was the Communist party, which had set itself in opposition to the republican government of President Chiang Kai-shek.

Most of our friends had fled while they could. Miss Leaman had repeatedly booked passage for America, but each time we had to cancel. In my weak and painful condition, I told her I didn't think it was possible for me to go anywhere. "But you go," I urged her. "Remember how the Japanese put you in the concentration camp. It may happen again with the changing government—or worse. I am Chinese. Somehow I will be all right."

"No!" she said firmly. "I will die here with you if necessary!

One day there was a knock on my door. An aggressive and good-looking young Chinese man asked to see me. He pushed his way in. "I am on a special errand. We want you to join our party," he demanded.

"Can't you see that I'm old and sick?" I replied. "What use would I be to any political party?"

He pulled out books and magazines and newspapers. "Is that your name?" He pushed them at me, showing me all the pamphlets and articles I had written after high school. "We want you to stay in China and write for our political party. You must join the party. I will come to see you again!"

He left, but the next day a different man came, repeating the same demand. The third day, still another man came. I notified my family and friends, and they answered as if with one voice, "Go! Get out of China! We would rather see you die on the ocean than to see you in their hands!"

I thought this over and prayed fervently for the Lord's wisdom. I was only one person. I should not stay and endanger my friends and my family. I asked Miss Leaman whether we should try to go to the American consulate to get our passports before we tried again to book passage on the boat. A friend of mine, who had a limousine, heard that I wanted to go to the consulate. We needed to ask the consul if we could take a servant along to America. If not, there would be no way I could survive there because of all the care that I required. The trip across town was complicated and exhausting.

At sixty-nine years of age, Miss Leaman was unusually energetic as she climbed the consulate steps. I thought to myself, *She is stronger than I; she will have many more years than I to serve the Lord. It will be all right if I am left behind and she continues to serve the Lord in America.* The consul flatly refused to let her take a servant along. She reported this to me, said that we should go home, and added, "You said that you would not consider leaving if you could not take a servant along. So we can't go."

"Wait," I said, "since we are here, it won't hurt if I go with you to see the consul." Miss Leaman, my servant, and another friend held me up so I could get on the elevator. The lady at the desk said, "You are very wise to go while you still can. But you must see the doctor first. He is the one to say whether you can go or not."

I had seen so many, many doctors. But this was the first one with such a long American face, chewing gum all the time. In his waiting room were about thirty people. Each one was loudly arguing with him about why he would not allow him to go. He paid no attention, but just kept chewing his gum. When my turn came, he told me to lie on a high, hard table. There was such a strong light above me that I could hardly stand it.

"What happened to your hair?" he barked. I wanted to tell everything truthfully. I told him that while ill with malaria and high fever I lost all my hair. "Why is your skin so yellow?" I told him it was from the antimalarial medicine I took during my long illness. He examined me carefully. "The first finger on your left hand and the thumb on your right hand both have fungus. You must go to a surgeon and have the nails taken away from the roots, then come back to see me."

Miss Leaman was shocked and wanted to argue with the doctor. But I waved at her and said in Chinese that we should not say anything. We went to see our good friend Dr. Woo, the atheist surgeon. He was very kind and told me that according to regulations I should go to the hospital, but he would try to operate on my fingers in my own room. Three friends came to see me in tears and went with Miss Leaman into another room to pray while I had my operation. I can't describe such intense pain! To have one's fingernails cut off was torture.

We returned and I passed the consul's exam and he approved my visa. How many papers we had to sign! When we came home, it was dark and we were exhausted. Evidently the bandages on my fingers had worked loose, and by bedtime sharp pains started in both of my hands. My servant, Little King, was with me all night long. I couldn't sleep a minute because of the pain. Miss Leaman and I both had phones in our rooms, but I did not want to disturb her. Just before daybreak she came to check on me, and I had to confess that I had not slept all night. She looked at my hands and turned pale. "Hurry! Send for the doctor!" she said.

The infection had gone right up into my arm about five inches, and it was swollen, white, and tight. The doctor could hardly talk when he saw it. His face was like a sheet. "Miss Tsai, I'm very sorry," he said. "You must go to the hospital quickly and have part of your arm amputated!"

Miss Leaman and I could neither talk nor cry. Others scolded the doctor, for being so bold as to think he could perform such a delicate and dangerous operation as removing my fingernails outside the hospital.

"Miss Tsai, there is only one other chance," Dr. Woo said. "If you are willing to cooperate, I can try to operate again. If the infection could be released downward instead of going up, there is a chance."

I agreed weakly, nauseated from the infection, and my head swimming with fever. The second operation was more terrible than the first! Again Miss Leaman went to her room in tears, pleading for the Lord's help. The pain was unbearable! The doctor made incisions in my flesh and immersed my fingers in water with strong medicine. "If the infection does not come down, we must rush you to the hospital," he warned.

Pooh, my faithful servant who was like a sister, held my hands in the basin all day and night. Every three hours for three days and three nights the doctor gave me penicillin injections. The Lord once more worked a miracle, and eventually we began to see the infection receding. Dear Pooh, never complaining or thinking of her own exhaustion, always saw to it that my hands never got out of the medicine solution. It took many weeks for my hands to recover, during which the rumors of war increased.

Finally, our passports were ready. So much time had elapsed that the next boat to leave would be the last. Miss Leaman called the manager of the steamship lines. "Miss Leaman, there are three hundred on the waiting list," he said. "There is no chance!" She asked him to try his best and said she would pray.

Not too much later, the phone rang. "Miss Leaman, two passengers could not go because of illness," the manager reported. "I feel I should let you two sick people have the first chance, and I'm going to bypass the waiting list. There may be six people in your cabin, however."

"I will pray, as you try your best," Miss Leaman encouraged him. "Because we are sick, we don't want to bother others. If you could get a cabin for two, we would be very grateful."

"Impossible. Impossible," muttered the manager.

The Lord worked another miracle—we had a cabin, to ourselves!

Many of our Christian Chinese friends could not leave, and they were eventually put in prison. One by one they went to be with the Lord after enduring very bravely and standing for the Lord through unimaginable trials. Many of those very friends had escorted us to the boat.

It was not easy parting from those whom we knew we would never see again on this earth. Pooh had come to me when she was only nineteen. She had served me for an additional eighteen years. As far as I remember, she never said a discourteous word to me. As we were parting, she said, "Miss Tsai, may I arrange your pillows?" choking back her sobs.

I looked at her through my own tears and whispered, "Pooh, who will arrange pillows for me after you go?" Her hot tears, big as peas, dropped on me. She had been like a sister to me. She may still be living somewhere. I often wonder—did she escape the terrors of the war and the changes that followed? Three doctors carried me to the boat.

Dr. Woo also had tears in his eyes as he held my hand. When he saw me off at the boat, he whispered, "I really hate to see you go." With so many friends around, and so much commotion, did I have time to speak a last word about the Lord to him? Yes, cost what it may, I would!

"Here is a Bible for you," I said. "I hope you will read it and that Jesus will speak to you. If you believe in Jesus, someday we will meet again in heaven." Was it any use to say once more what I had told him over and over and he had not heeded? I sent up one more earnest prayer to the Lord on his behalf and then said good-bye.

Miss Leaman and I took a last tearful farewell look at our beloved China as we were half pushed, half dragged, up the

It was our last farewell to our beloved China.

gangplank. Most presumed we would quietly fade away, and frankly I'm not sure we hoped for anything more, either. It was January 19, 1949, and we were two old, invalid women. I was fifty-nine and Miss Leaman sixty-nine.

Chapter 10

Paradise

Several weeks later, after a stop in Honolulu and deboarding in San Francisco exhausted and ill, Miss Leaman and I traveled cross-country by train. We arrived in the predawn light of a winter's morning, and the porter swooped us off and deposited us with our baggage on the long, cold platform in Pennsylvania. Snow swirled around us, and the train pulled away, leaving us shivering and deserted. An unbelievably long flight of stairs led up to the station, and neither of us could imagine climbing them. There was nothing to do but wait and pray to be rescued.

I thought, what a difference from my first visit to America in the 1920s when Miss Leaman invited me to accompany her on one of her infrequent furloughs. Invitations came from the Presbyterian Board, asking me to make an extensive speaking tour throughout the United States. I was booked in prominent churches, Bible colleges, before the General Assembly of the Presbyterian Church, at Moody Bible Institute, to address prisoners at Sing Sing, and for an audience with President Harding, who invited me on a tour of the White House. For three years I rode on the crest of the wave of popularity and saw, with great admiration, the wide scope of Christian work everywhere in America. We stayed in mansions of wealthy Christians, and in humble homes of ordinary folk. Everywhere we traveled, crowds were on hand to greet us and arrange for our comfort. The days we spent with the family at the Leaman home in Paradise were precious ones.

During that furlough there were two Mary Leamans at the old homestead, the other being a cousin. The name "China Mary" was used to distinguish the missionary Mary, the one born in China. It was particularly appropriate, because she was indeed more Chinese than American from the inside out.

Now here we were, more than two decades later, deposited like abandoned freight along the railroad tracks. After a long while, two men appeared with two wheelchairs. Thinking they were for each of us, we gladly staggered toward them. But they put me in one and our baggage in the other, evidently sizing up the situation and assuming that at least the American lady seemed to be able to walk. China Mary tottered weakly beside me, holding me up and steadying herself. I was very dizzy as usual and could easily have tumbled out of the chair. The men pushed us and our baggage in and out of two elevators, finally reaching the baggage room. Then they disappeared. I was ready to collapse. A good friend had arranged to pick us up in her car at seven o'clock. "We will be dead by that time," I whispered. "We must get a taxi at once."

After the ten-mile ride to the village of Leaman Place in Paradise, Pennsylvania, we saw the great old house lighted up from end to end to welcome us. The driveway was heaped with snow. China Mary's sister Lucy and their cousin Mary were waiting at the door. Lucy hugged and kissed us ecstatically. Cousin Mary laughed excitedly, "Welcome to Paradise!"

We had a glimpse of the front parlor full of antique furniture accumulated by the Leamans. The spacious old- fashioned kitchen with its wood-burning stove was at the back, but I was too tired to stay up. With help, I sank into the high-backed antique bed and asked for the shades to be pulled. I felt literally and figuratively in Paradise! Our days of refugeeing were over, our hardships at an end. We could rest at last. But a disturbing thought suddenly crossed my mind. Perhaps our lives of usefulness to the Lord were really at an end. What could we do for Him in this remote corner of the world?

The big, brown more than two-hundred-year-old house at Paradise was weathered but still sturdy. It nestled in a rich, rolling "garden spot" of America, Lancaster County, Pennsylvania. Christian Leaman had purchased it and an adjacent tract of land from General William Reynolds of Revolutionary War fame. He persuaded relatives and friends to build there also, and the government was so pleased that it named the village Leaman Place.

That put us on the map. This house had once been an inn where horseback riders on their way from Philadelphia to Lancaster stopped to switch horses. Lincoln Highway, Route 30, now runs past our door. It cut back our land, shaving off the front yard right up to the front porch. Oh, how I had loved the beautiful apple trees that always seemed to wave us a welcome when we got off the trolley in front of the Leaman house on our first trip to America! Now we were exposed day and night to a bombardment of trailers, ponderous trucks, and zooming motor cars which stormed up one hill and down the other in a thundering, never-ending stream.

Next door was a red brick country store, behind us a lumber yard and feed mill. A hundred yards behind our house was a freight station on the Pennsylvania Railroad, with long lines of freight cars rattling by at frequent intervals. Now speeding passenger trains zip along the gleaming tracks of the Pennsylvania main line, no longer stopping at the small Leaman Place station as they did a generation ago.

All around us was the lush, rolling countryside studded with clusters of gleaming white farm buildings, houses with large barns and silos. All this set in emerald green fields of waving corn, rippling wheat, and broad-leafed tobacco. Sky and earth met along the wooded ridges that shut in our world.

This was the country of the pink-cheeked, white-capped Mennonite women. Here also lived the somber, bearded, black-garbed Amish men and the bonneted, long-skirted women. Children still dressed as miniature adults, complete with black-brimmed hats and bonnets. Even today they are frequently seen and heard clopping along in horse-drawn carriages past our door, even on the traffic-laden Highway 30. Both religious groups are quiet, peace-loving, and conservative folk whose farms are their showcases. They still cling to the honest pioneer tradition of plain living and good, hard work. We get plenty of fresh fruit from their orchards, vegetables from their gardens, and creamy milk from their Holstein and Guernsey herds. Baked goods are brought to our door, and other homegrown produce abounds in the country store. We seemed to be in a Garden of Eden, and the pain and war of China were far away.

But our hearts were still in China with those we loved and with whom we shared Christ. My thoughts turned often to those I'd left behind, my relatives and friends, as little iron filings follow the magnet.

Not very long after we arrived, an airmail letter came from Dr. Woo in China. I opened the letter anxiously. There was a drawing of a birthday cake with candles and a figure with a Bible kneeling beside the cake. What could that mean?

> Dear Miss Tsai: After we said good-bye, I went home. As you advised me, I asked the Holy Spirit to be my Teacher and immediately opened the Bible. I read and read and read; I even forgot to go to bed. Never a day passed that I didn't read it. The Lord must have heard the prayers of you and Miss Leaman. Thank you for your patience. The Bible taught me that I am a sinner. I read that there is only one way to go to Heaven and that is by believing in Jesus. That picture I drew is of me, kneeling by the Bible. I have accepted Jesus Christ as my Savior. I just wanted to let you know: that is your birthday gift! I know that probably I will never be able to come to America to see you, and you will not be able to return to China. But, as you said when we parted, one day we will meet in Heaven!

Oh, may the Lord help me, in season and out of season, when

I feel like it or not, whether it is convenient or not, to tell people about Jesus. I must sow the seed—then the Lord sees to the harvest!

A year later, yet another letter arrived for me indirectly from one of my brothers left behind the bamboo curtain. He had been one who opposed my faith fiercely. He had torn up my Bible and hymnbook after my conversion and had persecuted me bitterly when I left Buddhism. He had resisted Christ for a long time. Who could have been more hardened than he?

But as he watched how the Lord tenderly led me through the severe suffering of prolonged illness in 1947, and how I faced it without complaining, the Holy Spirit began to touch his heart. The letter recounted how he had asked members of our family to gather around him. He announced, "From watching our sister's long suffering and seeing how she was given indescribable strength to bear it all, I know there must be a God! Therefore, I ask Him to forgive my sins. I decide now to follow Him and accept Him as my everlasting Saviour!"

Praise Almighty God! Churches in China may be forced to close, but the Head of the church, Jesus Christ, can never be closed out of the hearts of His true believers. Missionaries may have been driven from the visible China, but the Holy Spirit can never be driven out of His own children.

Chapter 11

The Lily

China Mary and I felt like fish out of water. We were in our pleasant American home with its many conveniences, but we were used to China ways. Housekeeping here with the help of experienced, capable women, who had good minds of their own, was a contrast to China where ignorant country folk were content to be our hands and feet.

Neither of us knew much about cooking nor had the strength to do heavy chores. Missionaries in China, as in other lands, did not usually do many of their own household tasks. They were in the country by the call of the Lord to give priority to their ministry among the people. It would not have been good stewardship of their time and efforts to spend large segments of each day in taking care of their homes while servant help was so willing, available, and inexpensive.

China Mary, although American, was indeed more Chinese in outlook and approach. She loved the Chinese people dearly. Like the Mary of Bethany in the Bible, she was deeply spiritual, devoting her life to prayer, personal counseling, and literary pursuits.

In China we always ate Chinese food, which I had our servants prepare. China Mary hardly cared what food was set before her and often forgot to eat if more important matters demanded her attention. It did not matter to her how food tasted, as long as it was nourishing. Now, as the eldest and least feeble of the four of us, she became head of our household and had to learn the role of Martha in the Bible. She had to be busy "about many things" (Luke 10:41). Yet her mind was always on the less common. Her hardest task was to remember that there was food cooking on the stove. How often it burned! She had to teach herself to cook, and her inclination toward things Chinese was revealed in the tasty dishes she prepared, even ordering ingredients from New York or Hong Kong.

China Mary often reminded Cousin Mary, Lucy, and me of Genesis 45:24, when the brothers of Joseph went to Egypt to buy food. Joseph sent the brothers back to their fathers, cautioning them, "See that ye fall not out by the way." The Chinese translation indicates that this means not to argue. We asked the Lord to help the four of us understand each other and not quarrel on our journey. So our code was simple: never criticize one another, never question motives, and never turn away an opportunity to witness for the Lord. God never failed to do His part by blessing His work through us.

Forced to put behind me all the comforts of my early wealth and luxury, I have learned to simplify my way of life. I have furnished my room with only bare essentials: a bed, small tables, night stand, sofa and chairs for guests, a bookcase, and lamps covered by dark cloth. There is one window with dark shades drawn. This dark chamber is my office, dining room, reception room, and sleeping quarters. It also becomes my meeting hall and sanctuary. My bed is the platform from which I speak when groups come to see me.

I have to set two stages every day, so in the morning I get my room ready for the public eye by putting away all night things, changing clothes, and washing up. Unexpected guests often pop in very early. At night I have to turn my chamber again into a hospital room with everything handy for me during the night when I am alone. Often in the morning, after a sleepless night and the continued pain of my illness, I have felt so weak that my tears have washed my face as I have arranged my stage for the day. Yet I did not dare to let China Mary know, lest she be anxious about me. Often a quiet voice seemed to whisper to me, "Just count your many blessings instead!"

When guests come, they are invited to sit on little wooden chairs, which we brought back from the kindergarten that Lucy taught in China. Everything has its appointed place, and I usually know where to find it. People even come to me to borrow what they need and are amazed when I generally can produce it. I still sit up in bed every morning, "waiting for biscuits" as I did when I was a child. China Mary always brought them to me with the morning mail. Before we opened our letters, we asked our heavenly Father to bless every sender and make us a blessing in our contacts with them.

This is Miss Tsai's dark chamber—all the windows were covered with black clothes and thick curtains. Bulbs were wrapped with lamp-chimneys, and her books were displayed on the shelf.

Letters and guests became our life. The buzz of voices and the hum of activity were a welcomed break from the deadly monotony of a shut-in's life. They were pleasant sounds that tended to drown out the nuisance kind. We welcomed each guest with open arms. China Mary and I prayed each morning, "Lord, bring only those to us whom You desire, and keep away all who would only tax our strength and take our time away from Your ministry to the lives of those who need You."

When guests arrived, we enthusiastically received them, standing on God's promise that they were the exact ones He had sent.

Interruptions made up the business of our lives. The neighbor who dropped in at mealtime and the stranger driving by who wanted to meet us, might both have parked their cars under the old apple tree before ringing our bell. Hundreds of guests have opened doors and windows to us on an ever-widening world. Invalids like us, full of aches and pains, could have been overcome by self-pity unless we had concentrated on helping others. We soon realized that we were faced with either giving way to our symptoms and shutting out the world, or of rising above them and welcoming the interruptions, even capitalizing on them.

Though having set our feet in the latter direction, times would come when I would doubt that I could serve the Lord in my solitary room so far away from the traffic of life. I was hidden away in a dark, unknown corner. Then the Lord, to encourage me, brought to my mind an early experience that happened soon after my conversion.

By my doctor's orders, I was to take walks every day on the hilltops of Kuling, in Kiukiang, China, one of China's most beautiful summer resorts.

Early every morning I said good-bye to my spiritual mother, China Mary, and started my walk with my young maid. I wore straw sandals and carried a staff. My maid brought a little package of food, a small teakettle, and a box of matches. When we came to a stream where the clear water rippled quietly down from its fountain in the hills, we made a little fireplace with stones,

In the midst of that dirty, solitary dump stood an exquisite lily.

gathered some twigs and branches, lighted the fire, and cooked our breakfast.

How the morning star shone brightly and beautifully! The rustling pines and topmost branches of stately trees joyously bowed to each other above the sparkling streams to welcome the rising of the gorgeous, glorious sun. "O my Creator, Maker of heaven and earth, I adore Thee, I worship Thee!" was the prayer of my young heart, newly awakened to Christ's love.

One morning my maid lingered to examine some of the odd stones. I went on, wading through a cool stream and climbing some rocks to a narrow path. The sound of a waterfall spoke to my heart that I was not alone—I felt aware of the companionship of my Lord. He was indeed altogether lovely! I walked along, lifting my face to the blue skies, singing, "He Leadeth Me." Suddenly an indescribable sweet fragrance made me turn to discover its source. I searched and found only an ugly rubbish pile with broken pieces of stone discarded by stone workers in that hidden, unkept, and unfrequented spot. To my surprise, in the midst of that dirty, solitary dump stood an exquisite lily, incomparable in its stately beauty. It shared its fragrance freely for the joy of a chance passerby like myself.

May the God of all circumstances help me to diffuse His fragrance right here where I am! "Now thanks be to God, which always causeth us to triumph in Christ, and maketh manifest the savour of his knowledge by us in every place" (2 Corinthians 2:14). Through heavy burdens, prolonged pain and sickness, people's misunderstandings, failing health and strength, uncertainty about the future and financial straits, may my Lord's own sweet fragrance flow in and out of this little darkened corner.

Chapter 12

Queen of the Dark Chamber

China Mary and I were just two trickles that leaked out from China and dribbled down into a hollow in Pennsylvania. But we were a strange puddle that refused to dry up. Something had to happen here. The setting was both impossible and ideal. There was the big, brown house, secure but restricting. And there were four invalids—companionable but helpless.

We sensed a call to draw all Chinese exiles together. Old friends from China (exiles like us) passing along the road, stopped often to chat with us. We had a common faith in divine providence that makes all believers in Jesus Christ children of God and brothers and sisters in Him, regardless of race, tongue, or profession.

A common love of the Chinese way of life, with its excellent traditions of courtesy and hospitality, woke memories of good things and good times shared in the past. They were doubly precious because they were behind us and far from us. We had a common loyalty to a world we appreciated and loved, now at least temporarily lost; a mutual sorrow for the tragic plight of the Christian friends we had left behind in China; a deep concern for the dark, agonizing ordeal of China's millions. This opened up the fountains of love in our hearts. We never stopped wondering what happened to the friendly, smiling multitudes we loved. What madness of change had come over changeless China?

China was in our blood, embedded in our bones, crystalized in our thoughts, and echoing from our lips. How could we forget the latticed windows, the vermilion walls, the turned-up temple roofs, the jade green rice fields, the blue hills, the winding canals crossed by artistic arched bridges, the patched sails of the gliding junks?

How could we blot out the memory of the jolly rickshaw boy with his eagerness for passengers, the song of the toiling coolie with his backbreaking load, the elegant, witty scholar with his nimble brush, the slender woman with her sleek black hair and her chubby children staring at us with solemn eyes? Just as real to us as our new friends were memories of smiling, wrinkled, old village folk, wiley merchants, the ever-present throngs, the confusion of dialects, the rags and riches that are China.

"What is happening to our own friends in China?" That was the question ever springing from our anxious hearts. But it was a question no one could answer. We dared not write to any friends and relatives over there for fear of reprisals upon them. Every little scrap of information plucked from the Hong Kong grapevine was eagerly discussed and passed on. Yet the sometimes unspoken but keenly sensed questions that finally impelled me to write my first book were, "Was it worth it to send missionaries to China? Was it all in vain: the money spent, the lives invested, the earnest prayers, and the blood shed?" I had to witness! I had to confirm, to declare, to encourage, to shout that it was! Praise God, it was worth it!

But I must confess that after we were finally somewhat settled in the old Leaman homestead, and some of our personal effects were unpacked, the reality of my isolation began to grip me. I faced an "open end" confinement in a room about twelve feet wide and fifteen feet long. I had promised the Lord that as long as I had breath I would serve Him, and at every opportunity I would witness to the gospel. I found myself with breath, but no opportunity to go anywhere to witness about Him. This poem echoed my feelings:

> "Father, where shall I work today?"
> And my love flowed warm and free.
> Then He pointed me toward a tiny spot
> And said, "Tend that for me."

I answered quickly, "Oh, no, not that!
Why, no one would ever see.
No matter how well my work is done:
Not that little place for me!"
And the word He spoke it was not stern:
He answered me tenderly:
"Ah, little one, search that heart of thine
Art thou working for them or for Me?
Nazareth was a little place,
And so was Galilee!"

And so was Paradise, Pennsylvania! Driving through it either from the east or west on Highway 30, a person could miss it and be far beyond before realizing it. Having lived in teeming cities in China much of my life, I felt I was now in the middle of nowhere. How could I *go* with the gospel when I was a shut-in who could not even walk? I laid the problem before the Lord. I rested contentedly, because it was His problem and not mine.

Then He began to speak through friends who knew my story and were repeating it over and over to others. Clearer came the conviction of His call: "Write a book to witness of Me and reach the world."

"Lord, how can I write? And who would read it? I am nobody. Who knows my name? In China, years ago, I was known. But after so many years, who knows Christiana Tsai?"

It was as if the Lord gently rebuked me by saying, "You are not to write a book about what you did but what *I* did. My name is important, not yours!"

Two years passed before I could do anything about giving wings to my witness. I was often ill with recurrent attacks of malaria. My head would ache so that I felt it would burst. My dizziness swayed the room until I was seasick with nausea. I could neither eat nor sleep. Any slight noise would jar me into a painful consciousness. I used to dream of my old Chinese servant. "If only Pooh were here to rub my arms!" I sighed. "She would keep up my courage in the face of the endless pain and boredom of lying in bed alone." In my better moments I tried to sing hymns and keep my mind stayed upon the Lord.

I recognized God's hand of training and preparation upon me. In moments when I was somewhat free from pain, I began to jot down in a notebook an outline of my early life and the events of the Lord's working through the years. Many months passed and my notebook grew full. One day about two years after we had left China, Ellen Drummond, another missionary exile from our own area, arrived in our hollow. We were old friends and our bonds were close in Christ. We had lived in the same war-scarred house in Shanghai during the two years before we came to the United States. We had been grateful that in that jam-packed city we had a roof over our heads and four walls around us.

Miss Drummond also was a second-generation missionary, her parents having come to Nanking, China, later than the Leamans. She now also shared with us the dubious distinction of ill health—one more cripple, though not a shut-in.

When I told her my decision to write my life story, she offered to. help. Ellen was retired now and so had leisure time. Above all, she knew us intimately, as well as the setting and scenes of our lives from childhood. For me, cooped up in that dark room, it seemed that my only contribution to spreading the gospel from this point on could be my personal testimony. I could recount the great things God had done for me, my family, and fellow Chinese countrymen through the Christian missionaries.

While I was unable to realize my heart's desire to travel around America as I had done in the 1920s testifying of God's grace, I could still express my gratitude to Him through the written page. The story of my life would be carried into the homes and hearts of people everywhere. Perhaps this book would encourage many faithful believers who had prayed so fervently and given so sacrificially for mission work in China in the past, and who were now asking whether all the labor there had been in vain.

The theme of my story would center around the mighty work of God wrought by His Spirit in the place of greatest darkness. I would testify that although I was privileged to come from a wealthy, aristocratic family of imperial China, a product of its ancient historic culture and pride, Buddhism did not hold the answer to my heart's need. As a young girl I had no inner peace, no enlightenment. I was almost ready to take my vows to enter the Lin-yin Convent and become a nun. My superior nun had already given me a new name. The day had been set for shaving my hair and entering the "gates of emptiness." But the God whom I did not yet know had other plans. He had prepared a new name for me, too, to be written in the Lamb's book of life. He detoured me around the rocks of Buddhism and guided me directly to the Rock of Ages.

Since coming to know Christ, my greatest joy became to win others to Him, beginning with the members of my own big family. I knew there were many in America who also had no peace, in spite of materialistic abundance; many who suffered without hope; many lonely souls who felt they were no longer wanted. I knew they could all find peace in Christ. My story would help them. So with Ellen's help, we set upon our demanding task.

It seemed impossible, but with God's ever-present help and nearly round-the-clock writing, we finished the first draft in two short months. The first great step had been taken in a chain of events that was to grow in ever-widening circles—spreading to more and more parts of the world even to this day. However, the manuscript was far from ready to be submitted to a publisher. We needed line-by-line correction and polish, to which the four of us shut-ins applied ourselves every day for a whole year. After a quick breakfast, we would all gather in my room and pray for God's guidance in each word, each thought, each paragraph! Then we would spend hour after hour working with care on accuracy and continuity. We wanted every event to be recorded to the glory of God and not man. Cousin Mary often remarked, "If this book is ever published, it will be a book of prayer!" My eyes could not read continually, so the three Leamans patiently took turns reading each paragraph to me. So often I said, "Please read it again."

Finally we reached the point of needing an expert typist for the final draft. One spry, ninety-two-year-old judge's wife and resident of Lancaster had been writing down historical notes about Lancaster. She came to see us once in a while, always chauffeured by her niece. This young lady was a meticulous businesswoman, charming to look at, and dressed in the most attractive fashion. As she sat on the little kindergarten chair by my bed, I talked with her about missions. She coldly and brusquely stated, "I am not a Christian. I am not interested in missions."

At this rebuff I prayed silently, *Fisher of men, perhaps I am not the right bait for this fish*, and I did not press her further. She left me and went into the parlor to join the others.

Later, China Mary hurried breathlessly into my room with the news. "That young lady has offered to type your manuscript free of charge! She says she can come every Saturday to go over it with you!"

The following Saturday and each Saturday thereafter, she arrived, beautifully dressed in a different stylish outfit each time. She carefully and expertly went over every comma, period, and quotation mark in the manuscript. Later, much to my great surprise, she said, "Your story is interesting. The people in my office gather around my table and ask me to read it aloud."

Another week a missionary, who accompanied her out of my room, heard her remark, "Anyone who did not believe in Jesus before could not help believing after reading that book."

Later, she made an even more electrifying announcement. "I have already asked to be baptized," she said, quickly adding, "But I don't want to be a missionary. I don't want to leave my country."

"Dear lady, we are all missionaries," I said.

She opened her eyes wide and asked plaintively, "Do I have to be one?"

"Yes!" I said, but then inquired, "Do you love your husband?"

"Of course," she replied, puzzled.

"As long as you do, you will work in the kitchen. And you can start by being an in-kitchen missionary," I told her. "I myself cannot go traveling around the country, but I am still an in-bed missionary."

By God's grace we had now completed the manuscript, but we had not decided on a publisher. I had always admired Moody Bible Institute since I studied Moody correspondence courses years ago in China. My first choice was to send it to Moody Press. A pastor who had been a salesman for seven years in a well-known bookstore, said, "Publishing is a gamble. The life of such a book is short—six months to a year. Moody Press only publishes books by well-known people. Nobody knows you," he warned.

"People may not know me," I said, "but my God knows me. I heard that when Queen Elizabeth and Princess Margaret were children, they lost their way and landed at an old folks home. 'Who are you?' an old man asked them. 'We are nobodies,' they replied, 'but our father is king!' " China Mary and I prayed about it and mailed the manuscript to Moody Press. Two months later the acceptance came! In August 1953, *Queen of the Dark Chamber* was off the press. Seven months later it had already been reprinted three times.

Chapter 13

Best Seller

From 1953 to 1976, *Queen of the Dark Chamber* was reprinted thirty-six times in English by Moody Press and translated into more than thirty forms of publication and two braille editions. Many best sellers have had far greater circulation, but we had the assurance that God was sending this particular witness to every individual whose heart He had already prepared.

The Lord's gift to us was a renewed interest in life and many friends. I am busy from morning until night. Countless friends from far and near—in fact, from all over the world—have made my life richer, sweeter, and brighter. Because some message in my book stirred their hearts, they have been drawn over the highways and down into our hollow.

As book sales mounted, enthusiastic reviews appeared in magazines. The postman began stuffing our box full of "fan mail." One letter was from John F. Kullgren of Washington, D.C.:

> Dear Miss Tsai:
>
> I saw your book, *Queen of the Dark Chamber*. And as I read, it suddenly dawned upon me that here I was meeting once again that childhood "Queen" of the lighted temple: an unforgettable, charming, persuasive, no less than dramatic messenger of the Gospel, who suddenly appeared in my small-children circle, who conquered me wholly—and then, somehow, disappeared among the 450 million Chinese, not to reappear before now. Yes, I conclude from reading the book about you, that you must be that person.

I thought you might like to read about our last meeting: It must have been about 1915 or 1916, when I was a 10-year-old schoolboy at the Swedish School in Ichang, Hupeh Province. At the time, my parents, of the Swedish Missionary Society, were in Wuchang, and I was at the school in Ichang, living with Rev. Fernstrom and his wife, who were in charge of us children. One day this beautiful Chinese young lady appeared, living with us at the mission while conducting an evangelistic campaign.

You not only aroused the Chinese congregation of the various Swedish and British missions in Ichang, you roused us Swedish children as well to a new desire to confess our sins and become "living" Christians. You used to sit down by the organ in the parlor of the "Ladies House," and teach us a song which you liked. And we learned your song by routine, the way Chinese school children learned their characters by endless repetition. And I'm not sure now that I know the meaning of all the words in the song, no more than the Chinese children necessarily knew the meaning of all the characters they repeated. But your song has stuck in my memory all these years, and that should show a good teacher as well as a willing student.

These were sounding words, written and sung for a people who still largely went to their Buddhist and Taoist temples and had to be given the reassurance of Christian, heavenly protection in order to desist from their tradition-bound ways. Not that we children went praying to these temples! The point of learning the song was that it was your song, and when you led, we followed gladly. We were all, and I for certain, caught by that evangelistic revival spirit of yours. But most of all, that refreshing memory of you has never dimmed. To the boy, you were a princess from a Chinese fairyland, brought up-to-date in a twentieth century reality. Aptly, in the book about you, you are now a queen.

> Reading the book about you not only recalls that China from World War I and before World War II which we loved so much. It also provides a personal inspiration, retracing your life of devotion to your people and unswerving faith in the gospel of Christ, a faith I know will continue to sustain you in this period of trials you have sustained through these many late years of sickness. It is so sad to read this part of your book, but though our science lacks means of healing you, it is clear that your spirit and your faith are sustaining you to bear these sufferings without a waver of your enthusiasm for life and the furtherance of the fellowship of man under Christ.

Suddenly life was transformed. The prayer that China Mary and I first offered when we began serving the Lord together many years ago became an even greater heart cry now that we faced the throngs of people the Lord was bringing to us. Now we prayed, "May the Lord whom we love and serve together this day, suggest, direct, and control all that we say and do for Him and for His children."

We were no longer just overage freighters, rusting away at our anchors. We soon had to have our driveway enlarged. Many visitors were old missionary friends, delighted to find us again. They dropped in without ceremony as they were passing by. Many church delegations phoned for engagements. Sometimes Sunday school youngsters came to sing for us. Whole families stopped by to say hello and then stayed for a meal. Travelers saw the JESUS SAVES sign in both English and Chinese in our yard and wanted to talk over their problems. Groups of college students on vacation arrived. Church leaders on the way to conferences enjoyed refreshment at our home.

A little boy of ten, who came with his grandfather, a retired general of the United States Army, promised to send me a dollar a month. I called him "president of my mission board." I told

Unspoken testimony

my boy president, "Hereafter I cannot say that since 1919 I serve my Lord only by faith since I expect to receive one dollar a month regularly from you!"

We were honored that numerous dignitaries—political, educational, military, and religious—visited us. Indians, Japanese, Koreans, and many from the Philippines have taken the trouble to find us. Visitors come in the front door and the back door. Sometimes we have one guest at a time, although frequently we have several groups in the house at once. On special occasions the hall, sitting room, and kitchen have been full, and there has barely been standing room in my bedroom, with the overflow gathering at my door.

An interested friend examined our guest books over a period of a month and figured our average to be about forty-three guests daily!

Many were earnest Christians who had much to give us in inspiration and fellowship. Some were sick, searching for health, and some were burdened, asking for prayer, while a number were just curious "to see the little Chinese girl" they had heard about. Wide-eyed children asked to see this mysterious "queen" who lived in a dark room. To tell the truth, my life, while unusual, has had more downs than ups, but to them it sounded exotic and glamorous. I was surely no longer a girl, nor a queen, just an ordinary person, and well into my sixties.

A bilingual sign in Chinese and English that read "Jesus Saves" on Leaman house's lawn was perhaps the most unique scene on Route 30 in PA a half century ago.

Visitors were a challenge that we could not refuse, but you can imagine that we were taxed to the utmost. Often I trembled to answer the phone. Lucy was under doctor's orders to keep quiet. Cousin Mary had been sheltered all her life. Only China Mary, a strange blend of iron determination and simple faith, never wavered. She decreed that we would receive and entertain, in the best Christian and Leaman family tradition, everyone who came. Nothing was too good for our guests.

Fortunately, we all enjoyed meeting people. So we rose little by little to meet the challenge, each entertaining in her own way. Such interesting and worthwhile guests they proved to be! They have done far more for us than we could have done for them. Each of our shut-in quartet rallied at the sound of the doorbell and found untapped resources of spiritual power and physical stamina to bear up under the strain. Many neighbors pitched in and helped to serve refreshments. Food had to be stocked so we could be ready at a moment's notice. The dining room table usually remained extended to accommodate perpetual guests. Then, after the meal, the inevitable dishes had to be washed.

China Mary was busy from morning till night. She still wore Chinese clothes, usually of navy blue, and rarely had time to take off her apron in an entire day. Always quiet, always smiling, always unhurried, she devoted herself to each individual, no matter who he was. Butcher, baker, truck driver, or repairman, was always prayed with at the door before he left. Though they were busy people, most appreciated it. With all visitors she was the perfect hostess, greeting them warmly, sitting down with them quietly, conversing about the Lord. If they arrived at mealtime, they were simply included, and when they had to go, she urged them to return soon. "Restful availability" was China Mary's motto—available to the Lord for His gentle leading through her to touch the lives of others for His glory.

One man driving by had noticed our sign. He was an alcoholic. "Your sign said that Jesus saves. Can this Jesus save me?" he asked. China Mary sat down in the parlor and talked and prayed with this absolute stranger for two hours. He came back the next day to thank her. "It worked! It worked!" he reported gratefully. "I gave my problem to Jesus!"

I am often cautioned by my doctor to keep the flow of visitors to a minimum so as not to overtax my frail body and mind. But he has begun to realize through many years of caring for me that God's Spirit in me is still vigorous, although very evidently my "outer man" is wasting away. When China Mary would come into my room to say, "Dear, there are some visitors who want to see you," no matter how weary I had been the moment before, no matter how I ached, I would come to life and begin to organize: I would comb my hair, change into my black velvet jacket, spread out my silken coverlet over my work on the bed, and ask to have chairs arranged. Then I would set out my Bible and books and other things that I might want to refer to, and genuinely welcome the visitors and treat them like long-lost friends.

I am not blind, but since bright light hurts my eyes, there is a covered light by my bed and another shaded one by the window. I cannot see people's faces very clearly as they come in, only their shadowy outlines. At most, only thirty can be seated in my room on folding chairs, but on frequent occasions forty or more are squeezed in. More than once the over one-hundred-year-old bed has cracked with the weight of extra guests sitting beside me! Many other guests stand in the dining room looking in.

But whether my guests are adults or children, men or women, important people or simple folk, we like to have them talk about themselves and tell us what is on their hearts. Interesting discussions develop, and all kinds of questions are asked—some on theology, world affairs, spiritual subjects, and even medical matters.

Even in my advanced age, I still get nervous and apprehensive when people I don't know descend upon me. In myself I know that I have nothing to give them. I often feel inadequate to share Christ with those who are well educated, knowledgeable in world affairs, and probably preachers and teachers themselves. But the Lord reminds me that it is not myself I am to present to them, but Himself. Then He takes care of the butterflies in my stomach that are flitting about because of my lifelong fear of strangers. Has not God's Word declared, "Be not afraid of their faces" (Jeremiah 1:8)?

One spring I had accepted an appointment with twenty-two medical doctors and nurses from hospitals in the Philadelphia area. One doctor had been here before. After only a short time of fellowship in the Lord, we all became warm friends as if we had known each other all our lives. They bought one hundred and twenty copies of my book to share with their friends. They were convinced that many of their patients and suffering ones, after reading my testimony of God's keeping power, would be moved by the Lord to courageously go on.

Three days later, twenty-five members and campus leaders of Inter-Varsity Christian Fellowship spent some time with me. Although none of us had ever met before, again we were wonderfully united in the Lord.

Menno Simon, one of our dear Mennonite friends and a well-known businessman, was critically ill in the hospital some distance from us in Pennsylvania. China Mary phoned him every day to pray with him. For three weeks his pain grew so severe that he could hardly stand it.

China Mary asked me, "Do you feel led to pray not only for his freedom from pain, but also for his healing?" He had been praying that the Lord would show him if there was anything in his life that had caused this suffering, that he might deal with it before the Lord, or else that his pain might be relieved.

I answered, "Yes, but he must agree in faith with us." We phoned him with our proposal and he agreed. We three formed a prayer circle. He had not slept through the night for many weeks because of the pain, always depending on tranquilizers and injections to get any rest at all. Then China Mary and I prayed for him through the night, pleading God's promises according to His Word and according to His will.

Menno phoned us the next day, relating this wonderful story:

"Last night, although still in intense pain, I suddenly fell sound asleep. But soon I woke up and lay quietly, not daring to believe that my pain was gone! The nurse came in to give me my usual injection to relieve the pain and I refused it. 'I have no more pain,' I insisted. She could hardly believe it when I got right out of bed and walked around. Later the doctor came in. 'I have bad news for you,' he said, shaking his head seriously. 'We don't know what is wrong with you, but we know that we can't give you the every-four-hour pain killer any longer because your system can't take it.' I told the astonished doctor, 'That's all right. I don't need it—I'm perfectly well!'"

We thanked the Lord together on the phone for His healing. In two days he was discharged from the hospital, and the pain has never returned. Menno Simon, a sincere, hardworking Christian before, rededicated his life and all that he had from the Lord to serve Him even more faithfully.

Miss Tsai in the dark chamber—bed cannot prison me but is where God disciplines me. The Holy Spirit is my mentor, and welcoming visitors is my homework.

Chapter 14

My Co-workers

A house is not self-cleaning. Meals don't appear out of thin air. Dishes don't jump up and wash themselves. How could all these activities go on with crowds of extra guests in a house of invalids? We can invite people to a meal, but someone has to buy the food, prepare and serve it. When people drop in at all hours of the day and night, someone must give extra time to attend to them.

It is the dear friends and co-workers among the Mennonites who have touched our lives so deeply since we settled in America, and without whom we would not have survived. When any guests have visited us, they are first met by Mennonites who help us in our home. Often they are also entertained in Mennonite homes and taken to their places of worship. Their testimonies have made a lasting impression on many of our friends, especially the Chinese students and military officers.

The Mennonite women have been "ministering angels" to us. They have expressed the serenity and peace of the Lord not only in their faces but in their hearts. They have the kind of happiness, peace, and assurance in their lives that most people desire. They are well-known for their orderly and spotless houses and their neat buildings, yards, fences, and gardens. Because they are not afraid of hard work and center their interest in home tasks, they immediately came to our rescue. They helped us at every turn with cooking, cleaning, physical care, and their generous hospitality to the many visitors whom the Lord brought to us. They lived a Christlike life before our guests and ministered God's Word to them as well.

In China, a friend who knew our circumstances said firmly, even prophetically, "I am praying that God will provide you with some Mennonites in America who will work with you." That is just what happened!

Miss Susanna Eshleman, our neighbor, is a Mennonite lady and faithful follower of the Lord Jesus who recognized our need and came to help us with housekeeping. She soon learned our Chinese ways of living and became accustomed to meeting internationals and people from different walks of life. Friends often tell me how kind and thoughtful she is. Hostess, companion, prayer partner, nurse, cook, and housekeeper are only a few of her many ministries. Whenever unexpected callers drop in around mealtime, it is Susanna who has to leave her work and prepare a meal for them. Having had much experience in nursing members of her own family in the past, she helped nurse each of us invalid four with faithful dedication.

After my book was published, I desperately needed someone to help me with my exploding correspondence. The Lord provided a second Mennonite friend, Mrs. Frances Stoltzfus, a farmer's wife and busy mother of three daughters. She drives the sixteen-mile round trip to our home several times a week, no matter what the weather, to do my secretarial work. Her sacrificial devotion has made possible the extensive correspondence related to the worldwide distribution of my book and its various printings and foreign editions. She sits at the foot of my bed in the semi-darkness and takes dictation. She writes faster than I can dictate and then transcribes my letters in the parlor on a portable typewriter. She has attended to the packing and mailing of thousands of book orders through the years, and as a personal secretary she handles much of my business. In the early days of our working together, as she would leave, I would hand her a used envelope, saying, "This is for your gasoline." At times I could only give her forty-six cents. I was embarrassed at the sum, but it was all I had to offer then.

One day, to my great surprise, she handed me a clean envelope. In it I found sixty-six dollars. She said that her Sunday school class had learned that even in my weakness I was serving the Lord by faith. They had baked and canned food to sell, and the proceeds were designated to help our work. This was the first time I ever received such a love gift. It truly encouraged me to continue working in the Lord's vineyard. However, I was more surprised and encouraged to receive the following lines from her own pen, after we had been working together for more than fifteen years:

A TRIBUTE TO MY QUEEN

Her chamber may seem very dark
When first you enter it,
But soon the Saviour's face you'll see
As by her side you sit.

I thank my Heavenly Father
For all to me she's meant—
For trials and for joys we've shared
Since I to her was sent.

In her I have seen patience,
Faith, contentment, love so true:
Of God she's asked again and again,
"What wilt Thou have me do?"

My prayer is that I may be
More like this one I love.
Won't it be just wonderful
To see her crowned above?

And so I beg, "Dear Father,

Be merciful and bless
Her remaining days and years
Just as Thou seest best."

Praise the Lord that all the time, as we have worked so closely, we have never had any harsh words or misunderstandings. Many times we have carried separate personal burdens that we could share with no one, not even each other. These could have disturbed our work for Him each time when we came together. But instead, we prayed and laid these burdens on the Lord and proceeded to work in harmony. Then we found we did not want to pick them up again. We left them with our burden Bearer, Jesus Christ.

Later on, the Lord miraculously brought to us a very talented Chinese friend to join us in serving Him. Grace Ng was the president of a Christian school for about twenty years in the Philippines. She had led her whole family to follow the Lord.

Three intimate co-workers in the dark chamber:
Secretary Mrs. Fu Situ (first to the left) who worked with Miss Tsai for 30 years;
Mrs Enci Huang (second to the left) worked with Miss Tsai for 23 years;
Miss Susanna (first to the right), was a good housekeeper to Miss Tsai for more than 30 years who passed away ten months earlier than Miss Tsai on Oct. 5, 1983.

She is truly a woman of prayer. Very, very often long distance phone calls come to ask her for prayer for difficult problems and for spiritual advice. Nothing can hinder her from spending an hour in prayer on her knees morning and evening. She longs for everyone who enters this house to know Jesus Christ and helps them to have a clear understanding of being born again.

For extra cleaning chores we have sometimes employed some traditional Amish women to help. They would arrive, promptly roll up the long black sleeves of their billowy dresses, and attack the most difficult tasks of scrubbing, polishing, and cleaning. They accomplished wonders with non-automatic brooms, scrub pails, mops, and their own skillful hands. This helped me wonderfully because they worked so fast and silently, not jarring my sensitive ears with the whir of vacuum cleaners, but working with the quietness of well-seasoned muscles.

One day an Amish lady appeared, alighting from her carriage and tying her horse to our tree. She declared, "Miss Tsai, I just read your book and so I came to see you." After a most interesting conversation, she took from her pocket a well-worn small bag. She counted out her pennies one by one on my bed, fifty-six cents in all, and said, "Miss Tsai, I want to help you in your work." I never forgot her warm smile and sincerity.

For lighter, routine tasks of washing dishes, helping to get us settled for the night after our evening meal, and other work that should be done by younger legs, China Mary engaged neighborhood high school girls. Knowing that young high school girls often had school events cropping up at unexpected times, she hired several different girls to help us, teaching them each the same work. When we had extra guests, meetings, or health emergencies, she had a reservoir of help at her beck and call.

But her primary desire was that she might reach these young girls for the Lord. She often set aside some of their regular tasks to call them into her room, asking them to read some Bible passage to her, especially after her eyesight was failing. Sometimes it was to read an article from a Christian magazine, or to listen to a radio sermon, or to take home a Christian record or cassette and later report to her about it. She invested her prayers and her time in these girls, believing that God's Word would not return void but in due season would come to harvest. We Chinese say, "The bamboo shoots all of a sudden spring up."

The Lord took China Mary to her heavenly home before some of the seed had sprouted. Later, one by one, five of them could hardly wait to come to tell me how Christ came into their hearts and how they longed for others to know Jesus and follow Him. Others told me how these girls had already influenced their parents, friends, relatives, and even a boyfriend. One of the girls wrote a tribute to China Mary: "She was one of the most admired people that I have ever known. Her life was an example for every Christian, completely devoted to the Lord. I always felt that being with her each day was a new experience in Christ. Though I was a teenager and she was 92, her faith did not seem old to me because she renewed it every day of her life."

On some of the big occasions when our parlor overflowed with Chinese friends, officers, and students, I was aware that without our Christian friends from the community and churches, this would never have been possible. These friends have been like a treasure from the Lord. Not only have they worked with us, but they have encouraged me by their visits and letters.

Chapter 15
Holiday Haven

Chinese students by the thousands are scattered in nearly all of the universities and colleges of this land, and at holiday time most of them do not get to go home as do their American classmates. Gradually, as they heard about us and "the little bit of China" that was in Paradise, many of them began to make our home their home on Thanksgiving, Christmas, Easter, and other holidays.

At Thanksgiving they learned how to roast and carve the traditional turkey and bake pumpkin pies and other goodies. More than that, they learned that the true meaning of the celebration is to give thanks and praise to God for their many blessings.

Christmas found the Chinese students decorating our rooms with colored lights and the Christmas tree with tinsel and bulbs. The girls put on their best Chinese dresses and the young men put on their ties to welcome group after group who came in to sing Christmas carols. They stood in a row to welcome them, bowing when they left. On Christmas Eve when carolers came from far and near, the students would hurry to turn on the floodlight at the doorway and invite them in to have a hot drink. Most of all, they learned that Christ who was born in a manger in Bethlehem had come into the world to bring salvation to all men.

One Easter I was asked to speak to a large group of students about Jesus' resurrection. A pretty young Chinese girl, a PhD candidate, and daughter of a very wealthy Philippine businessman, suddenly exclaimed, "Why, I have been in this country for seven years, but just this morning the Holy Spirit convinced me that I need to confess before others that I am a sinner. I want

Chinese students decorated our rooms for Christmas.

to believe in Jesus and receive baptism!" Her baptism took place not long after, on a very quiet and beautiful Sunday afternoon. I was helped by two strong friends out of my darkened room to sit on the chaise lounge. It was the very first time I had left my room to participate in a service. I felt like Lazarus raised from the tomb!

After the message, China Mary accompanied the young lady to the front as she knelt to receive baptism. Her face was radiant. It seemed like a host of angels was worshipping Jesus and giving Him the glory because a lost sheep had been brought back to the fold. Her step took real courage because she would soon return to her unbelieving family to face much opposition. This was only the beginning of many more students, seamen, and military men accepting the Lord and being baptized in our home.

Our home was also the setting for the first Christian Chinese wedding in Lancaster County. Nearly two hundred guests assembled in our parlor to attend the ceremony. China Mary had the floor structure and basement beams of our over 250-year-old house reinforced in anticipation of the large crowds now assembling regularly in our home. We usually borrowed folding chairs from the local funeral parlor to seat so many friends. Preceding the service an international quartet from Westminster College was sent as a special favor from the president of the school. Our local Presbyterian pastor officiated at the double-ring cremony in front of the palm-banked altar in our parlor.

The bride-to-be volunteered her recollections: "It was on Christmas 1949, the year that Miss Tsai and Miss Leaman returned from China, that I first visited the Leaman home. My mother had called on them in Shanghai and was impressed with their love and work. Because they were in such poor health, Mother urged that we go to visit them and give them any help we could. But over twenty-five years have passed since then and we haven't helped them one bit. On the contrary, we so often received their help and encouragement.

"During the time I was a student at Princeton, whenever

there was a vacation, members of our family and friends took off for Paradise. In 1954 I met the man I was one day to marry. In January 1955 my fiance accepted Christ right in the Leaman living room. We dedicated our lives to the Lord together. On February 19th of that year we were married in the Leaman home, with preparation and responsibility being cared for by these two elderly folk. A deep spiritual impression was left on each one who attended.

"As our three children came along, they were loved by these dear old folks as much as by their own grandparents. When we visited them, there were always toys for the children to play with. When they grew a bit bigger, there were candies on hand for them. After the children went to school, the dear folks read Bible story books to them and sent the books home as gifts. Afterward, when Miss Leaman's eyes became poor, she wrote her last letter to the children, urging them to love their parents and to lead others to the Lord. On our last visits, when she couldn't see at all, she still touched each one and called their names, sang with them, repeated Bible verses, and asked each one about his school. She told them when they went home to write and tell her all that they had seen on their excursion.

"When news reached us of Miss Leaman's home-call, the three children decided they must go to her memorial service and they volunteered a musical number. We had always gone to the Leaman home on festive occasions with gladness in our hearts. This time it was a funeral—but somehow still a festive occasion. It was the joyous celebration of a faithful child of God entering the gates of Heaven amid happy shouts of the angelic hosts! As we left the cemetery, our oldest said, 'I'm happy! At least we could do this much for Grandma!' None of us could be sad at her departure— not for her, only for us that we would miss her Christlike love and care for us."

Chinese students felt at home in PA.

Chapter 16

Responses

I am a native-born Chinese. But I wrote my book in English. My Chinese friends gave me no peace until the Chinese translation was under way. The Chinese edition came out in 1955 and has become one of the best sellers.

One day I received a letter from a Chinese woman that revealed a story stranger than fiction. She had been a secretary for the Communists in China for six years. Eventually she escaped to Hong Kong. Lonely and depressed, she refused to have anything to do with church or Christianity. She would not read any Christian literature, and twice she was found just in time by her neighbors as she tried to commit suicide. A woman called on her and casually left a copy of my book on her bureau, hurrying off before it could be refused.

Still determined to end her life, she prepared a double dose of poison. When she was ready to take it, a voice seemed to say to her, "Read that book before you take the poison." She did. She read it through twice without stopping. Her terrible sins were revealed to her. Crawling on the floor, she sobbed for hours in repentance. Her letter said, "My doubts all disappeared. Before, this Jesus had seemed far away—just a myth. Suddenly He was very, very real. My heart brimmed over with unspeakable gratitude and I determined to accept Him as my Savior." She learned of my whereabouts through a church, and we carried on an extensive correspondence. Not only did she become an earnest Christian, but she also started a Bible class which later became a Christian church.

When the Communists occupied China, they wanted to destroy every kind of religion, and that included the lamas. Temples were burned, idols destroyed, and lamas killed. Some tried to escape to India over the Himalaya Mountains. Most of these refugees died on this dangerous trip, although some got as far as the border of India. They were exhausted and their feet were one mass of blisters from climbing the rugged mountains.

At the foot of the Himalaya Mountains there is a little chapel of the Moravian Christian Church where some missionaries live. They came upon the lamas lying half-dead on the ground—a pitiful sight. They gave them water and food. A number of children among them were almost starved. The missionaries made an offer to the adults, saying, "We would like to help your children if you will permit us to feed them and teach them free."

Among the children was a certain seven-year-old. He was old enough by custom to enter the lama temple, and his mother had already determined that he should do so. But since he was starving to death and there was an opportunity for his life to be saved, the mother allowed him to go with the missionaries. At the age of eleven, this very bright boy, who studied well, decided to accept Christ as his Saviour. He learned to read the Indian language, and an Indian translation of my book came to his hands. The Holy Spirit evidently touched his heart. He thought, *When I finish my education, if the Lord would guide me, I would like to translate that book into the Tibetan language. Our people do not have books or literature to read except the religious books of the lamas and repeated prayers.* He recalled seeing much Christian literature and Bibles in some homes. He longed for his people to have such books to read.

Another missionary managed to help the boy come to Canada to study in a Bible college. In his leisure time he actually translated my book into Tibetan. As I am writing this, I have just received a letter from him saying that he has finished it. He knew a friend in India who had a publishing house and wrote to him asking if he would consider publishing this book. The friend agreed to publish one thousand copies. He writes, "My people are poor.

They came upon the lamas lying half-dead on the ground.

They don't have money to buy a book, so we may have to give it to them. Pray that the Lord will guide my people to read the book and accept Christ as you did."

One of the most touching reactions to the book was a letter from my own nephew in Taiwan. Woodrow grew up amid the scenes in my book. I trembled when I sent him one of the first copies. He is one of the few remaining Tsai relatives with whom I have any contact. He wrote,

> Your book just arrived. Congratulations, Auntie! It is beautiful—a beautiful name and so very beautifully written. I had an engagement last night, but before the dinner was finished, I thanked my host and came back home hurriedly to meet "the Queen." I went through your book in three hours. It is much richer than the luscious food I had! You must have received many flattering remarks from all your readers, but myself, "Ever-Cheer" in your book, knows you well from the inside, and is glad to verify that everything you mentioned in it is true and to the point. That is the important thing for any autobiography. You said you wrote it as if you were telling your story to a friend—I think rather that you have prepared a report to your Lord. The Lord will judge your achievement through all those you have led to believe in Him. You shall surely win the first prize!

One day I got a surprise letter from Canada on stationery from the famous missionary-minded church, The Peoples Church in Toronto. It was from their noted pastor, Dr. Oswald J. Smith. Among other things, he wrote:

> So stirred was I to read your book that I was hardly able to lay it down when once I had started reading it. When I think of all that you have come through for

Christ, I feel that I have done so little. He has undertaken for you in a marvelous way and you have been most faithful to Him. You have won many souls and you are assured of a crown. I think of your suffering and my heart goes out to you....I want you to know that I have been praying definitely for you. Your book has given me a new understanding of Chinese life among the wealthy classes. I do so want to bring about a reconciliation between the people of China and the people of America. We and the Chinese ought to be the best of friends. Your book will help heal that wound. It will free us from prejudice against the Chinese. Our hatred of Communism has poisoned our minds and hearts toward these lovely people, who, when Jesus lives in their hearts, are unsurpassed for their simple, beautiful saintliness. In you we see them as they can be and as the noblest of them are....Sometime ago I wrote a little poem for you to show you how greatly my heart was stirred by your story. Here it is:

I WANT YOU TO KNOW

I want you to know you are never forgotten,
The Savior is with you, He sees all your grief;
Remember, He cares, He will never forsake you,
And soon He is coming to bring you relief.

I think of you daily and pray for you always,
How often I see you in darkness and pain;
But though you must suffer, His grace is sufficient,
And someday with Jesus forever you'll reign.

The Lord will be with you, dear Queen of the darkness,
And all of earth's shadows will soon pass away;
For you have been faithful and many in Heaven

Will praise you for turning their darkness to day.

Your book has brought blessing, it makes me unworthy,
For you have accomplished so much by His grace;
Someday you will step from your chamber of darkness,
For Jesus remembers; you'll see His dear face!

With Christian affection, my sister from China,
I send you this message—your prayers He will hear;
I want you to know that God's mercy is o'er you—
Forgotten? No, never! Your Savior is near!

OSWALD J. SMITH

Chapter 17

Stupid Donkey

When Major Chang arrived from Taiwan at Aberdeen, Maryland, to learn the techniques of modern warfare at the Proving Grounds there, he realized that his English was inadequate to understand his classwork. An American officer's wife offered to tutor him. She used *Queen of the Dark Chamber* for a text. He soon realized it was written by a Chinese and when he learned that I lived within driving distance, he asked her, "Will you take me to meet this lady?"

Later, he wrote about his visit to us in a Chinese magazine.

> I stepped into a dark chamber to meet Miss Tsai who had been bedridden for so many years. Forgetting my rank, I sat by her bed on a small kindergarten chair and chatted with her. Deep down in my heart I experienced a sudden upsurging of peace, joy, and hope. Right there I was born again and really saved. From that time I have tried to live a real Christian life inspired by Miss Tsai, not because of her own strength, but by the Holy Spirit who spoke to my heart through her lips.

How God used this very first contact with the Chinese military to enlarge the circle of witness even to other shores.

Back at the base, he excitedly reported his visit to fellow Chinese officers. A week later, a consecrated Christian secretary at the Proving Grounds, Miss Edna Hill, who had also read the book and wanted to meet us, drove over with five more Chinese officers. They were all high-ranking military personnel, carefully chosen for their exceptional qualifications. We sensed the importance of these contacts. Each man won for Christ could influence his own family and many men under him and they, in turn, could reach their relatives and friends. What a wonderful "army of the cross" that might be! Each officer won for Christ would be an important victory for the Lord of Hosts in His eternal war to save the world from sin and death. And as for us in this remote corner of rural America, it spelled opportunity—now we could still carry on our missionary work among the Chinese!

One copy of my book had started the ball rolling. These and subsequent groups of officers visited us time and again and invited their friends to come along. Faithful Edna Hill and others often brought them over in their cars. We urged them to think of our house as their home away from home and of us as their relatives here in America.

China Mary became "Great Aunt" to them and I, "Seventh Aunt." We always presented a Christian message, had prayer with them, and taught the Bible. We never insisted that they join a particular church. Each one who made a decision for Christ and asked for baptism did so of his own free will. After his baptism, each man wrote his own testimony of why he had believed. Then he made a tape recording of his experience and a prayer. In this way, other military men coming later could hear the testimonies of their fellow officers and be helped and blessed.

For years, almost every holiday and on many weekends, groups of two, three, four, or more officers came to our house to spend the day. Their course of military training would usually last only a few months, and the groups became much smaller. But each group visited us many times before they returned to Taiwan. They said, "Formosa [Taiwan] means 'Beautiful,' and we would be interested to see the beautiful things in America, too, but we prefer to come to you and find out what the Bible teaches." So they came every possible weekend. Nine different pastors baptized about seventy-two of these men through the fifteen years of this particular military program at Aberdeen.

What gives us the deepest satisfaction is the knowledge that many of these men have become missionaries to their own countrymen. Although the foreign missionaries have been withdrawn from the China mainland, these Chinese leaders are effectively ministering in His name. The army of the Lord for China is marching on!

God has given us a special respect for these brave men who are committed to the task of defending their country. We prayed that through us they would feel a certainty of an unseen Power above and beyond our own that was sustaining us, that they would find in us love transcending human affection, shining through clay, and that as a result they would find a faith in a heavenly Father more real than the material facts of existence. They had come here to learn how to use the most frightful weapons ever devised by man. They knew the indescribable horrors their use would let loose upon the world. And, more personal to them, they knew they were the ones who would train others to be sent to the front lines to be the first victims in any attack. They were being taught how to fight and how to kill, but not how to live or how to die. What they needed most was not a skill to fight, but a faith to live and to die for. They needed most of all to know the love of God.

Most of these officers were not battle-scarred veterans who had tasted blood, but youths torn from their families and forced to flee their native land. They were desperately lonely boys without their wives or children and only the barest pittance to live on. They knew the suffering of those back on the mainland of China, and yet they were helpless to deliver them. Only minutes away by plane across the straits of Taiwan were bombers that could pour down a rain of death. And entrenched on mainland China was the Red Army with its missiles trained on the island.

So to these men, the message of a heavenly Father who loved and watched over them, a gracious Lord who died for them, a Holy Spirit abiding forever in their hearts, a heavenly home awaiting them, and the exceedingly great and precious promises of God to comfort them in all their trials—this faith was able to melt their bitterness, relieve their frustrations, and fill them with joy. It also drew them together in a new brotherly fellowship. It set before them a better way of life, and gave them a cause worth dying for.

Just why did these colonels, majors, and captains of the Chinese army seek the society of four crippled old ladies like us? They summed it up in the term they so often used: warmth. Though they knew we were doing this for the Lord, they also knew we truly loved and understood them. They felt at home with us. It was as simple as that. Their intellectual attainments were far above ours, but they sat at my bedside and listened eagerly as I tried to introduce them to Christ. The simple illustrations made the deepest impressions. I tried to see things through their eyes, to show them what it meant to be "a soldier of the cross."

This work, though exhausting and demanding, was very sweet. I was glad I was old! Had I been young, I could never have done it. Because of my age they looked upon me as an aunt and treated me with the deference the Chinese so graciously accord their elders. But the pupils soon outstripped their teacher. They kept asking so many searching questions that I began to worry. The climax came when they said they wanted to come and study the Bible with me.

Me, a Bible teacher? Here was an opportunity but I felt unequal to the challenge. At night with tears I told my Lord, "I'm not a Bible teacher, and besides, I haven't been able to use my eyes for so many years. How can I teach them? I am just a stupid donkey!"

The Lord's answer was clear. "I used a donkey to speak to Balaam. I can use you!"

Praise His name, He did! He used this stupid donkey. When I met with the men to study God's Word, the Holy Spirit manifested Himself by taking control and teaching us together. Many friends also helped make this possible by their prayers and their loving service. The long, drawn-out, sustained effort for over fifteen years of those officers' contacts had drained our life's blood, but oh, the rewards!

Chapter 18

Before the Footlights

One night just before Chinese New Year, a colonel phoned to tell me that a special class of Chinese officers from Taiwan at the Proving Grounds said they wanted to call on me the next day to offer their New Year's greetings. "Tomorrow?" I gasped. "How many?"

"About forty."

I covered the phone and held a whispered conversation with China Mary, who answered without hesitation, "They have offered to spend Chinese New Year with us. It is of the Lord. We can't refuse the honor. Tell them to come."

I resumed, "We will be delighted. Come early and spend the day with us."

These men had the same forlorn feeling as American GIs finding themselves stationed in a foreign land on Christmas Day. Away from everyone they loved and from every fond memory that made that season so dear, the officers were delighted to learn that there were four old ladies near Lancaster who understood what Chinese New Year meant to a Chinese.

I am sure it never occurred to them that they had presented us with an appalling task. We were to serve a New Year's feast, including two meals, to forty officers with twelve hours notice! They wouldn't ever think that it was an imposition! In China all heavy tasks are performed by well-trained servants, with the mistress of the family merely giving them orders and supervising their efforts. But here in America we were four old cripples, dependent on the kindness and availability of others for even our basic needs. We were living in a land where it is a tradition for every woman to take pride in doing her own housework. Here no one wants to be thought of as a servant. Modern conveniences and ingenious gadgets are the servants available.

However, we had long since ceased to ask God why He let people impose on our weaknesses or invade our privacy at all kinds of inconvenient times. This anticipated day especially was an unparalleled honor and a marvelous opportunity that could not be lost, no matter what the cost.

"Oh, just give them hot dogs and ice cream," a friend advised, hoping to simplify the work. China Mary did not answer but vanished to her cubbyhole office-bedroom. She shut the door and began to make out a list of all the food we would need. It was nearly ten o'clock when she picked up the phone to rouse the storekeeper. She dared to ask him to deliver everything we needed that very night. After all, the next day was Sunday! Then she called the turkey farm for huge turkeys and called the dairy for ice cream. She had decided it was going to be a real New Year's feast with all the trimmings!

Even at that late hour I phoned some other friends to come and help us entertain. One exclaimed incredulously, "You can't be serious! You can't possibly do it. This doesn't make sense!" No, it didn't make sense, but it was for Christ. I phoned another Christian Chinese friend in New Jersey. She answered cheerfully, "We just got back from Chinatown and bought all kinds of Chinese food. I won't need to sleep tonight. It is Chinese New Year's eve, anyway, and I am going to start cooking right away! I'll come early tomorrow morning."

Despite their misgivings, our friends rallied loyally. In addition to the feast, we had to arrange for a Christian service. Since most of the officers knew little or no English, we had to find a leader who could speak Chinese. Next we called on our neighbors, asking them to help prepare and serve the feast and, of course, to wash the anticipated piles of dishes! Fortunately the Leamans had cupboards and cupboards of beautiful dishes inherited from earlier generations. The neighbors not only agreed to come, but they also contributed large dishes of delicacies which they had hurriedly prepared. Besides all this, we invited interested friends from as far away as Philadelphia. We wanted them to join the party and meet our Chinese guests. Two other essential jobs were to charter a bus to convey the officers and to borrow folding chairs for the service.

It was well after midnight when we turned off the lights and tried to sleep. We had burned the telephone wires, roused sleepy people out of bed, and answered a chorus of incredulous whats, whys, and hows. Even that night the table was already set and preparations under way. The next day we didn't serve five thousand, but we did serve over one hundred, and not for one meal but two!

When the bus rolled into our yard, the driver found it already full of parked cars. When he opened the bus door, colonels, majors, captains, and lieutenants all trooped out in their natty olive drab uniforms and proud insignia. Bowing and smiling with caps in hand, they entered our humble home. They were not stiff and formal, though they observed strict military protocol among themselves. To us they were more like a lot of boys who were home on leave. They greeted us like old friends. Some were from Hunan, some from Peking, others from Shanghai and many other places. Each spoke his own peculiar dialect of Chinese, which only the experienced ear can differentiate. Some were veterans of the war with Japan, but most were young men who had fled Communist China and had joined the army on Formosa.

The table was laden with a typical American turkey dinner. We couldn't provide a Chinese feast out of a magic hat on such short notice. But still there were ample Chinese foods and the typical Chinese New Year's array of fruits, nuts, dates, cakes, and other delicacies. Each signified a traditional New Year's wish for happiness, long life, health, prosperity, many sons, family unity, and so forth. China Mary explained the Christian symbolism of

Bowing and smiling with caps in hand, they entered our humble home.

each item, and because it came from such a motherly person, they enjoyed her injunction to be “the heavenly Father’s good, obedient boys.” Later, before a large group of friends, the colonel said, “I know how to order my ten thousand soldiers to obey me. Now I want to learn to obey my heavenly Father’s order.”

Our big house was crowded to capacity with guests and volunteer workers, who almost stepped on each other’s toes as they elbowed their way through the crowd. The officers were tremendously impressed with this display of Christian love and hospitality. This was Christianity in action, and they appreciated seeing the ladies hurrying around to give their time and service for Christ's sake. When they sat down to eat, personal evangelism started. Each Christian, with his or her tray, sat beside an officer to be friends and to share his faith. One of our friends presented each officer with a copy of *Queen of the Dark Chamber*, and the Gideons gave them each a New Testament.

After the service, with only one exception, they all held up their hands to signify their desire to believe in Jesus. At first I did not put much stock in this public expression, thinking it might only be a courteous gesture on their part in return for our hospitality. Only a few had any previous knowledge of Christianity. But later, their commanding officer, a Christian, handed me a long list of those who had voluntarily signed their names, declaring their sincere desire to accept Christ. We did not see many of these men again, but some have written from Taiwan and have told me they now go to church. Some take their families with them, and some have actually joined a church. I know that the Spirit of God was present at our party. It was He who spoke to many on that New Year's Day.

"How do you know that those who say they accept the Lord in your dark chamber are really saved?" friends sometimes ask. This is never for me to judge. I am only to be faithful in proclaiming Christ to them. Let me share an example with you.

In China in 1919 when I started to serve the Lord by faith, I wrote articles for Chinese magazines and for a daily newspaper. A Miss Chen was my able Chinese secretary. But no matter how much I witnessed to her about Christ, she refused to believe in Him.

Once when I went to Pei-ta-ho for a conference, she secretly ran off to Shanghai and put an advertisement for a husband in the newspaper. A man answered and before long they were married. She gave him all her worldly possessions. On their honeymoon he took her to a famous place called Ging-san in Chin Kiang. In a

Miss Leaman with Chinese military officials like a family.

secluded spot, he put his arms around her and said, "Look at this beautiful river." While they gazed at it, he violently pushed her into the river. She lived to later tell me this story.

As she was nearly drowning in the water, unable to swim, her whole past seemed to come before her. She remembered my witness about Christ and His willingness to save any sinner. She made a dying decision to accept Christ, though at the same time she was shrieking, "Revenge! Revenge!" As she was going down for the third time and at death's very door, men in a fishing boat suddenly saw her and she was quickly rescued. Nearly dead, she could not talk but made signs that she wanted to write. She gave the name and address of a certain hotel, writing that her husband of three days had attempted to murder her. Policemen were sent to the hotel and found him frantically moving out all his belongings. They arrested him on the spot. When Miss Chen was asked to testify in court against him, because of Christ newly in her heart, she reversed her attitude of vengeance. She stated before the court that because God had forgiven her sins, she would forgive this scoundrel. All she asked was that he return everything she had given him. This experience was the turning point in her life. From that moment she lived wholly for the Lord.

How do any of us know if a person is saved when his lips confess Christ? How do we know but that through our witness he will someday in the future come to Christ? If my secretary had drowned, of course she would have belonged to Christ. But to this day I would not have known that in her dying moment, like the thief on the cross, she had accepted Him. We must faithfully sow the seed of His Word in the Spirit and leave the results in His hand.

Expenses ran high for the fifteen or sixteen years that our opportunity with the officers was at its peak. One night as I was thinking and praying about this, I remembered a Christian man who headed a large corporation. Only once had he called on me. I decided to write him a letter, asking him if he would like to have a share in financing this work.

As I polished up the letter, I suddenly felt a restraint from the Lord. "Since 1919 you have served Me by faith," the Lord reminded me. "Do you want to beg now? This is My work. I will take care of it." Puzzled, but obedient, I tore up the letter. Again I was tempted to write him as bills piled up. Five times I wrote and five times I tore up the letters. "Daughter, sit still," the Lord assured.

A few months later, I was surprised to receive a letter from this same gentleman. He said, "From reading different periodicals, and from friends who have been helping in your work with the Chinese officers, I have come to see the value of your ministry. I have decided to have a little financial share."

In reply, to express our appreciation for how the Lord had moved his heart, I told him about the five letters that I had written to him and destroyed. He answered that this showed to him the Lord's seal of approval on his decision to help our work. But he went on to say that if I had mailed those letters, he would not have been able to give to the work. He asked me to make a bargain with him. I was to tell no one except Miss Leaman that he was contributing to our ministry. If I did, he would not be able to continue it.

As the work expanded, this gentleman suggested to China Mary and me that we incorporate our work so that others could contribute to it with tax benefits. We backed away from such a complication. We knew it would involve at least a secretary, treasurer, office work, and much red tape of accountability to the government and public. "I will pay for your accountant and secretary," he offered.

But we declared, "We really have no 'work.' God only brings us opportunities which come and go according to His good pleasure." This kind friend was summoned to his heavenly home just four months before China Mary.

Miss Tsai and Miss Leaman took a picture together in the dark chamber.

Chapter 19

Ministry Multiplies

One December afternoon, three Chinese officers enroute to the West Coast gazed spellbound from the windows of their express train. It sped away in the glowing sunset, leaving the wintry Lancaster County landscape behind. For a moment the train clicked along the shining railway tracks winding between the long, clean lines of modern factories, then for a few miles it paralleled a busy highway bordered with neat rows of cottages screened behind the bare branches of maples. Next it roared through the stillness of rolling fields dotted with dazzling white clusters of farmhouses, with here and there a slender church spire piercing the sky.

"What a beautiful, happy corner of the earth! Lancaster, we are proud of you, we will always bless you!" one of them murmured.

"Yesterday we said good-by to Great Aunt [Mary Leaman] and Seventh Aunt [me]. Two weeks ago we were baptized in their home. Today we are on our way back to Taiwan. What a change these few weeks have brought!" said another man. "We will never be the same."

"Even a heart of steel would have melted at that parting yesterday," said the third man. "I still feel the glow of God's love filling my heart."

"I have an idea," the first man said. "Let's each write a poem to Great Aunt and Seventh Aunt and ask them to translate the verses into English for our American friends to read."

"Splendid!" they all agreed. So each took out pencil and paper and began composing what they called "free lines." In China, when friends part, "like the morning and evening star, never to meet again," it is a time-honored custom to exchange poems rather than letters. Here are the three poems they sent us, translated freely:

Lieutenant Colonel H. wrote:

> Lancaster,[1] you are a beautiful, bountiful, wonderful
> land!
> Churches, farms and factories glitter on your breast
> like medals!
> Even a passing stranger would be deeply impressed,
> How much more we who came and went so often!
> Here is an open-handed, open-hearted Meng-Chang![2]
> Here is mankind's most perfect, friendly warmth!
> Although we come from a far distant land,
> To be here is like returning home.
>
> Here is a bridge leading to Heaven,
> Ah, Heaven, Heaven we can see with our own eyes,
> Not one a million miles away!
>
> For you, friends, who live in this happy corner of
> earth,
> We reverently and sincerely pray.
> May God give you joy and preserve your bodies
> and souls forever.

---

1 By "Lancaster" they meant to refer to Leaman Place, Paradise, Pennsylvania, and their associations with us.

2 Meng-chang is known in Chinese history for his lavish hospitality. He is said to have entertained as many as one hundred guests at a time, many of whom were persons of distinction. His home was surrounded by trees, but he loved his guests so much he couldn't bear to have them go, and so he cut down the trees in order to watch them until they were out of sight.

Today we are parted for a while.
Yet at some future day we will joyfully meet again.
Lancaster, we will always praise you.
Lancaster, we will always bless you.

Lieutenant Colonel T. wrote:

Lancaster, the spot where people love to linger!
Here are kind hearts and friendly homes,
That have entertained many officers from China.
These days though few and brief in time
Have wrought a change in our lives so great
They'll never be forgotten.

We were a flock of lost sheep
But we have found shelter in the Shepherd's fold;
The angel of the Lord beckoned us
To leave darkness and be born again.
We want to share in the joy of those kind old people there!

Ah, Great Aunt and Seventh Aunt, how kind and good you are,
May God give you happiness, long life and peace!
His the power to bestow, His the dominion forever and ever.
Lancaster, we are proud of you,
Lancaster, we will spread abroad your fame.

Major L. wrote:

Lancaster, you are our heaven on earth.
You hold the keys of Jesus Christ to open our closed and locked hearts.

Let us enjoy this heavenly place together,
May we never, never, NEVER forget each other!

May this parting be but for a while,
Our hearts o'er flow with children's love and devotion.
God, bind our hearts together,
God, cause these few kind old people
To live forever in that heaven on earth!
Ah, Lancaster, you are the place where I was born
again.
I'll remember you, I'll keep you always in my heart
So I may ever behold those rays of heavenly light.
I want to imitate you, I want to take the keys of God
To the four corners of the earth,
To open ten thousand times ten thousand hearts
That are still locked and sealed in darkness.

When Colonel Peter walked into my room, he had already rehearsed his lines well. He stood straight and proud and declared, "I am from Taiwan. I heard from Colonel B. what a remarkable woman you are. I have come to visit you. But I am an atheist. I don't believe in Christianity. You can never make a Christian out of me!"

With such an introduction, no words I could have prepared would have reached his heart. I prayed silently, then asked him, "Did you come directly from Taiwan?"

"Yes."

"What did you eat for breakfast?"

He replied, "Rice."

"And what for lunch?"

"Rice."

"And for supper?"

He replied impatiently, "You are a Chinese. You know we always eat rice!"

I asked, "Don't you get tired of eating rice three times a day?"

"Of course not! If we got tired of eating rice we would be sick!"

This gave me an opportunity, and I said, "I am a Christian. If I did not talk about Jesus, the bread of life, I would be sick!" He laughed, and the ice was broken. I knew the Holy Spirit could now go on to do His work. And He did! Recording his testimony later, Colonel Peter confessed,

> Not only had I not believed in Jesus, but had never given a thought about whether I would go to heaven when I died. My only hope was that in this life I could do something to serve my country and be a dutiful citizen. I used the strength and energy and wisdom that God gave me, but I never thought of obeying His command to serve Him. I was aimless and ignorant, just lost sheep, unable to direct my own steps, not knowing whether to turn to the east or to the west.
>
> Not until my third visit to America did I meet Great Aunt and Seventh Aunt, two of God's kindly old people. All the time they talked about salvation and the love of Jesus, things I had never heard about before. It was a revelation to me and caused my darkened heart to turn to the light. For the first time, I knew that I was a sinner, that I had only thought about my own way and never asked God's guidance. No wonder I went astray and failed to find happiness. These two old people are certainly God's "hunting dogs" who brought me into His sheepfold. I accepted Christ in Leaman Place and was baptized. From then on, my heart has been filled with joy. "Look unto Jesus, exalt Him and be faithful until death" is my motto.

Two Chinese colonels, a Muslim and an atheist, were among those sent to Aberdeen for training. After finding out about us, they came to our home every possible weekend, although motivated mostly by a desire for fellowship with their own countrymen. Gradually the Lord began to touch their hearts and they became more open to His Spirit. They asked to come and study the Word of God with us on as many weekends as we could spare.

I helped arrange for them to go to a Billy Graham crusade in New York. When they returned they rushed to my room, asking, "Seventh Aunt, please explain to us what this Billy Graham means by 'believe, repent, and be born again.'" I was thrilled to be able to point them to Christ.

When the officers' work first started, China Mary wrote to a friend,

> To think that right here in our old homestead, right where my father was born over a hundred years ago, here where as a child he heard people praying for an open door to China, here where he said good-bye to home and loved ones more than eighty years ago to spend a lifetime of missionary service in China, here, now that China Mainland's doors are again closed, the Lord, in His matchless grace and loving kindness is sending Chinese officers of the Free China army to hear the gospel!

The opportunity never ceased to amaze us!

Some American friends wonder at the emphasis that we and the new converts put on the rite of baptism after persons have made decisions to accept Christ. It is not that we believe baptism is essential for salvation. It is an outward sign of what has already happened in their spirits—they have passed from eternal death to the gift of eternal life. But coming from an Oriental background, the outward sign of baptism is a serious expression for all the world to see. The new believer declares that he has made a once-for-all commitment—a clear confession to follow Christ. It has almost the same importance as a wedding ceremony, "Forsaking all others, I cleave unto Him alone." That is why so many of those who finally made decisions for Christ immediately thought of being baptized to give expression to their new faith. In their hearts they meant, *No turning back. I give myself without reserve to my Saviour and Lord.* Baptism for repentance of sins is taught in the Scripture. We do not insist on any specific manner of administering the baptism, but leave it to the convictions of each believer as he interprets it for himself from Scripture.

We always regarded follow-up work for the officers returning to Taiwan as urgent. I often counseled them, "You received Christ in America. You may think that after you return home nobody will know what you do there. So your 'fox tail' might come out in your home. You may have a bad temper or treat your family unkindly. You must pray to Jesus to help you be a real Christian right in your home, which may be the hardest place to live for Him."

Praise the Lord! We heard that thirteen families of those converted officers were brought to the Lord in Formosa. The one whom God used was a beloved pastor, Dr. Chen Wei-Ping. He wrote us by his own hand at the age of ninety-three, "In spite of being advanced in age, I am still preaching the gospel. I am closely associated with the officers who came to the Lord at Leaman Place. Your works are permanent and glorious."

As further follow-up, we sent the officers subscriptions to Christian magazines, introduced them to Christians abroad, and even tried to find Christian wives for some of them. Now every Christmas we receive a beautiful array of greeting cards which I string up in my room.

I wrote to President and Madame Chiang Kai-shek in Taiwan, enclosing a copy of my book and telling about these men who had confessed Christ. Madame Chiang sent me the following letter:

Chinese seamen are welcomed by friends from Paradise.

OFFICE OF THE PRESIDENT REPUBLIC OF CHINA

Taipei, Taiwan
May 1956

Dear Miss Tsai:

It was good of you and Miss Leaman to entertain so many of our officers from Aberdeen. I am sure it meant a great deal to them to be in a home during their first lonely days in America. Through our prayer groups our chaplains who work with the armed forces can be informed about these officers who become Christians while in America so that they will progress in their spiritual life when they return.

With all good wishes,
Yours sincerely,
May-ling Soong Chiang
(Madame Chiang Kai-Shek)

Many Chinese cargo boats come from Taiwan to Philadelphia and Baltimore. Faithful Yun Yong, who started the seamen's work, kindly brought seamen to see me from time to time. Reverend Maynard Lu shepherded the seamen diligently and ministered to them and their families in Baltimore. Over the years we had the privilege to witness to them. A number of them received baptism in our home, and many were baptized on the boat and other places.

These Christian seamen planned all kinds of ways to lead other seamen and their families to follow the Lord. They held a weekly service on the boat for those who had not believed, they collected good Chinese books for the seamen, and they made brass boxes for collections, not only to help in the seamen's work, but also for mission work.

A Captain Shih accepted the Lord in my dark chamber. He led his chief engineer, some officers, many crewmen, and his wife to believe and to receive baptism.

Within a week, three Chinese captains of cargo boats either called on me in person or by telephone. Captain C. encouraged me by saying, "Seven years ago I was in your home and had my picture taken with Miss China Mary Leaman in your sitting room. The Lord spoke through both of you. My heart was very much touched and I became a Christian. I am sending you my tiny offering for the Lord's work. I am really a debtor to you for your spiritual help. I will try to come to see you when my boat returns to America." This helped me realize that when we follow the Lord's direction in sowing the seed, we should trust the Holy Spirit to water it and give the increase. We may not see any result, but we should not be disappointed. If we do see results, it may be because someone else sowed the seed years ago and God gave us the privilege of reaping.

Chapter 20

Understudies

The thousands of Chinese students in America and Canada have been much in our hearts, prayers, and ministry. "But at your advanced age, how can you relate to today's young people?" I have often been asked. "Don't you feel some kind of generation gap?"

Not at all, I'm happy to say! Chronological age has little to do with it.

The Chinese students come from Taiwan, Hong Kong, and other places in Southeast Asia, seeking the knowledge of this world in universities and colleges from coast to coast. Some were born on the China mainland and fled with their parents from the oppressors. A great many are professing Christians, children of Christian Chinese families, the fruit of faithful missionary labor. But some of their loving Christian parents have hesitated to allow their children to study in the United States. The stories they have heard and read about the godless university campuses, with riots, drugs, violence, and loose living make them fearful. But God's Spirit continues to hover over these Christian Chinese students in a very special way and is preserving them for purposes of His own "in the midst of a crooked and perverse nation" (Philippians 2:15).

Several special ministries, such as Ambassadors for Christ, Inc., Chinese Christian Mission, and others have been burdened with the spiritual welfare of Chinese students, and the Lord has used them fruitfully in America in the last couple of decades. He has given them a great field to work in. They have had the vision of evangelizing and building up the faith of the Chinese students in this land so they will not only stand firm for Christ, but also return to their homelands to witness for Him.

The circles these ministries have started continue to widen. They have established Chinese Bible study groups on college campuses, published Christian Chinese literature especially for the intellectuals, initiated missionary outreach by Chinese, and organized Christian retreats and conferences. They are pleasing the Lord by shepherding the Chinese students in this country. How happy we have been to have a part!

Much of our ministry in China was with students. As a young convert, while a student myself, I knew well the problems of fellow students. I was invited from school to school to speak to crowds of students about Christ. I usually spoke to non-Christians when I was associated with Miss Ruth Paxson, and she spoke to the Christians. I remember that some of the Christian students in True Light Middle School in Canton, China, went to the servants who worked in the school, urging them to come to my meetings. To make sure that the servants came to hear the gospel, they did their work during the meetings. After a few days, nearly every one of the servants accepted the Lord. How happy it made those girls!

In the early days of Christianity in China it was considered a very great success to persuade any girl or woman to accept a Bible. Later, girls and women were willing even to go without a new dress or other luxuries to wear at Chinese New Year, in order to save enough money to buy a Bible. We always encouraged them to purchase their Bibles rather than to accept those distributed freely. We found that when they paid for them, they valued them greatly. Of course, many of the girls in our Bible study classes had to buy their Bibles on the installment plan! Their families did not want them to have a Bible and often would not give them money for that purpose. The girls and women would come to class with red or green paper covers or some newspaper covering the Bibles in their hands. They loved them! Before they went home they usually wrapped up their Bibles carefully in their handkerchiefs so they would be protected during their walk home.

I rely heavily on the Lord Jesus Christ and His Word, the Bible, when I deal with the students who come to my bedside. I cannot possibly approach them on the same level as their academic training. It would be out of my field. Besides, the Christian life is not founded upon the intellect, but upon the response of the heart to the Holy Spirit's dealings. The Bible must be the basis.

"But do you understand every word of the Bible? Do you know the whole thing?" I have been asked. Of course I do not. The Bible has sixty-six books and I can't say that I understand the whole Bible. But I can say that the Bible understands me and knows me. Here is an illustration which has helped me understand about the Bible:

My parents had twenty-four children: my father's first wife bore him seven before she died, my mother fifteen, and a concubine had two children. In all, there were thirteen girls and eleven boys. Father was given a beautiful safe made in London, with twenty-six letters in the combination. Under the letter *U*, when my mother put in the key, it began to "sing"; when it stopped, the door opened automatically.

According to Chinese custom, at Chinese New Year, Dragon Festival, Full Moon Festival, and Father's and Mother's birthdays, all the children would wear new outfits. The girls put on pearl flowers, rings, bracelets, and other jewelry. Mother opened the safe only at night when the children went to bed. Then the next morning she would give the jewelry to us, saying, "You wear this or that." In the evening we would have to return it all to Mother. After we went to bed, Mother put the things back in the safe. I never questioned why Mother never allowed us girls even to see what was inside the safe.

Years went by and all my brothers and sisters were married. I was left alone with my mother. I remember very clearly one afternoon when she and I were alone, she suddenly put the key to the safe in my hand. "Daughter, you keep it," she said.

I did not know why. She went on, "All your brothers and

"Whatever is inside belongs to you."

sisters are married, and you alone are left with me. Open the safe. Whatever is inside belongs to you." No one could ever understand how I felt at that moment. I held the key in my hand reverently, trembling. I had never seen the inside of the safe, nor had I questioned my mother's love for withholding it. Suddenly I had the key to open it!

The Holy Spirit revealed to me a deep truth which helped me very much. The Bible, surely more important than this safe, and all the jewels inside the Bible are very precious. Some things we do understand, many things we don't, Deuteronomy 29:29 tells us. It taught me that when we read God's Word, we must never doubt or question our heavenly Father's love. Some things we must just wait to understand. Like the safe full of jewels, the day finally came when Mother could trust me with the key. We must never doubt the Bible or question its teachings. When the Lord's time comes, He will reveal to us the particular truth from the Bible that He wants us to know. We may read one verse dozens of times. We know the words but we cannot grasp the real meaning for ourselves. One day the interpretation or application suddenly leaps out at us. How happy we are! That verse then becomes a living word in our hearts.

The Bible has lots of jewelry inside. We Christians must trust our Father in heaven. I believe that every word is inspired by the Holy Spirit, even though I don't understand the whole Bible yet. I share this especially with students. Moody and Spurgeon knew much about the Bible and trusted it, so God revealed much of it to them. So He will reveal it to us as His trusting children.

The day after Christmas one year we had several Chinese houseguests whom we had entertained over Christmas. That morning when the mail was delivered, I received a package from a very kind friend whom I had met only twice. As our guests were preparing to leave, I put aside the package to devote myself to them. In the evening after these friends had gone, I rested on my pillows and let my thoughts fly back to my loved ones and friends in China. I wondered whether we would ever meet again in this world. While my thoughts roamed far and wide, my eyes fell upon my neglected package and I hurried to open it. Inside I found a box of writing paper, delicately scented and bearing the imprint of roses. There was a Scripture text on every sheet. Also enclosed were several airmail envelopes and even a sheet of stamps. How thoughtful! I was pleased by the paper's lovely scent and delicate appearance. Before putting away the box, I felt enticed to count the sheets of paper to see how many letters I could write; This was something I never bothered to do before. How surprised I was to find several crisp, new dollar bills between the pages! Immediately I was reminded of God's Book. Between its pages and in every line are hidden treasures. But alas! How often I neglect the Book; how much of the treasure I fail to gather up!

Sometimes students have come to me in groups. For about eighteen years, Chinese students from an annual summer conference sponsored by Ambassadors for Christ, Inc., have come to visit us each June. Sometimes I feel as if I am looking into a sea of faces as they crowd into my dark chamber. What can I share with these young intellectuals who are studying space, physics, mathematics, engineering, philosophy, or medicine? I, who never finished college! Yet I am so amazed that time after time students have lingered, tears in their eyes, touched as the Holy Spirit illuminated some bit of truth that He led me to share with them. I still receive many letters from Chinese students who were moved through reading my book. God seems to use my background of Chinese education and family status to give this humble vessel a hearing with these young intellectuals. May He alone receive the glory! At times I have had a PhD kneeling at my bedside or sitting in the kindergarten chair beside me. In God's sight, we are all His children, learning in His school. Sometimes we think we are ready for graduation, and then we find we need to go back to kindergarten to learn some elementary lesson.

One of the often repeated lessons I have learned from the

Lord in my school of suffering is that when I have come to the absolute end of my strength, I can rest in the Lord and trust Him to use me. Every few weeks I must take medicine for the malaria that flares in my bone marrow. This medicine is very toxic and makes me feel so ill that it is impossible for me to talk to visitors. I am just unable to think or concentrate.

One day just after taking this medicine, when I was hardly able to raise my head, China Mary suddenly appeared to report that a busload of Chinese students from one of the conferences had arrived to visit me. In a daze, I murmured that it was impossible to see them. She knew it well, but she said that they would be very disappointed if they could not just come in and say hello before going on their way. I weakly consented, wondering how I could even open my eyes. Then I remembered that evangelist Billy Graham had said that wherever he went, people recognized him and wanted to speak to him, so he always tried to make himself available. My spirit was willing but my flesh was weak—I did not even feel physically available!

China Mary and Grace Ng, my co-worker, directed the group to my room and went out to the kitchen to prepare some refreshments. I still have no idea what I said because my mind was not clear. I remotely remember something about "commit" and "rest."

With the group was a brilliant Chinese professor, Dr. Lit- Sen Chang, who was a well-known writer on philosophy and theology and special lecturer in missions at a divinity school. He had held a high official position with the Chinese government before the Lord saved him. As he was leaving, he grasped my hand warmly and said, "It was not you who was speaking today, but the Holy Spirit!"

Soon I was startled to hear loud cries coming from the sitting room. Pheobe Chua, who had come from Manila that morning was resting upstairs, but when she heard the cries, she stumbled down the stairs and rushed into my room, certain that I was passing away! It turned out to be some students weeping because

Professor Chang humbly testified to them that he had seen a sick person able to speak in the strength of the Holy Spirit. Although he was a theology teacher and the author of many books, that day he had been convicted of serving the Lord in his own strength and wisdom. His witness caused many to realize how much they also had failed to trust the Lord, and they sobbed with him, promising the Lord that from henceforth they would rely on the Holy Spirit. Then they all prayed and cried again. It truly proved the motto that hangs on the wall of my dark chamber, "Not I, but Christ!"

Our Sunday morning quiet in the Leaman home was shattered by the jangle of the phone one winter day. It was a friend who had received a long-distance call from New York City.

"There are two Chinese students from Canada coming on the bus this evening. They want to see you tomorrow," she announced. "I told them you had not been well and it was a risk to come without an appointment, but I could not convince them. They declared, 'We'll take our chances—*we must* see her!'

I had been feeling especially weak and ill, and the doctor had cautioned me that I should see no one. I felt there was no way that I could see these men. "Tell them really not to come," I instructed my friend.

"I can't. They were in a phone booth in the station, had their tickets, and were about to get on the bus!"

I sighed, resigning myself to an ordeal that would surely overtax my strength. Then I remembered again China Mary's watchword: "restful availability" to whatever the Lord planned for our day. "If God sends someone, we must receive him from Him" was her motto, even when she was nearly exhausted. *There must be some special purpose for the coming of these young men,* I thought to myself, and called my co-workers in to pray with me about it.

"Here we are!" announced a voice on the phone at 8 p.m. that cold winter night. "We are along the highway in Paradise where the bus dropped us off." Our friends picked them up, discovering that they were very young Chinese university students from Canada. They were dressed in hiking togs and boots, with bedrolls and knapsacks on their backs. They looked for all the world like Canadian woodsmen, except for their beaming Chinese faces.

They stayed overnight with our friends, warming themselves before the fireplace and consuming large quantities of Chinese noodles after our friends discovered that they had been trying to save money and had not eaten all day. But they soon came to the point.

"We have waited six months to visit the 'Queen of the Dark Chamber.' We spent all our money to make this trip during our vacation and barely have enough to get back. Our visas to re-enter Canada expire in two days, and we have to hurry back or else we will lose our immigration status. Tell us, what is the queen like? Do you have a photo? We are so excited to see her that we shall not be able to sleep all night!"

When our friends produced a photo, they passed it back and forth laughingly, nervous with anticipation. "Now that the time has come, we are almost afraid to go and see her!" one of them said.

"Actually, for what purpose did you want to see Miss Tsai?" our friends inquired.

"We really don't know," they said, shaking their heads. "We only know that we were supposed to come. God must have brought us." The next morning they were up with the dawn. "Today is the day!" they said as they hurried through breakfast.

When they walked into my room, I wondered why such handsome young men would want to see an old invalid lady who could be their great-grandmother. As soon as they introduced themselves, I made a short prayer with them, asking Jesus to guide our conversation that His name might be exalted. Then I asked them what made them come such a long way to see me. They explained that they had heard my name mentioned by their friends so often that it made them determined to come and see me for themselves.

I shared with them Philippians 3:8 in the Chinese translation: " 'I count it the most important thing to *know Christ.*' My name is not important," I told them. " 'As for man, his days are as grass,' " I reminded them from Psalm 103:15. "We Chinese always ask a person first of all, 'What is your name?' But even our names are not important. We will be given new names in heaven, according to Revelation 2:17. Even famous and important people may fail you. But the most important thing is to know Jesus Christ. He will never disappoint you. He is the only One who can satisfy you. He can help you solve all your problems and difficulties."

I told them this illustration: "Once a rich man had a tea party. A famous actor was asked to dramatize Psalm 23. There was loud applause at his talent. Then the host asked an old pastor to act out Psalm 23. He stood up and read it from the Bible slowly, reverently, and with meaning. Everything was quiet. No applause. The actor went over to the pastor with tears in his eyes and said, 'I know the words of Psalm 23 but you know the Shepherd.' "

I told those boys how honored I was for them to come so far to see me, but the best thing was for them to know Jesus.

"How was your visit?" the young men were asked as they flung their packs once more to their shoulders, preparing to return that night by train to Canada.

They were too choked with emotion to reply immediately. "I wept to leave her!" the older finally offered unashamedly.

"God talked to us through her," the other added. "She talked to us as if she were as young as we—like our sister, or friend. And yet she advised and taught us like a mother and a revered grandmother. We will never forget this day. Our lives are changed!"

Chapter 21

Cameras Roll

For many years I had placed the idea of my story being made into a movie on God's altar if it would please Him. Not long after, Dr. Micah Leo, a Christian Chinese writer, put my story into dramatic form. Meanwhile, the Chinese Christian Mission had a burden from the Lord to make their first gospel movie in Chinese to reach the unchurched masses. They had no previous movie-making experience, no equipment, no actors, no professional staff or producer—only the vision to serve God. They approached me as to whether I would be willing for my book to be their first attempt at a Christian movie. After much prayer, I believed that the Lord was leading me to approve. Dr. William Culbertson, president of Moody Bible Institute, visited me one morning and agreed that a gospel movie was the thing to do.

A member of the staff of the Chinese Christian Mission, Andrew Ho, had been a radio singer in Taiwan for seventeen years and knew many people. He began to contact pastors and other Christians to enlist their prayers and help. They found Christians willing to learn the parts, regardless of whether they had acting experience or not. To my knowledge, few, if any, of them were professionals. They were simply believers in the Lord who wanted to serve Him. The drama by Dr. Leo was adapted into an an abbreviated movie script, and the project was launched with many prayers and an empty budget. Through many hardships, it was filmed on location in Taiwan. I do not appear in the movie myself. The soundtrack was in Chinese, the Mandarin dialect, with English subtitles. Later it was dubbed in English. It ran about an hour. This Christian mission had done its best for the Lord with its first venture, an amateur production. Indeed, the spiritual results from the showing of this humble film were as the water turned into wine by the Lord Jesus. Because He stoops to use "the weak things of the world to confound the things which are mighty" (1 Corinthians 1:27), it is the Lord and not men who receives the glory. In the written reports by the mission that made the film, it was stated,

> Our first gospel film in Asia, "Queen of the Dark Chamber," brought an enormous response. During the first few months there were seventy-two showings to 11,092 people, and 606 decisions for Christ were made, and 778 Christians dedicated their lives to serve the Lord. Many who otherwise would never have attended church have been reached. Others who had long been absent were challenged. Drama and film are indeed effective tools in reaching out to the unchurched people.

In the same issue, Jonathan Cheung stated his impression of the film:

> After watching the "Queen" film, we can clearly see three unreliable things: fame, status, wealth. We also see the three most crucial trials Christiana Tsai went through after she believed in the Lord, persecution by her family, desertion of her loved one, and the loss of health. Yes, but she said, "I have had the Lord Jesus Christ as my Saviour." She lost her companion, but she gained an everlasting, ever-abiding friend. She lost her health, but to the Lord, she is the most exuberant Christian.

Wen Chuan Wang of Vancouver, B.C., wrote of the film showing in his area:

It was a spectacular sight: the hall was fully packed with people, cars filled all the parking spaces of the nearby streets, and people were still coming! Never had we seen anything like this before. What was happening? The "Queen" was coming! The first color gospel film in Chinese was to be presented that night by the Chinese Christian Mission. Most of the Chinese Christians were present, and many had brought along several nonbelieving friends, there was quite a number of Canadian friends too, being attracted by the posters all over town. The seats were occupied in no time.

What really amazed us was the response to the showing of the film in the coffee shop in the basement of the Salvation Army. The audience was a group of hippies. It turned a smoky dirty den suddenly into a quiet and respectable meeting place.

There are many incidents of how the Lord used the "Queen" movie to draw people to Himself. In San Francisco, the Chinese newspapers publicized the movie. The Chinese owner of a big business in Chinatown saw the advertisement. He rushed to see it. When he got there, he could hardly find a place to stand. This was the fifth time that the movie had been shown that day. Later Mr. T. wrote to me:

"I never heard of you nor read your book. But when I was looking at the movie, I could not restrain my tears. Finally I stood up to accept the Lord. When I looked around, I saw over one hundred standing to express their acceptance of our Saviour Jesus Christ."

Mr. T. borrowed a copy of my book from a friend and read it to his family. The members of his family also accepted the Lord. Somehow he found my address. He said that he did not know where to buy the book, so he was copying it!

Miss W., the president of a seminary in Singapore, wrote,

> "I remembered that when you spoke in Ku-lang-su, a beautiful island across from Amoy, China, about 1918, I heard you, and many others believed because of your witness. When I was in America in 1968, I wanted to see you so I could report to friends in Singapore, but I could not make it. Praise the Lord, your movie came here and was shown to different groups who were inspired by it. Then it came right to our seminary! The whole school was greatly moved. We did not know how to express our appreciation, so we are sending you a little love gift. We will continue to pray for you, asking our Heavenly Father to use you."

A Chinese university student came to have an interview with me in preparation for showing the movie in various university centers on the East Coast. He asked me, "How does it make you feel to have your biography made into a movie?"

"It makes me feel humble," I answered. "I pray that the Lord may help me so to live that I may not disgrace Him, nor disappoint my friends."

I shared with him a little story about humility. For years the Lord has been teaching me about the biblical principle of dying to self. It is wonderful when one puts himself on the cross and Christ on the throne. A dead man has no feelings and cares not what others say, for he is dead. How I long that I may learn to exalt Jesus in every way and to lead every one who enters my darkened room to meet the Lord Himself.

Years ago in Kuling, a beautiful summer mountain resort in China, there was a spring of clear water in the garden of our home. Because it was some distance from our kitchen, we brought some hollowed-out bamboo poles and fitted them end to end to pipe the water to our kitchen door. One day when we were expecting guests for dinner, the cook suddenly rushed in to say that there was no water coming from the pipe. I hurried up the side of the hill to the spring to find out the reason. The cool, fresh water was still bubbling up from the ground, and the bamboo poles were still carefully fitted together, lying on the green grass. 1 started to pull the poles apart, and there I found a large, fat green frog firmly wedged inside one of the poles. It completely blocked the way so that no water could get through.

When I saw that proud, fat frog, my heart immediately bowed at my Lord's feet and I cried, "My Rock, my Saviour, search me and see if there be any hidden sin, any swelling pride blocking the pipeline of my heart and stopping the overflow of Your Spirit." Later, remembering this incident, I composed the following lines that may be sung to the tune "Nettleton," commonly used with "Come, Thou Fount of Every Blessing."

> Saviour, make me always humble,
> Not for honor, not for fame,
> Saviour, fill me, empty vessel,
> Full of praises to Thy name.
> Never let me hide Thy glory,
> Idle words Thy truth conceal,
> Save me from all pride; before Thee,
> Worthy Lamb, I humbly kneel.

Mrs. Torrey Shih, a well-known Chinese writer, carried *Queen of the Dark Chamber* day and night for three months,. Then she wrote a Chinese play of it. It was first dramatized in Manila, Philippines, in 1964, then in the United States and Canada. The following is a brief report from Manila:

> You must be very anxious to hear about the presentation of our drama last January 3. Well, here it is!
>
> There was a big crowd of more than five hundred people, each dressed in his or her best, in that large air-conditioned auditorium, waiting to witness one of the greatest dramas ever presented in local church history, if not the

local Chinese dramatic life. The curtain opened promptly at 8:00, the atmosphere was very good, the actors and actresses were ready after four solid months of training and prayer, the lighting was the best in the country—and on top of all this, the free and liberal working of the Holy Spirit made the 2½ hour presentation a success. Praise and glory to Him who both began and accomplished it. Your prayers as well as those of people all over the world did not go in vain.

Do you know that over DZAS, the most powerful station in the South East Asia, otherwise known as the Far East Broadcasting Company, your biography has been narrated in a weekly, fifteen-minute program? It started January 1, and will probably be through in three or four months. The narrator, Mr. Teddy Young, is an active youth leader of our church. Do pray that this may become a blessing to many listeners."

Several years ago the Lord called a lady to join The Evangelical Alliance Mission radio station in Taiwan. It gave her a wonderful opportunity to dedicate her pen to the Lord to write for gospel broadcasts every day. She had always had a secret longing to work on my book for broadcasting. It had to be carefully rewritten to adapt the story for radio listeners so they could visualize the living witness. She reports,

There were many difficulties. At the beginning of this year, God gave me the courage to see it through. While I was writing, I shed tears again many times for the witness of your life. This summer my co-workers and I were overjoyed to have the unexpected surprise of actually corresponding with you. We never dreamed it was possible to receive a handwritten letter from you! We now feel like partakers with you in your glorious spiritual fight and are

Queen of the Dark Chamber English version was published in 1953, the Chinese version was published in 1957. Over 30 different versions were published afterwards, as well as braille, screenplay, tape, and film.
This brought many Chinese and international visitors.
Quite a few officials from Taiwan came for further study in the U.S. accepted the Lord here,
got baptized and attended Bible study fellowships,
about which Lancaster newspaper made special reports.

> one heart with you. All in all, we unite in praise to the Lord that we have been given a little part by the Lord in such a great opportunity to introduce this chosen vessel, you, as a handmaid for the Lord, to inspire brothers and sisters behind the bamboo curtain in China!

The TEAM radio station broadcast to mainland China the drama form of *Queen of the Dark Chamber* in eighty-six broadcasts of fifteen minutes each, commencing in June 1973.

Chapter 22

More Dramas Unfold

One Sunday morning a Chinese friend stayed with us while Susanna went to church. Suddenly the quiet was shattered by a fierce ringing of the back doorbell. Our friend said, "There is a tall American with a terrible face demanding to come in to see you. He has come all the way from Maine. I'm afraid to let him in!"

I said, "Let us just trust the Lord. Let him in."

When he strode into my chamber, I thought our hour to meet the Lord had come. "I have read your book, so I came to see you. I am going to kill my wife and my six children and myself!" he ranted.

As a helpless invalid in bed, unable to defend myself, I was sure he was going to kill us, too. I put our defense in the hands of the Lord and cried out to Him in my heart for wisdom for what to tell this man. I softly answered, "If I talked to you for three days, it wouldn't answer your questions. Let us each take a Bible. Ask the Lord to speak to you." For three or four hours God guided my dizzy head to point him to one Scripture after another to show him his condition and the way out through Christ, not through murder and suicide.

Finally I sensed a breakthrough as he asked me pointedly, "Why are you smiling all the time? What are you so happy about being old and sick so long and lying in bed?"

"It is Jesus who lives in my heart. He gives me joy." I told him that when I opened my heart to Christ even the leaves and grass and flowers all seemed to change color. The whole world was transformed. "Your life is black and terrible to you because you don't have Jesus in your heart."

His intense face finally broke into a smile. He rose and declared, "Miss Tsai, I want Jesus to come into my heart. I will follow His teaching. I promise I won't kill myself and my family. I will trust in God and go to church!"

After we prayed, he held my hand and with tears said, "May I give you a kiss?"

Since I was almost eighty years old and unable to answer no under such circumstances, I accepted it as a "holy kiss." As he left my stage and marched out the door, I could only lie there exhausted and praise God, not only for preserving our lives to serve Him a little longer, but also for the privilege of pointing another soul, who had been going in the direction of darkness, to turn to His light.

Another time, prison doors swung open for two cars full of women prisoners with their guards to drive four hours from Muncy, Pennsylvania, to visit me. One of the guards told us that it was the first time such a group was allowed to visit in a private home. After I spoke to them, the prisoners crowded around me in parting, saying that they wanted Jesus to live in their hearts forever.

Standing at the back of the room while I talked to the prisoners were five Chinese, most of whom had been born in Tanzania, Africa. They had come to Paradise as the result of a visit to Africa by Reverend Moses Chow, executive director of Ambassadors for Christ, Inc. Right after the prisoners walked out, they came to my bedside and said, "All five of us want to accept Jesus as our Saviour." Not long afterward they were baptized, and since then they have been faithful in attending church.

Three days before Easter 1958, the American Bible Society called from New York and told us the following cable had been received from Hong Kong: "Chinese Phonetic account urgently requires remittance U.S. dollars six thousand (6,000)." At last the phonetic Bible would be off the press!

I wish you could have been here with us when we were going

to sign the check. I asked China Mary to sign, and she asked me to sign it. We were scared, because it was the biggest check we had ever signed in our lives. After we prayed at least a dozen times, asking God to bless everyone who had helped in preparing the Bible, we both signed the check.

On the night of a great snowstorm one year, cars were stalled all along Lincoln Highway in front of our house. Unfortunate travelers were suffering from exposure, so we opened our doors, inviting them in. Soon our house was full. Because of electric failure, we had no light, no heat, and no water. Among the travelers was an elderly grandmother, as well as a baby with pneumonia, who was crying all night outside my room.

Susanna gathered up all the supplies she could find and cooked a whole pot of food for the snowbound travelers. Just as the truck drivers were ready to lie down to sleep on the floor in our big parlor, a phone call came saying that Pequea Valley High School was kindly opening its doors and wanted the truck drivers to go there. The snowstorm actually lasted a whole week.

One young man, a "rock and roller," danced around to amuse the guests. At last he came into my room and pleaded, "Let me show you some rock and roll."

Was my room really going to become his stage? "All right," I answered; "but I want to make a bargain with you. You can rock and roll for me if you will promise to go out and read my book afterward."

"It's a deal!" he cried. He really rocked and rolled more than half an hour. I was his only audience! Then he settled down and started to read my book. The next morning his manner had changed completely. "I want to accept Jesus," he said. Later, he came back as a sincere Christian to visit me from Pittsburgh.

"Oh, Miss Tsai, do you remember my mother, Mayhill?" one visitor eagerly began. "She was one of the seven normal school pupils in China who were expelled by the dean, Miss Plum, for going to your home to study the Bible. You wrote in your book

Among the travelers was an elderly grandmother and a baby.

how she and over seventy pupils believed in the Lord. Well, now my wife and I and two daughters also love the Lord. Do you know that Miss Plum, who turned to the Lord and served Him so fervently, was kept in a Communist prison for eighteen years and died there? She witnessed that she would rather die than compromise her faith in the Lord. What a brave soldier of the cross! We want to follow her example!"

How my heart was lifted. My praise overflowed to the Lord as I remembered. It had been a difficult decision I had made so many years ago in China that made possible the story of salvation which this Chinese brother in Christ and his family were bringing me.

China Mary had double pneumonia a little over a year before she went to be with the Lord. She was almost unconscious one day as I was taking care of her, when a woman asked to see her. The woman came in and told the following story which had been unknown to me. "My husband was an alcoholic. China Mary quietly helped us. She also helped my husband enter Keswick Colony for alcoholics to break his awful appetite. Praise the Lord! He is now free from it and has become a very earnest Christian. Here is sixty dollars for China Mary. I owe her a very great deal! I will remember her all my life with unspeakable gratitude. We will try to live like her!"

Later, a Mr. B. suddenly appeared at our back door. He was very anxious to see China Mary, so we requested that because of her weakness, he stay only five minutes. He held her hand and choked with emotion. Tears came to his eyes as he spoke gently, telling her that she had helped him so much spiritually. He also told her that he owed her a great deal of money and that because of her real Christian love, all of his children were following the Lord. He gave her one hundred dollars as he left, promising that by the Lord's power he would try to follow China Mary's example and help others. Both he and his oldest son are now pastors!

A pastor from another state had asked me repeatedly if I would see the parents of his church secretary. They had rejected her. Three times I had to refuse to see them because of prior engagements, but this time they came anyway.

It was very difficult to talk with the couple, because the father monopolized the conversation. He seemed to know everything, just like an encyclopedia. As is my custom with talkative people, I let him talk on, praying silently until he was all talked out. Finally he became quiet. Then he asked me abruptly, "If people believe in Jesus secretly in their hearts, isn't that enough? Why is it necessary to make it known publicly?"

I prayed and answered him simply, "It is like marriage. When you want to get married, why should you have a ceremony and guests and a public occasion? Will that increase the love between two people?"

"No," he answered.

"In a wedding ceremony you are announcing to your relatives and friends that you and your wife have become one person," I continued. "Conversion or being born again truly takes place in your heart, privately. Please read Matthew 10:32-33."

He read it aloud very distinctly: "Whosoever therefore shall confess me before men, him will I confess also before my Father which is in heaven. But whosoever shall deny me before men, him will I also deny before my Father which is in heaven."

"Confessing Christ by being baptized and joining a local church is letting people know you are united with Christ, that you are on His side," I stressed.

Later, the pastor came back for this couple. To my surprise, the father stood up and asked the pastor, "When is your church going to have a baptismal service again?"

"In November," the pastor answered.

"Then put down the names of my wife and myself," the father said. "We want to publicly confess Jesus Christ as our Lord and Saviour."

I was told later that the father was truly born again. Nothing could keep him from telling others about salvation in Jesus Christ.

A certain group had come from New Jersey so I could speak to them. When I finished, most of them went into another room to buy books. I noticed a man who had been sitting in the back of my room, silently listening to every word I spoke. While the leader of the group was talking to me about some church business, this man suddenly came to my bedside, demanding, "Who taught you Buddhism?"

I answered him promptly, "Yang Ren-san." He surprised me by bowing low to me.

"It is unbelievable that anyone indoctrinated by Yang would become a Christian!" He shook his head.

It was true. Yang Ren-san was a former Chinese ambassador to France and well educated in many fields. An ardent and well-trained Buddhist, he turned his mansion into a center to teach Buddhism. He had a print shop in his home where he published Buddhist materials, and he built a temple in his back yard, where devotees lived. I remember staying there many nights with my friends, eating only vegetarian foods. Three of us girls especially used to pray day and night. It was our custom to go to Ambassador Yang's home every Sunday afternoon to learn about Buddhism. We were well brainwashed.

This gentleman confessed, "I actually came here today as a spy. I was far from Christianity. I wanted to catch you in some error or expose you by proving that you did not know what you were talking about. I could not catch you. When I came I was far, far away from following Jesus. Now maybe I am one inch away."

I replied, "One inch or one mile, it doesn't matter how far away you are, if you aren't in!" Then I witnessed further about my Lord to him. Later, my co-worker Grace took him into another room and led him to an open acceptance of the Lord.

Chapter 23

The Chase to Philadelphia

My hand shook as I reached for the phone in the predawn of a cold November morning and dialed the number of our friend Leona Choy in Silver Spring, Maryland. I breathed a prayer. The telephone continued to ring. If our friend were not available, we would surely not be able to make the long trip to the hospital by ambulance.

A sleepy "Hello," then an enthusiastic and willing agreement, hasty arrangements, and our friend was on her way to us. She drove the 125-mile trip in record time.

The anticipated worst had happened. For two days, China Mary had had excruciating eye pain and a headache which she had tried, in her accustomed manner, to hide from us all. When her suffering and pain became no longer bearable, we found out and called the doctor. He had warned us several years before that if China Mary developed acute pain in her eye, the glaucoma would be out of hand and any delay might prove fatal. In less than four hours we made all the arrangements on our side and were on our way.

I say "we" advisedly, because Leona's station wagon, one of the largest models, was loaded to capacity with not only China Mary, the patient, but our co-worker Susanna *and* myself. Leona had scant visibility through the rear window because of the "essentials" we had to take with us. In China, literally everything that one would need had to be taken along to the hospital. Families would even bring in food for the patient's meals and care for him. We had no experience with hospitals in America, so we wanted to be prepared. Our Chinese eye specialist, Dr. Huang, on the staff of Wills Eye Hospital in Philadelphia, knew us well. He did not try to dissuade me when I insisted I was coming along to the hospital with China Mary. We had not been separated for a single day or night in the twenty-three years since returning to America. There was just no way I would let her—aged, nearly blind, and in pain—out of my sight to go to the hospital by herself!

Dr. Huang miraculously (it was he who used the word!) succeeded in having me admitted simultaneously as a patient with China Mary, though the hospital was already overcrowded. The records showed that I was to have extensive tests with specialized optical equipment, which he had felt for a long time was necessary. The second miracle was to get permission from the hospital administration to allow Susanna to stay in the same room with us as a "nurse's aid." We agreed to pay the patient's rate for her as well. To obtain an empty room for *three* was the final miracle, but our Lord is used to doing the impossible.

The doctor had instructed that eye drops be put into China Mary's eyes every fifteen minutes to ease the pressure and pain. This had to be continued even during the journey to the hospital. As for me, I had left the Leaman home for such a long ride only once in those twenty-three years, and that was to appear for my American permanent residence exam in Philadelphia. I could not even sit or be pushed in a wheelchair, because motion sickness would immediately set in. To contemplate riding in a car as far as Philadelphia again was like a trip to the moon without the benefit of a pressurized capsule to offset my nausea.

I implored Leona, "Drive ever so slowly. Stop by the side of the road every fifteen minutes so I can recover my balance."

I did not fully grasp her tactful attempt to explain about "regulations on the expressway" and something about "minimum speed." I only knew that I might die before we got there! Dutifully, she kept the speed to a rapid crawl and regularly signaled to pull aside on the four-lane highway to allow me to rest and have Susanna put the eye drops in China Mary's eyes. All of us were perspiring with tension as the trip progressed. We prayed continually, sometimes aloud, sometimes under our breath, that the Lord would see us through.

When Leona reached the final junction spilling the Pennsylvania Turnpike traffic into the Schuylkill Expressway to inner city Philadelphia, she parked in an area marked "Emergency stopping only." We applied the eye drops again, and I clung to the seat in front of me to keep the world from swimming by as the heavy trucks and madly rushing cars zoomed close to our windows. To shield both of us from the intense light, we had put cardboard on the side windows. The light snow that had fallen a few days previously reflected an unbearable glare. Leona had not shared with us her lack of familiarity with how to get to the hospital once within the inner city. Indeed, she didn't have time to consult a map or ask for directions, for we called her out of bed and from her home and family at 5 a.m. She had committed it to the Lord, trusting that when the time came, God would provide.

Before she got the car in gear again, the sound of a siren shrilled in our ears and two police cars screeched alongside. A burly policeman in natty uniform and dark glasses strode up pompously to Leona's window. "And just what do you think you are doing? You are parked in an emergency zone!"

"Officer," Leona replied, "this *is* an emergency. I am taking these elderly friends to the hospital as fast as I can get them there."

Immediately sizing up the situation with sympathetic understanding, after Leona had confided to him that she wasn't sure of the way, he motioned his fellow officer to proceed to other calls, and beckoned, saying, "Just follow me. Ignore the stoplights and the speed limit as long as you stay right behind me. I'll guide you to the hospital."

We took off—literally, I thought! At least I felt as if I were in an airplane, for he had not given Leona a chance to explain that we had to drive at a snail's pace for the sake of my nausea. For the first time in my life I saw the flashing, rotating red light in action on top of a police car. For the last half hour of our trip, the officer sped us straight through the morning rush-hour traffic, zooming through red lights and weaving in and out of lanes of cars. I believe I must have fallen into a daze or faint. I expected that my next waking vision would be that of my heavenly Father at the gate of heaven!

We screamed to a halt, right at the admitting door of the hospital. After he found our Chinese Dr. Huang, the officer tipped his hat to acknowledge our gratitude, and disappeared. The policeman had been our angel sent by the Lord! For God has promised, "For he shall give his angels charge over thee, to keep thee in all thy ways…lest thou dash thy foot against a stone" (Psalm 91:11-12). Or, in our case, "lest we get lost in the maze of downtown Philadelphia!"

The entrance elevator was only a few yards from the admitting door, and Leona ordered two wheelchairs. Interns helped us out of the car to the elevator. Leona had to remain with the car, temporarily double-parked at the entrance, with our baggage. At the same time she requested that the elevator operator return for our "essentials." As instructed, the old man returned to the main floor entrance, anticipating a little overnight bag for each of the three "grandmas" as he called us. When Leona began pulling out armload after armload of paraphernalia, equipment, and "strange things tied up in bundles like from the old country," he could hardly believe his eyes.

"You're putting me on!" he said, aghast. Besides innumerable suitcases and boxes, there were armrests, a walker, teapot, herb tea, thermos bottles, foodstuffs, pillows, blankets, and other things. "No one, but *no one* has ever come into the hospital with all this gear! They won't allow it upstairs, and then I'll have to take it all the way down again. Come on, lady, give it up!" he pleaded.

After Leona had finally convinced him that each bulky item was critical to the survival of the three "grandmas" and a substantial tip had been given to deaden the pain, Leona began her ascent by elevator to the floor where we had been assigned a room. Still shaking his head and clicking his tongue, the elevator operator deposited everything in the hall, which was now full of nurses, interns, and orderlies, who had been alerted that there was an invasion of some sort. Somewhere along the line it was noised abroad in the hospital that there was a Chinese queen and her attendants moving into a private suite!

But everything was far from under regal control in the hospital room to which we had been ushered. The room was big, in a corner by the elevator, and was set up with two regulation single hospital beds, and one low camp cot by the wall prepared for the "nurse's aide" who was to be in the room with us. I was wheeled in after China Mary had already been lifted to one of the single beds. I motioned for the nurse to push me over to the camp cot. "That's the one I want to sleep on," I declared.

"But that's for your helper," argued the young nurse. "That is not for a patient. I can't put you there!"

"I *must* stay there," I said. "I can never lie on a high bed. I have a balance problem. I would be dizzy and fall off!" "There are bars at the side of the bed," she pleaded nervously.

"I don't want bars. I want to sleep on the low cot!" "Sorry, lady, I can't let you!"

"Oh, but you *must* !" I insisted.

"I have to call the supervisor!" she said weakly, parking me near the bed and running off.

In a moment, a buxom, commanding lady in white appeared with a clipboard and papers, which she checked over swiftly, peering over her bifocals. She turned to Susanna. "And just which ones are the patients?" she demanded.

"They are," Susanna said, pointing to China Mary and me. "I am their companion. I've come along to help." "Patients can *only* stay in regulation hospital beds. Any violation will be cause for insurance coverage cancellation, and then all of us will be in for a big heap of trouble!" she thundered.

By that time Dr. Huang had appeared on the scene and surveyed the mounting drama. He tenderly but firmly explained to me that I had to stay in the hospital bed. I agreed finally, asking the Lord to preserve me on that white mountain as He had in many valleys before. The head nurse was so pleased to avoid a further scene that she kissed me and thanked me for complying.

The examinations started almost immediately for both of us. We were wheeled downstairs where, in room after room, eye-testing machines stared menacingly at us. They were indeed a testing and a torture for both of us. For China Mary was suffering from her weakness and pain, and I from my motion sickness, fatigue, and disruption of any semblance of my usual schedule. That night we were not returned to our room until 10:30—we who always prepared for bed at 6 p.m.

The next day China Mary and I went through even more detailed examinations. They continued all day, until at 11 p.m. the head surgeon pulled my wheelchair aside and said, "I am sorry to tell you that Miss Leaman had a stroke once in her eye which left scar tissue; this prevents us from operating on her after all."

"What would happen if she were operated on?" I asked fearfully.

"She might have a massive hemorrhage and die on the operating table," the doctor answered soberly.

"What will happen if she does not have the operation?" I ventured.

"She will die in terrible pain and suffering," the doctor answered reluctantly.

As the astronauts enroute to the moon kept constant contact with their Houston, Texas, headquarters for directions and corrections, so I kept my heart turned by prayer to my headquarters, the Lord Jesus. I asked Him now to give me His clear direction. He did. I concluded, "Well, if she has to face death one way or the other, I would rather have her go to the Lord on the operating table than to die in lingering pain and suffering."

"Very well," the chief surgeon said. "Let me call some of the other doctors for a consultation." It was 11:30 p.m. Three American doctors joined her for a whispered discussion.

After what seemed like a long time, I was again called, as if to a courtroom. "Are you willing to sign the paper of responsibility in case of a hemorrhage on the operating table?"

My Lord clearly guided me to say, "Yes, I am ready to sign."

It was almost one o'clock in the morning by the time we were wheeled back to our room. During the night various nurses came in to prepare China Mary for surgery. I truly felt my merciful Lord Jesus' constant companionship.

Early next morning, Leona returned from her place of lodging. At once we prayed together, asking our Lord to be the Great Physician. Soon the attendants came to transfer China Mary to the operating room. I was amazed how smoothly they moved her to the rolling table from her bed. It was so skillfully, quickly, and quietly done. During my long illness, I had entered seven different hospitals in China and St. Barbar's Hospital in Osaka, Japan. But I had not seen such tender handling before. Leona followed the rolling bed but had to stop about ten feet away from the final swinging door, on the other side of which patients were waiting their turns for surgery.

Again my heart checked in with my heavenly headquarters. "Everything under control." Yes, all was under my Lord's control!

China Mary was operated on. After four hours, Dr. Huang, still in his surgical gown, rushed breathlessly to our room: "Praise the Lord!" he said. "The operation is a success!" Skillful doctors had performed the needed repair which the Great Physician had taken care of. China Mary would have to be most careful, and the emergency could recur, but we thanked the Lord again for His providence that we were able to get there on time. My examinations gave the doctors a much better diagnosis of my eye problems and enabled them to preserve what sight I do have.

We had requested not to have visitors, as we needed our full rest. Nevertheless, we were besieged with calls and inquiries from kind friends. One dear old friend did get past the hospital vigilance to our bedside, anyway. It was Dr. William Miller, officially retired after being a missionary for forty years, but far from stopping his work for the Lord. He was responsible for preparing the Iranian translation of *Queen of the Dark Chamber*. I was told that each time he rode on the hospital elevator he witnessed to the people around him and gave them tracts. Once a missionary, always a missionary!

We stayed in the hospital for ten days. As I was about to leave, I gave a copy of my book to the surgeon and one to the head nurse. Somehow the news got around, and before we left the hospital, thirty-five resident doctors and nurses requested copies. I could not count how many came asking me to autograph their books.

The trip home to Leaman Place was less eventful and more joyous. The Lord had seen us through another lesson in His classroom, entitled "Trust Me, even to Philadelphia!"

Chapter 24

My Godmother's Hands

When my godmother and I were in fairly good health, we often speculated about our future. I always insisted, "If the Lord should tarry and we have to be separated, I want you to pray that God will allow me to go to heaven first. I would never survive without you! You are the one with such strong faith in the Lord. I am weak."

China Mary would always gently reprove me, "You must not say that, dear. You have to let the Lord decide whatever He sees best."

When she was taken ill for the last time, I realized it was serious. I not only prayed myself, but repeated to her, "Godmother, please pray that God may take me first, because you can face troubles and I can't." I also told her, "If the Lord should take you first, I want you to know that I will refuse to see people; I will not write; I will not do anything. I will just sit and wait! I will 'close my store,' as we Chinese say."

Sick as she was, she whispered patiently, "Christiana, take it back. Take it back! You must follow His will."

On the night of January 19, 1972, my heart was pounding with apprehension. I sensed that she was slipping fast. I insisted, against literally everyone's orders, that she lie in my bed with me. We could not be separated at such a precious time. During her whole illness she lay beside me on my bed, often semiconsciously tossing and turning so that I was almost pushed off the bed. Day and night, week after week, she had become increasingly ill. On this night the kind nurse held one hand and I held the other.

Her hand had been our only means of communication for

some time. She could not see anymore and could only mumble a few words, but her hand reached over constantly to touch me. It was my godmother's hands that had lovingly and patiently cared for me for forty-one long years while I was bedridden. For those first sixteen years that the doctors had not been able to diagnose my illness, when I was sick with fever, all my knuckles had cracked open and eight fingernails disappeared. My godmother had soaked my hands in lukewarm water and gently rubbed my fingers day after day. In order to force-feed me and save my life when I could not swallow, she had fed me orange juice a drop at a time, gently stroking it down my throat for a whole month. Even to the day when she was suddenly taken sick, her warm hand reached to my icy-cold hands as my persistent malaria chills came on every day. She would take my cold hands in her soft warm hands, saying, "Let me *wu-wu* them" (*wu-wu* means "to warm up" in Chinese). Above all, those dear hands had prepared the whole phonetic Bible for my illiterate countrymen in China so they could read and understand the Word of God. And when we came to the United States, her hands had prepared many meals and ministered to the Chinese officers, seamen, and students. It would take pages more to tell what those dear hands did for me and others all those years.

As I held her hand on that final night, the nurse repeatedly tried to listen to her faint heartbeat. Suddenly China Mary became very quiet She raised her shoulders just a little. I whispered hoarsely, "Godmother, Godmother!"

She answered, "Um."

I called to her again. Everything became quiet. No answer.

The nurse said, "She has gone from us. I am sending for the doctor."

What a thunderbolt! When her hand finally stopped reaching toward me, I knew she was in the presence of the Lord, as Paul said, "absent from the body…present with the Lord" (2 Corinthians 5:8).

Dr. Robert Snader arrived. After his examination, he said sternly to me, "Christiana, I insist that you leave this room. She has gone. You must take care of yourself now. You have to get some rest!" This doctor was very kind and thoughtful of me. He had taken care of both of us for more than twenty years. I told him that I wanted to stay with her for a while, even though her spirit was in heaven. He answered very strictly, "No such thing! Go out and rest!"

While he was writing the death certificate in our sitting room, the thoughtful funeral director, Mr. Brown, who had heard the doctor's remark, privately whispered to me, "Christiana, I understand. Never mind. It will take me two hours to make preparations to come back for her." His place was nearby, almost within sight of our home, so I knew it actually might have taken him only ten minutes to return. But he knew my aching heart and that I needed to spend more time with her. He was a church elder and had been our good friend for many years. When we worked with the officers, seamen, and students, he brought his folding chairs and set them up for the large meetings. He always said, "I want to share in what the Lord is doing."

It was late at night. Everyone was out of my room except my godmother and me, and she was now beholding her dear Saviour's face. I held her cold hand. We had worked together for the Lord fifty-eight years for His glory, separated only for the two years she was in the concentration camp after Pearl Harbor. Now she had entered heaven's gates. This parting scene brought back memories of when she entered the concentration camp in China. About fifty of our Chinese Christian friends came on bicycles to accompany her to the camp as she rode in a rickshaw. I could not go along because I was not well enough, so I stayed back with my lonely tears, just watching her umbrella disappear in the distance. The Japanese guards stood at the gate. She got off the rickshaw, picked up her bundle, and passed through the gate all alone. All her friends watched tearfully as her shadow disappeared.

In all my eighty-two years, this was the first time I had ever seen the fearful power of death tearing away a loved one. I longed to take her place and die for her, but death paid no attention to me. As I looked at her hands, finally still, I praised the Lord Jesus Christ for His wonderful salvation. I knew my godmother was with Him forever. I thanked Him for the assurance that by His saving grace I would meet her in our heavenly home. I also understood now the utter terror of anyone facing death without believing in Jesus and of passing all alone into the great unknown.

Because of the hope of our resurrection and the assurance of eternal life through Jesus Christ, my separation from my godmother, although sorrowful for the time being, had in it the joyous seeds of victory and hope that we would be together again someday in His presence. So at this time I had no tears. I could not even pray.

Suddenly I seemed to see a vision of a vast wilderness, with dark clouds overhead. A figure appeared, walking very fast toward a bottomless pit. I was not able to distinguish the features. Then I seemed to hear a voice calling three times, "Christiana, stop that person!"

I suddenly woke from my vision and realized the Lord was patiently teaching me a lesson. There was still work for me to do for the Lord. I bowed my head and prayed, "Lord, forgive me for what I said. I do not want to hurt Thy feelings with my self-pity nor turn against my dear godmother's wishes. Lord, help me follow Thy leading, whatsoever Thou wouldst have me do."

Old folks really don't want new clothes. I was already eighty-two. Could I really expect a "new garment"? Did I dare pray that my godmother's Christlike life and winsome spiritual witness, like "Eiljah's mantle," might fall upon me, so that my hands also might in every way serve the risen and coming again Lord Jesus Christ?

Then the reality of the practical details of China Mary's funeral dawned upon me. In China I had never participated directly in any funerals. When my father had died, my brothers had taken charge of everything. I had been away when my mother died. What did I know of all the responsibilities for burial arrangements, estates, and legal matters in America? Here I was in a foreign country, unfamiliar with its traditions and customs. I could scarcely believe that the Lord put into my hands the management of all three of the funerals of those dearest to me: the Leaman sisters and Cousin Mary W. In the midst of my personal grief, I had to handle the estates, deal with lawyers and courts, act as executrix, and attend to legal matters! China Mary, previously capable and practical-minded to handle any emergency throughout my long illness, had been too physically weak to manage the home-going arrangements of both Cousin Mary and Sister Lucy, who had died eight and four years before, respectively. And, now, upon her departure, I was left alone without her wise counsel and patience to direct me. But the Lord was my "very present help in trouble" (Psalm 46:1) as always.

After the funeral, all my kind friends and helpers were tired. Suddenly the back doorbell rang. Our faithful co-worker Susanna opened it to confront a well-dressed American man. "Who are you?" she inquired.

He answered abruptly, "I'm not going to tell you my name." He walked through the dining room, where Miss Ng requested him to sign the guest book. Again he refused, saying, "I'm not going to sign my name."

When he walked into my room, I could tell with my dim eyes that he was handsome and young. The first thing I asked was his name. Refusing again to answer, he sat down right on the corner of the couch where my godmother used to sit early each morning. He covered his face with his hands and began to cry loudly. In all my life I had never seen a young man cry that hard. I thought that he must have known my godmother and he was crying with grief at her home-going. I tried asking him different questions, but there was no response. I prayed, "Lord, I don't know the heartaches of this gentleman. You know them. Speak to him and comfort him."

Meanwhile, my co-workers were suspicious that he was a bad man who had come to harm me. They sat outside my room, carefully watching him. Finally I said to him, by the help of the Holy Spirit, "Sir, we are all made to die once and after that the judgement" (see Hebrews 9:27). He paid no attention but kept on crying. The Spirit helped me to go on and explain to him what salvation is and what eternal life means to believers.

It was growing late and Miss Ng came in to say, "Sir, don't you want to come to the parlor and rest awhile?"

By that time he had stopped crying so loudly, but he was still quietly sobbing. He stood up, fixed his eyes on me for about a minute, then said, "Thank you. You have given me the key to salvation. Good-bye!" To this day I don't know who he was, nor have I ever seen him again. God knows.

As soon as he left, a friend came in and said, "What shall we do? I know how exhausted you are, but a group of American young people has come. They didn't even know that China Mary has gone to be with the Lord."

I answered, "We must let them come in." I remembered China Mary's constant attitude of "restful availability" for whatever the Lord brought into our lives. "I will just say hello to them."

Those precious young people quietly marched into my room. My eyes were so tired and dim I could hardly see them. I said to them, "Precious in the sight of the LORD is the death of his saints" (Psalm 116:15). Then I shared with them for about ten minutes how wonderful salvation is.

Later my friend asked me, "Did you see the hands of six young people raised to accept Christ when you invited them to believe?"

How patient and forgiving the Lord Jesus is! "He restoreth my soul" (Psalm 23:3). Although He had just led me through the valley of the shadow of death, His rod and staff not only were comforting me, but they were also lovingly forcing me to keep on comforting and ministering to others. He did not allow me to "close my store." "I must be about my Father's business" as usual!

Long-distance calls, telegrams, and letters of sympathy poured in from friends who were wondering what I was going to do without China Mary or any relatives in this country. Indeed, as my godmother, she had been more than a mother to me. Three years before, when we had put up a cemetery marker for China Mary's sister, Lucy, we had decided to put all three of our names on it. China Mary wanted the following words inscribed on the stone: "Jesus will never leave us" (see Hebrews 13:5). Yes, my godmother had to leave me, but Jesus will never leave me.

I asked my friends to kindly remember me in their prayers so that(1)I would not be anxious about the next step. My godmother used to remind me every morning, "As thou goest, step by step, I will open the way before thee" (Proverbs 4:12, Hebrew translation);(2)I would not anticipate the future. It is in the Lord's hand alone;(3)I would not choose my way, for His way is higher; and(4) I would not carry the heavy load of imaginary thoughts on my own back. He careth for me! I knew my Lord wanted me to go forward.

Chapter 25

Longing for Home

Life is like a train. There are many stops. One gets off here, another there, along the way. So many of my friends have gotten off already when the train arrived at their stations. When I came to this country in 1949, China Mary, her sister Lucy, Cousin Mary, a maid, a couple who came here to help us, and the family doctor were all aboard the first day. Now all seven have gone to be with the Lord. I, the weakest one, am still here. 1 do not ask why. I am among the few of my generation still left on the train. My ticket is in my heavenly Conductor's hand—He will let me know when I arrive at my stop. Meanwhile, the Lord must have a purpose for me to live so long.

In 1949, we had begun as a most joyful and harmonious quartet in Paradise, Pennsylvania: Cousin Mary W., Sister Lucy, Godmother China Mary, and me. We always served the Lord with one heart and one mind. Mary W.'s one wish was so often expressed: "all together." Whenever I held a meeting in my darkened room, the three prayer warriors never failed to quietly pray for me in the sitting room—we four were one.

In 1964, our dear "all together" Mary W. was the first of our quartet to enter glory. By the mercy of the Lord, the trio continued.

In 1968, Sister Lucy was summoned to be with the Lord. I often marvel at God's mercy and goodness. He continued to lead China Mary and me to play a duet. I must confess my weakness and say that I often "hanged my harp upon the willow" (see Psalm 137:2) and "sat down under a juniper tree" (1 Kings 19:4). But my godmother's devotion to the Lord never wavered and always kept me steady. Her prayer life was more important than her food. Only the Lord knows how she helped and encouraged me to go forward!

On January 19, 1972, exactly twenty-three years to the day since she and I had left China's shore, she was called to her "new job" in her heavenly home. Every four years one of us had dropped out of the quartet. We know there are no re-runs of the film of life. So here I am alone! I can only bow my head and say that I know my master Architect has guided my steps "by the skilfulness of his hands" (Psalm 78:72). By His grace, I take up my harp and go on playing a solo.

The day dawned like any other day. Though it was midwinter, the sun rose brilliantly, though late, and reflected against the new fallen snow. I could see its rays seeking entrance to my room through the cracks in the dark curtains around my windows. But I dared not look at it, blinking my sensitive eyes away from its glow.

That morning my eyes also blinked away a great flood of tears. I was trying to hold them back by a dam of self-control, though some trickles still made their way through my eyelids and splashed against my pillow. Today was the anniversary of the home-going of my dear godmother.

After she joined the Lord, I did not believe that I could survive if left alone. I did not want to go on. I begged the Lord to take me, too, right away, so that we would not be separated. How wonderful it would be to behold the glory of the face of the Lord side by side with my companion of a lifetime! How we would together enjoy finding out the mysterious things now revealed in His presence! She would be able to see and I would be able to walk! "Oh, let me leave this earthly tabernacle, Lord!" I had prayed. "It has been long enough! I cannot go further by myself!"

But the Holy Spirit, my Comforter, held me up moment by moment and day by day for weeks and months, and now it was five years since my godmother had left me. The love and the pain in my heart were not less than on that day five years ago. The longing to join her before the Lord was no less intense. But then the sweet peace of Jesus, "which passeth all understanding" (Philippians 4:7), swept over me once more.

And I sang this song unto the Lord:

> Thy cross all my refuge, Thy blood all my plea,
> None other I need, blessed Jesus, but Thee!
> I fear not the shadows at close of life's day,
> For Thou wilt go with me the rest of the way!

A message came one day that Mrs. Billy Graham; the Grahams' youngest son, Ned; their daughter Bunny and her husband, Dr. Dienert, were coming to visit me. The Lord sustained me in my weakness and gave me unusual strength and quietness in my heart for this unexpected pleasure. As soon as we were introduced to each other, I prayed, asking the Lord Jesus to bless our fellowship for His glory. He did!

Ruth Graham (Billy Graham's wife)
with children visited Miss Tsai several times

Mrs. Graham, who was born of missionary parents in China, told me she had read my book three times and that she was going to read it again. Strongly urging me to hurry and finish this sequel, she exclaimed, "Oh, Miss Tsai, you should stop all your meetings, keep people from coming to see you, and concentrate fully on finishing this witness! It will surely be used by the Lord to encourage many—even more than the meetings here in your dark chamber!"

I was led to ask her son-in-law to read the preface and the first chapter of this sequel. After he read it, he said, "This is what people want to read. They want to read actions of God's doings in a human being. Hurry and finish your sequel!"

In my human desire, this also would have been what I would have liked to do. But the Lord's call to me to be His "hunting dog" is still as clear as it was the day that I turned over my life to Him. "Mrs. Graham, you and I know that the coming of the Lord is near, even at the door!" I said. "If I refuse to see some person whose heart is prepared to accept Him, I would fail my Lord. I must be ready, by His help, to win people to Him and open the door into His sheepfold so that the lost sheep may find their way in. If it pleases the Lord that this little witness should be written, it must be done between the swinging of the doors while the lost sheep enter His fold and go 'in and out, and find pasture' " (John 10:9b).

Mrs. Graham kindly gave me permission to use this poem from her book:

> Test me, Lord, and give me strength
> to meet each test
>   unflinching, unafraid;
> not striving nervously to do my best,
> not self-assured, or careless as in jest,
>   but with Your aid.
>
> Purge me, Lord, and give me grace
> to bear the heat

of cleansing flame;
not bitter at my lowly lot, but meet
to bear my share of suffering and keep me sweet,
In Jesus' name.[1]

I keep a small magnet in my "miscellaneous drawer." Because of my poor eyesight and the darkened room, it is most difficult for me to rummage around to find exactly the tiny things that I want. I pull my magnet around, and all kinds of pins and objects jump to the magnet and cling there. It doesn't matter if they are crooked, bent, broken, small, or large. In 1 Thessalonians 4:17, believers are promised that at the coming of the Lord, we shall be "caught up....to meet the Lord in the air." In Chinese, the word translated "caught up" has the meaning of "pulled up" or "lifted up" like the action of a magnet. Not all the things in my drawer can be lifted up by my magnet—only those items which are magnetized. The other things just lie there with no response. So the Lord has reminded me that at His coming, whether new or old, bent, broken, or whatever—we who are His, and only those who are His—will be lifted up with Him.

Shall I only sit and wait for my King of light, my heavenly Bridegroom, to come and take me from the stage of my dark chamber so that my final curtain can come down? No! In His love and in His perfect plan revealed in His Word, He has said, "Occupy till I come" (Luke 19:13). So in spite of advanced age, infirmity, weakness, and increasing limitations, I joyously agree with Him that I must go on!

Dr. Oswald J. Smith has graciously allowed me to use his poem, "We Must Go On," which expresses my continued heart commitment to my Lord:

---

1 From *Sitting By My Laughing Fine*, by Ruth Bell Graham, Copyright, 1977, Ruth Bell Graham, Word Books. Used by permission of Word Books, Publisher, Waco, Texas.

WE MUST GO ON

We must go on, the night is fast approaching,
The past is gone, we cannot change it now;
We weep, we pray, and yet forget we cannot,
O God, forgive, as at Thy Throne we bow.

We must go on, atone ourselves, we cannot,
Thy blood alone can make us clean within;
There is no hope except Thy love and mercy,
Then pardon, Lord, and take away our sin.

We must go on, the future still awaits us,
The present, too, is ours to live for Thee;
Our past, dear Lord, oh help us to forget it,
And by Thy power, come now and set us free.

We must go on, although our tears are falling,
For all our work on earth will soon be o'er;
Our prayers, our toils will someday be rewarded,
And we shall dwell with Thee forevermore.

We must go on, the Day will soon be dawning,
The future calls, we cannot change the past;
Thy plan is best and though our hearts are breaking,
We must go on, 'twill all be plain at last!

Christiana Tsai with visitors, 1973

JEWELS FROM THE QUEEN OF THE DARK CHAMBER

Contents

Dedication

I dedicate this book to the memory of my godmother, Mary A. Leaman (China Mary), who led me to follow the living God when I was a young student in China. Because of her witness and teaching, fifty- five members of my family in China came to know Him too.

Mary Leaman first met me at the door of Ming Deh, the first girls' school in Nanking, which was established by her parents. My classroom experience in God's school of daily living began there.

Without my godmother's patient guidance, unfailing prayers, physical care, and great sacrifice I would not have been able to serve God these many years.

I dedicate this book most of all to the glory of God, whose Son, Jesus Christ, for these scores of years, has been "my light and my salvation; whom shall I fear? the LORD is the defense of my life; whom shall I dread?" (Psalm 27:1).

Acknowledgments

I wish to acknowledge the encouragement of the three founders of AMBASSADORS FOR CHRIST, INC: Rev. Moses Chow, Mr. Ted Choy, and Mrs. Leona Choy. Rev. Chow first suggested I put my little illustrations into a booklet to share with my friends, and Mrs. Choy helped to compile and shape them up.

I would like to thank Mrs. C. P. (Margie) Wright, my longtime friend, who offered suggestions and prepared the Bible verses.

If I were to mention every friend who touched my life as these stories unfolded through the years and who were God's instruments to help teach me the lessons God wanted me to learn, it would take many pages. I ask the Lord to bless each one who had a share in helping me to complete this manuscript to the glory of God.

Because I am a part of all the people I have met who shared their stories with me, I realize that some of the illustrations in this book do not originate with me. But because I may have heard or read them long ago, I may not remember where. I wish to acknowledge my debt to their authors, though unknown.

Last, but not least important, I thank my three special coworkers: Miss Susanna Eshleman, who has lovingly cared for my needs since we first met in 1949; Miss Grace Ng, who has been my companion and helper since 1961; and Mrs. Frances Stoltzfus, who has been like my right hand to assist me in my writing and correspondence since 1954.

Foreword

How bizarre to think of a tiny Chinese woman, born into wealth in 1890, only to become a Christian at a girls' mission school, strike a lifelong friendship with the principal, and serve the cause of Christ with her friend (China Mary Leaman) until they were forty and fifty years old, respectively, traveling throughout China and the United States, speaking and writing.

Yet even the ravaging, mysterious illness, which relegated Christiana to bed in a dark room in 1931, failed to affect their ministry or their friendship. This woman continues to engage in outreach, even from her darkened chamber in Paradise, Pennsylvania. From this little room in the great old Leaman home emanates prayer, letter writing, and personal witnessing unparalleled by most who can walk.

Jerry Jenkins
Director, Moody Press

Chapter 1

My Classroom

Day by day I am learning lessons from my Lord Jesus, the great Teacher. I look upon my life as a school. I also learn from those who come to call on me, my fellow students.

When I was a young student in China, I had a teacher, Miss Helen Drake, who taught me English literature in the girls' school. She was very kind but very strict. When she assigned a composition, she was particular about every comma, period, and paragraph. If we made even the slightest mistake, she insisted, "Rewrite it."

One day she assigned us to change the book "The Lady of the Lake" from poetry into prose. Every morning we had to recite one paragraph and diagram it on a big blackboard. We had to rise early to do this, before breakfast and chapel, because the literature class was scheduled right after chapel. Miss Drake went over every detail of what we had done and demanded perfection. We even wished that our teacher would be sick for a day so we could take a vacation! But she was very strong and healthy. What little English I know is a credit to her efforts. Although at the time I did not appreciate Miss Drake and her demands, I am now very thankful for the discipline I endured.

In the same way the Lord trains me daily in my life classroom. It is an everyday affair— no skipping. The Lord is teaching me in each area of my life, through everyone with whom I come into contact, through all of the people who enter my dark chamber. Whatever happens is a lesson to me, something that my heavenly Teacher wants me to learn. I am privileged to be enrolled in His school.

Teach me, O LORD, the way of Thy statutes,
And I shall observe it to the end.
Psalm 119:33

Chapter 2

Big-Headed Silkworms

I constantly have to take care that I am faithful to pass on the blessings that the Lord has given me. It is so easy for Christians to attend many meetings, hear sound preaching, feed on the Word of God, and store up God's riches without sharing what they have learned with others.

China is famous for three products: Chinaware, tea, and silk. In the past, silk has been the number one specialty. It is not a synthetic product; it comes from the lives of the silkworms.

The area around Hangchow is famous for its mulberry trees, on which the worms feed. I used to see many young girls in the early mornings, singing on their way to gather the tender leaves. They assembled trays for the worms and then scattered the leaves on the trays for the worms to eat. The leaves and the hands that touched them had to be very clean.

The worms would eat until their bodies grew fat. It took forty days to complete that stage of the cycle. Toward the end of that time, the worms would start to spin large silk cocoons around themselves. Then their bodies would gradually become thin and dry and begin to shrivel. During this stage, the worm ate very much—not for its own enjoyment, but ultimately to produce the silk. Others than the worms themselves were to benefit from this process.

But every time, another variety of silkworms got mixed into the tray among the good ones. As soon as the mulberry leaves were scattered on the tray, these worms would invariably be the first to snatch the leaves and gobble them up. Their heads and bodies would get bigger and bigger, but they would not produce any silk. The attendants would have to pick them out and throw them away as intruders.

I often search my heart to see whether I am like the good silk worms, productively carrying out God's purpose to benefit others, or like the big-headed ones, taking in God's blessings for my own pleasures only.

> It is more blessed to give than to receive [Acts 20:35b].

> And from everyone who has been given much shall much be required; and to whom they entrusted much, of him they will ask all the more [Luke 12:48b].

> Freely you received, freely give [Matthew 10:8b].

Chapter 3

The Kindergarten Chair

Sometimes when I think it is time that I graduate from some lesson the Lord has been teaching me, I find that I have not passed yet, but need to study it all over again.

Mary Leaman's sister, Lucy, brought a small, wooden, kindergarten chair back from China, where she used to teach small children. The chair sits by my bedside as a constant reminder of our need for humility and a lowly spirit.

Many times I have had visitors sitting on that little chair—PhDs, college and seminary presidents, directors of great organizations, and other famous people. They have not come for me to teach them something. In God's sight, we are *all* children, learning in *His* school.

"Come...and learn from Me," invited our Master [Matthew 11:28-29].

And whoever exalts himself shall be humbled; and whoever humbles himself shall be exalted [Matthew 23:12].

Chapter 4

Secret Tapestry

We may say, "I do not understand the devious paths by which God is leading me. There are so many things in His dealings with me that are puzzling." I learned many lessons about this question from the Hanking tapestries.

During the Manchu Dynasty, the emperors and high courtiers wore gowns made of beautiful tapestries, all woven in Nanking, China. I often took visitors, especially American friends, to see the famous weaving process by which those tapestries were made.

The tapestries are woven on a hand loom by two weavers working closely together. One sits at the head of the loom and slides the shuttles of different colored threads through the warp. He weaves from the reverse side of the tapestry; since he cannot see the design he is creating, he must memorize the pattern. The other weaver sits above the loom, where he can pull up different groups of threads, so the various colored threads can slide between them. He, too, must do this from memory, and the two men must work in perfect harmony with each other. The patterns are highly secret, and each weaving company guards its own designs carefully against theft. Thus, the craftsmen must be careful, skilled, and trustworthy.

Although God's design for our lives may yet be a secret to *us*, we can be confident that it is fully known to Him; He has created the perfect pattern for each of our lives.

"For I know the plans that I have for you," declares the LORD, "plans for welfare and not for calamity to give you a future and a hope" [Jeremiah 29:11].

Chapter 5

Reflection in Silver

Nearly fifty years ago, just a few days before I was enrolled by the Lord in the school of pain and suffering, He prepared me through a precious illustration.

I was taken to a factory to observe the different phases of refining silver. In one department, the fire from the furnace felt unusually hot. A workman had fixed his eyes on the furnace. As I asked him a question, he acted as if he had not heard me.

A little later, as I continued to watch the fire with fascination, the same workman explained, "Madam, I am so sorry. I could not answer you just then, because I had to watch the silver very carefully. As soon as I can see my face reflected in the silver, the silver has to be taken out of the fire."

May the Lord help us to reflect His love, so that—wherever we go and whatever we must go through—people will see and know that we belong to Him.

> But we all, with unveiled face beholding as in a mirror the glory of the Lord, are being transformed into the same image from glory to glory, just as from the Lord, the Spirit [2 Corinthians 3:18].

Chapter 6

Like a Child

The Lord requires us to become like little children if we want to enter the kingdom of God.

One day the little son of a Chinese family that was visiting us sneaked downstairs very early in the morning. He crawled right into bed with me! This was the first time that this had ever happened! I wanted to keep him quiet, so his parents could sleep longer, and wondered how to entertain him. I decided to read him the story of Zaccheus from the Bible; then I taught him to repeat it to his parents.

During a meeting in my room with them that morning, I showed them an object lesson—really a simple chemistry experiment. I had two jars of water, one tinted with red color and the other clear. Then I made the red one clear by adding a chemical. I was demonstrating the analogy that Jesus makes our sins white as snow, after they have been red like crimson (Isaiah 1:18). The little boy watched, wide-eyed.

Before anyone knew what was happening, he jumped up from his chair and ran over to my table. He picked up the water jar in his chubby little hands and was going to drink the contents—with the chemical and all! "I believe in Jesus," he said. "I want to be clean *now!*"

I screamed at him just in time. "Stop!" I cried. "That is *poison!*" My little story almost turned into a tragedy. But the little boy had given his young heart to Jesus in the simplicity of child-like faith, even though he did not understand everything yet. The Lord requires the same faith of us all.

And He called a child to Himself and set him before them, and said, "Truly I say to you, unless you are converted and become like children, you shall not enter the kingdom of heaven. Whoever then humbles himself as this child, he is the greatest in the kingdom of heaven" [Matthew 18:2-4].

Chapter 7

Loving His Appearing

How real is my hope of meeting the Lord when He comes for His church!

I keep a small magnet in my "miscellaneous drawer" beside my bed. Because of my poor eyesight and the darkened room, it is most difficult for me to rummage around to find exactly what tiny things I want. I pull my magnet around in the drawer, and all kinds of pins and clips and objects jump to it and cling there. It doesn't matter if they are cracked or broken, small or large—they all cling to the magnet.

God's Word promises believers that, at the coming of the Lord, they shall be "caught up" to meet the Lord in the air. In the Chinese translation, *caught up* has the meaning of *pulled up* or *lifted up*, like the action of a magnet.

Not all of the things in my drawer are lifted up by my magnet—only those items that are magnetized. The other things just lie there still, with no response. The Lord has reminded me that it will be just so at His coming. Whether new or old, bent or broken, if we are His, we will respond to His coming—only those who are His will be able to respond.

The sunflower always turns its blossom (or head) toward the sun. So we must always keep looking to Jesus and loving His appearing. What a comfort it is to my heart to know that, although I am far from perfect, I do not need to depend upon *my own* righteousness to meet God, but only upon my simple faith in Christ and *His* righteousness. Only *that* qualifies me to be lifted up by His "big magnet" in that wonderful day to come!

For the Lord Himself will descend from heaven with a shout, with the voice of the archangel, and with the trumpet of God; and the dead in Christ shall rise first. Then we who are alive and remain shall be caught up together with them in the clouds to meet the Lord in the air, and thus we shall always be with the Lord [1 Thessalonians 4:16-17].

Chapter 8

The Choice

How strong is our determination to follow Jesus, if we are threatened with losing all—even our loved ones and life itself?

I have a picture on the wall of my dark chamber. It is a copy of the famous painting *Diana or Christ?*

The picture illustrates a story in the first-century record from the book of Acts, regarding the Ephesian goddess, Diana. The apostle Paul strongly opposed the worship of Diana; his opposition caused him a great deal of trouble with the authorities; he was nearly killed.

My picture shows a lovely girl, who has accepted Jesus Christ as her Savior. The people have discovered that she has refused to worship the idol, Diana, and the priest has given her an ultimatum: either worship the idol or be fed to the lions.

The girl has become engaged to a young man; he also appears in the picture, holding her hand and pleading with her to bow to Diana and live. Her parents, relatives, and friends are likewise pictured, begging her to do the same. What a difficult decision! How easy it would have been for her to give in!

To sacrifice money or position would not be as hard as to refuse the love of parents or the love of the man she was going to marry. To choose Christ would be to die.

In the picture, the girl looks up to heaven for strength. Then the priest offers a compromise: "Here is a picture of our goddess, Diana. Here is the incense burner. I'll let this boy hold the incense box. I will allow you to take some incense from the burner and place it before the goddess. That will show that you worship and follow her. You do not have to kneel."

Even with the priest's compromise, the girl would have had to yield to the worship of Diana.

Would I have had the strength to stand firm in my faith? Such things do not only happen in history, they happen all the time in many places of the world—even now.

We are daily faced with many decisions. Will we follow Jesus or go our own way? Let us ask Jesus to help us to be strongly determined to follow Him. He must have control over matters of our hearts and human love—and our lives as well.

> But Jesus said to him, "No one, after putting his hand to the plow and looking back, is fit for the kingdom of God" [Luke 9:62].

Chapter 9

Faithful Unto Death

Some of the greatest enemies of Christ have, like the apostle Paul, become the staunchest saints. Some have been honored by the Lord to give their lives for Him.

I have a delicate little blue Peking vase, which I always keep on the bureau in my dark chamber. It was given to me as a parting "Sayonara" gift by my friend, Miss Li Yuen-Ru, when China Mary and I were leaving China for the last time. I cautioned her, "Miss Li, what if those who do not believe in Christianity will hold a big sword to your neck to force you to renounce your faith?"

She answered, "We are all human. No one wants to face a cruel death. But if the Lord Jesus, who gave me grace and courage to accept Him as my Savior, is with me, I am sure He will give me the same kind of grace to face the big sword, if that time comes."

Who was this lady of such courageous faith? She was the very same teacher who, before her conversion, burned thirty-seven leather-bound Bibles that belonged to the Christian students. She expelled seven of the girls, because they had come to my home to study the Bible and, as a result, had believed in Jesus.

Later, for the sake of Christ, this lady was indeed cast into prison in China, where she was kept for eighteen years. She suffered much for Jesus and has now gone to be with the Lord whom she dearly loved.

> Therefore, my beloved brethren, be steadfast, immovable, always abounding in the work of the Lord, knowing that your toil is not in vain in the Lord [1 Corinthians 15:58].

Chapter 10

Shepherd or Butcher?

Many tired, discouraged, and burdened Christian workers have come to call on me. "I'm almost at the breaking point with overwork, " some have declared. I understand that feeling, because I have walked the same path.

One of my friends was making a tour of the Holy Land. When he returned, he reported a story to me. He was very interested in sheep and shepherds. The guide on the sightseeing tour bus explained that shepherds always lead their sheep, going before them, with the sheep following behind.

Suddenly, the bus passed a man who was driving some sheep before him. The man pointed it out to the guide. "Look at that!" he exclaimed. "I thought you told us that the shepherd always walked in front of the sheep."

The guide answered, "That's what I said. It's always true. That man is *not* the shepherd—he is a butcher!" When the sheep realize they are being driven, they become very nervous.

The Holy Spirit *leads* us gently, like a shepherd. Satan *drives* us, like the butcher. Many times we drive ourselves or are driven by others. We run around—even in Christian work—accomplishing little of eternal value, yet in the name of serving the Lord. Satan is driving us.

We should be *sure* that we are called to do a certain work for the Lord—before we embark. It is not enough to see a vacancy or need and then fill it. We must be sure that, in God's service, it will not be said of us that we just went but that we were really *sent* by the Lord.

The Lord has taught me that I could spend three whole days and nights preparing myself to preach or witness but if it is done in self or in the flesh, it will be of no avail. Yet if I say three sentences in the power of the Holy Spirit, souls can be converted.

> The LORD is my shepherd, I shall not want. He makes me lie down in green pastures; He leads me beside quiet waters [Psalm 23:1-2].

Chapter 11

What's in a Name?

Of what importance is one's name when measured against time and eternity? I remember when the Lord first taught me that lesson.

During the time I was touring the eleven provinces of China one year to witness for the Lord, I had occasion to visit the birthplace of Confucius. In the company of other missionaries, I was the only one in the group who was Chinese. The seventy-sixth generation of Confucius was living there, and we went for an audience with him.

We visited the famous Tai-Shan and then traveled to Chufu, about eighteen miles away, after a picnic lunch at the Temple Statue of Confucius.

Confucius' grave was said to be near there, and we went to seek it out. I was awed yet confused to see literally hundreds of grave markers—all labeled "Kung," which was Confucius' surname.

I inquired of the caretaker, as to which was *really* Confucius' grave.

He shrugged, "Who knows, lady, who knows?"

I thought of the words of the Old Testament: Moses had died and was buried, "but no man knows his burial place to this day" (Deuteronomy 34:6). No one really knows where such famous people as Confucius and even Moses are buried. What is a name? What does it matter *who* Christiana Tsai is?

I thought to myself, *How the world regards me is of no consequence after a generation or two, when our place is remembered no more. My purpose is only to fulfill whatever task the Lord wants me to do in my life and to glorify His name.*

Yet what a comfort it is to know that my Lord says He knows His sheep *by name* and that I am precious to *Him!*

> To him the doorkeeper opens, and the sheep hear his voice, and he calls his own sheep by name, and leads them out [John 10:3].

Chapter 12

The Complete Message

Things are not always what they seem. Above the dark clouds, the sun is always shining. The reverse side of sorrow is joy and victory.

I have been much encouraged by the following story. News of the historic battle of Waterloo was brought by a sailing vessel to the south coast of England. From there the tidings were passed by semaphore to London. In due course of time, the semaphore on Winchester Cathedral began to repeat the message.

Letter by letter, it spelled out: W-E-L-L-I-N-G-T-O-N D-E-F-E-A-T-E-D. Just then, a blanket of fog swept down and wrapped the signal away from sight. Far and wide across the land, the news began to spread that the battle had been lost. Later in the day, the fog lifted, and the despondent people saw to their surprise that the semaphore arms were moving again.

This time, it spelled out the complete message: W-E-L-L-I-N-G-T-O-N D-E-F-E-A-T-E-D T-H-E E-N-E-M-Y. For very joy, they could scarcely believe what they saw! But it was true, and soon the whole country rang with the gladness that apparent defeat had become actual victory!

The Easter story broke upon the world in a somewhat similar fashion. On Good Friday, the stark outline of a cross upon a hill and the cold finality of a sealed tomb proclaimed to the beholders: J-E-S-U-S D-E-F-E-A-T-E-D. All weekend, this was the message that hammered with cruel persistence upon the minds and spirits of Jesus' followers. But on Easter morning, the open grave and the risen Lord proclaimed the completed message:

J-E-S-U-S D-E-F-E-A-T-E-D T-H-E E-N-E-M-Y. Gloom gave way to gladness.

> "O death, where is your victory?
> O death, where is your sting?"
> ...but thanks be to God, who gives us the victory through our Lord Jesus Christ [1 Corinthians 15:55, 57].

Chapter 13

The Devil's Favorite Tool

Discouragement is a dangerous state of mind, because it leaves one open to every assault of the enemy of our soul.

Discouragement often comes sneaking around to weaken active people and to spoil their service for the Lord. I have seen men and women who had been greatly used by the Lord literally felled by discouragement—often right after great spiritual victories.

Great leaders in the Bible were not spared this experience: Elijah moped under the juniper tree; David often found himself in the throes of despair; Moses wallowed in self-pity.

How much more prone to discouragement are we shut-ins and invalids, who see ourselves as laid aside on a shelf after a busy life of service? When days stretch into weeks and then months and years and decades of weakness and suffering, I have often been tempted toward discouragement. I have wanted to turn my face to the wall and weep, like Hezekiah in his illness (see 2 Kings 20:2-3).

The devil, according to legend, once advertised some of his tools for sale at a public auction. When prospective buyers were assembled, they discovered one oddly-shaped tool, labeled "Not for Sale."

Asked to explain what it was, the devil answered, "I can spare my other tools, but I cannot spare this one. It is the most useful implement I have. It is called *discouragement,* and with it I can work my way into many hearts that would otherwise be inaccessible. When I get this tool into a man's heart, then I open the way to plant anything else there that I may desire."

When the evil one comes at me with his weapon of discouragement, I surely cannot defend myself. Everything he whispers into my ear may be true. But "greater is He who is in you than he who is in the world" (1 John 4:4).

I rebuke the enemy by claiming Revelation 12:11: "That by the blood of the Lamb, I rebuke you to leave me" (Chinese version). I could never trust my own strength to fight him, but I hide in my Rock, Christ Jesus, who is my refuge and my fortress and my high tower.

> Submit therefore to God. Resist the devil and he will flee from you. Draw near to God and He will draw near to you. Cleanse your hands, you sinners: and purify your hearts, you double-minded [James 4:7-8].

Chapter 14

Preparing Our Wedding Gown

A group of Chinese Christian students asked me, "How should the hope of the second coming of Christ affect us?"

"We must take great care in our daily walk as Christians," I told them. "We must live holy lives day by day, purifying ourselves, just as God is pure" (see 1 John 3:3).

In Revelation 19:7-8 we read that the Bride of Christ is preparing herself with a garment of the most beautiful, pure white linen. Since the book of Revelation was written nearly two thousand years ago, we can be sure that there were no electric sewing machines at that time! The bride had to use a needle and sew by hand. She had to wash her hands very thoroughly, so she would not soil the white cloth. She carefully prepared her wedding gown to wear when she met her beloved bridegroom.

In Scripture, Christians are represented by the Bride, waiting for the Bridegroom, Jesus Christ. Each Christian should be preparing his white robe carefully, as he waits to meet the Lord. Every day, stitch by stitch, by living holy lives, we are lovingly preparing ourselves for the second coming of Christ.

> Beloved, now we are children of God, and it has not appeared as yet what we shall be. We know that, when He appears, we shall be like Him, because we shall see Him just as He is. And everyone who has this hope fixed on Him purifies himself, just as He is pure [1 John 3:2-3].

Chapter 15

Anticipating Him

I often ask myself, "Am I really waiting for my Lord's return?" I often pray, "Lord, help me to be ready to welcome you, my King of Light!"

In our home in Nanking, there was an exquisite painting. The artist had depicted a beautiful azure sea with a seashore stretching into the distance. In the foreground, there was a pile of wood. A beautiful woman had lit the fire, and the wood was burning. A brilliant flame leaped skyward to send its light out into the ocean.

The woman was kneeling beside the fire. Her husband had left home by ship on business and had not returned yet. She was waiting and waiting for his return. Every night she lit a pile of wood, so that its light could lead him back to her. She knelt beside the fire, praying for his return.

The memory of that picture stirs my heart with expectation for my Lord.

> Looking for the blessed hope and the appearing of the glory of our great God and Savior, Christ Jesus [Titus 2:13].

Chapter 16

By Any Means

Did you ever hear of praying for people to make mistakes? That was precisely what Mary Leaman did in China!

"Dear Lord, please let someone dial the wrong number!"

China Mary believed in using every means at her disposal to witness for the Lord. She recognized that the telephone, newly invented at that time, could be a marvelous means of communicating the gospel.

In China, she wanted a telephone so that she could do many things that, as an invalid herself, she could not get out to do. Telephones were.very scarce, and none was available to her. Finally, another Christian let her have her telephone, because she felt China Mary's need for it was greater than her own.

Out of thanksgiving for the phone, China Mary did a thing I have never known another person to think of or have the courage to do. She prayed that, if there were people in Shanghai who needed her witness for Christ, they might get her—either by dialing the wrong number or by some other mistake! Her prayer was quite wonderfully and often answered, and she was actually able to lead some to Christ over the telephone and encourage the hearts of many.

For "Whoever will call upon the name of the Lord will be saved." How then shall they call upon Him in whom they have not believed? And how shall they believe in Him whom they have not heard? And how shall they hear without a preacher? [Romans 10:13-14].

Chapter 17

Identification and Robins

"How can I preach to my family when I return to my home?"

A young Chinese graduate had just received her PhD and was preparing to return overseas. Being a zealous new Christian, she was burdened for the salvation of her family. That was *just* what they were afraid of! From her sincere but aggressive letters, her parents sensed that, when she came home, she would press upon them how holy she had become since she had accepted Christ in America. Though they loved her, they were apprehensive about her attitude.

I sensed the delicate situation. I prayed for wisdom and then gave this advice to the girl. "I believe you should help with the household tasks—cooking, clearing the dishes, mopping floors."

Her eyes grew wide with shock at my "unspiritual advice." But the Holy Spirit gradually enlightened her about acting too far above her loved ones because of their ignorance of the Christian faith.

"Have you ever seen a robin jumping about on the lawn?" I asked her. "I instinctively want to get close to it, reach out and touch and care for it. But if I try to do so, the bird becomes frightened and flutters away. How can I reach that robin? Only another robin can get close to it. I would have to become a robin to understand robins and be accepted by them. The secret is to identify. As Christ became flesh (John 1:14) and identified with humanity to reach us, so we must identify with people to reach them for Christ."

But it is not so among you, but whoever wishes to become great among you shall be your servant; and whoever wishes to be first among you shall be slave of all. For even the Son of Man did not come to be served, but to serve and to give His life a ransom for many [Mark 10:43-45].

Chapter 18

The Long Road

Most older people, and some young ones too, have difficulty sleeping at times. During some nights, I am hardly able to sleep at all. Other nights, I am thankful to sleep three or four hours.

The Lord is good to me. He has been my real Companion, not only during all my days, but during the many long nights as well. When I am awake at night, I visualize Abraham walking on his way to Mount Moriah. The Bible says that the journey took three days. In those days the roads must have been quite primitive—with steep hills, thorns, thistles, bits of broken pottery, and sharp stones along the way.

What a wonderful picture of obedience! Abraham never argued with God or complained about the rough path. God had asked him to surrender his only son as a sacrifice when he arrived at his destination. How Abraham must have suffered to keep this intention to himself and not even mention it, as he walked with his precious young son along the way! Abraham was a frail human being; he undoubtedly had the same emotions we all share. Although his heart must have been torn with anguish, he walked steadfastly forward.

During my sleepless nights, I often review my long road before the Lord. He is teaching me not to question His direction and to accept as perfect His plan for my life. No matter how long and rough the road, I must walk patiently with Him toward my own Mount Moriah. I am absolutely sure that some day I will see my Lord face to face "and tell the story—saved by grace." [1]

That I may know Him, and the power of His resurrection and the fellowship of His sufferings, being conformed to His death [Philippians 3:10].

1 Fanny Crosby, "Saved by Grace," (Carol Stream, IL Hope, 1957).

Chapter 19

Reaction To Heat

When I am tempted to self-pity, the Lord lovingly brings me examples of others who are far worse off than I am. I have discovered that it is my reaction to suffering that is all-important.

A pastor who became my friend through corresponding with me and reading my book visited me one day. I could hardly believe he had made it to my room. He was completely paralyzed, with the exception of one hand and his head. His wife literally carried him like a baby from the automobile, then strapped him into a wheelchair so he would not fall over.

But the light of Christ shone beautifully from his face! He expressed no bitterness, but accepted his condition as having been lovingly and perfectly appointed by God for His purposes.

Two things can happen as a result of heat: the hot sun can beat on a path and harden it. Yet that same heat can melt ice or butter. Likewise, the heat of pain or suffering can either harden our hearts toward the Lord and our fellowmen, or it can melt our hearts in tenderness and obedience to God's will.

The choice is ours—we can become sweeter or more bitter. We should have no doubt as to which reaction glorifies the Lord.

In everything give thanks; for this is God's will for you in Christ Jesus [1 Thessalonians 5:18].

Chapter 20

The Ultimate Test

Our daily relationships with people are a test of the sincerity of our faith in God. Our faith must be echoed in our conduct.

Once a pastor spoke to a large congregation about the love of God. He was an eloquent speaker, as he described how we should love God, our families, wives, husbands, children, friends, neighbors—all kinds of people. He spoke very movingly. The audience was so pleased with his oratory that they all sat perfectly still, attentive to his discourse.

After he had finished, as he prepared to descend from the platform, a woman rushed forward and grasped him by the hand, pleading, "Pastor, please don't come down! I want my husband to remain a 'platform husband,' not a 'home husband'! You just preached so well about loving your wife and children, but your actions do not coincide with your words. There is no love in our home. Please remain on the platform!"

If I speak with the tongues of men and of angels, but do not have love, I have become a noisy gong or a clanging cymbal [1 Corinthians 13:1].

Chapter 21

Contentment

Humanly speaking, I would certainly not have chosen to spend the last fifty years as a bed-ridden invalid, confined to my dark chamber. Should I doubt God's choice for me?

The legend says that there was once a Chinese ruler who went for a walk in his garden, anxious to see the beautiful trees. He noticed that one after another had fallen to the ground. "What happened?" he asked each of them in turn.

"Oh, some think I'm not as good as the others," said one.

Another replied, "I'm disappointed with the spot where I am planted."

Others complained, "I'm not as beautiful or stately or tall or fruitful as some others."

Then he came to a tiny plant, growing under an obscure tree. It was named *An Hsin Tsou*, "the peaceful heart plant."

"Why are you so happy and flourishing?" the ruler inquired.

"I'm satisfied to be planted where the gardener put me. I am sure that this place must have been his best choice."

For me, I know that where I am planted has been the Master Gardener's perfect choice for me.

Not that I speak from want; for I have learned to be content in whatever circumstances I am [Philippians 4:11].

Chapter 22

Another Roll of Paper

Sometimes one is tempted to despair because life seems spoiled or marred for one reason or another—illness, adverse circumstances, tragedies, and the like. God is able to reverse and retrieve the situation for His children who trust and call upon Him.

In the examination halls of early China, young men had to intensely prepare to take the literary examinations that opened the way for civil service and official appointments. It was a totally impartial system whereby each student was shut into a narrow cell the size of a telephone booth for three days and nights. He was allowed only one roll of paper to write upon. If he spoiled that, he could not have another. If he failed the examination, he often died of disappointment or committed suicide, rather than facing his family and a demoralized future.

My father, who passed the examinations in his early years and won many important posts, eventually became the head of the examination halls in Nanking. Clothed in the ostentatious robes and wearing the insignia of the highest official degree, he manned the tower overlooking the roofs of endless rows of examination cells. He would arrive in his green sedan chair with eight bearers and horsemen fore and aft.

My father had deep sympathy for the poor, as his own early life after the tragic death of his father had been a struggle from poverty. Since he had been through the rigorous examinations himself, his heart was tender toward the students and what they had to face.

One night he changed his fine robes for the coarse ones that the attendants usually wore and went down to the examination halls to see how things were going. There, crouched against a cell, was a student from a poor family; he had barely scraped up enough money to be sent to take the examinations. When my disguised father asked him what was wrong, the student sobbed, "My essay slipped out of my gown and fell into the night soil! I have no more paper and don't dare return to tell my poor widowed mother that I have failed—I want to kill myself!"

My father was deeply touched and, against the strict rules, got the boy another roll of paper to rewrite his essay. The student passed his examination and later, upon recognizing my father as the chief examiner, bowed low and cried, "Sir, I shall remember you with gratitude for the rest of my days!"

I, too, felt like that despairing student when sickness came upon me. I was in my prime; I was one of the first Chinese women to be educated; I was in the midst of exploding opportunities to serve God after my conversion. Suddenly, all hopes seemed to be dashed. My roll of paper was ruined by illness, and I would not have another chance.

But my Chief Examiner, the Master of the classroom of my life, the very Son of God, came down from the splendor of heaven to my level. My Savior and Lord, who became a man by His birth and then died on the cross for my redemption, came to me in my discouragement and weakness. He gave me another roll of paper, as it were, on which to write. He gently led me and taught me Himself, from one lesson to the next, in my classroom of suffering— until I learned to write on that second roll of paper as on the first.

This time the words were not written so quickly. They were shaped often with pen dipped in tears, under the dim light of the lamp in my dark chamber. But they wrote the same story as on the first roll during my active life of service: "Glory to God in the highest! Come unto the Lord and be saved!"

Have this attitude in yourselves which was also in Christ Jesus, who, although He existed in the form of God, did not regard equality with God a thing to be grasped, but emptied Himself, taking the form of a bondservant, and being made in the likeness of men [Philippians 2:5-7].

Chapter 23

Scattered for a Purpose

What use are small, crushed stones when the job is so great?

Long ago, when we were preaching in the countryside of China, we had to walk wherever we wanted to go. One day, in the company of a missionary, we set off for a village, carrying with us a guitar and some gospel literature. We passed a place where many workmen were breaking rocks and singing at their work, cracking large rocks into small stones.

"Why are you doing that?" I stopped to ask, as a naive city girl.

"Lady, don't you understand?" laughed the men over the noise of their sledge hammers. "We are preparing the road for the railroad tracks that will bring big, important trains to this area. If we leave the big rocks there, the train won't be able to go over smoothly. We have to break them into small pieces to lay the proper foundation."

Those men taught me a lesson. Many Chinese Christians have been broken off from the big rock of the church in China. Because of the difficulties there, they have been scattered as little stones throughout many parts of the world. The disciples and early Christians faced a similar situation, being scattered after our Lord was crucified and after persecution beset the early church. "Therefore, those who had been scattered went about preaching the word" (Acts 8:4).

My prayer is that all the scattered Chinese Christians throughout the world might unite their hearts with the desire to "prepare the way" for the Lord so that the gospel might flourish in China again in God's due season. These little stones must be close together so that the great train can pass over.

How wonderful of the Lord to let little crushed stones like me be a part of His big plan to carry the gospel to all the world!

As it is written in Isaiah the prophet,

> Behold, I send my messenger
> before your face,
> who will prepare your way:
> The voice of one crying
> in the wilderness,
> "Make ready the way of the Lord,
> make his paths straight."
>
> Mark 1:2-3

Chapter 24

A Doctorate in Prayer

Old people have sometimes come to visit me, complaining, "We are old. We are useless, and nobody pays any attention to us."

We can continue to be useful at every stage of life. In the Lord's work, there should be no retirement. We must go on until the time comes for us to go to our eternal home, or until the Lord Jesus comes to receive us.

How can we still be useful? Maybe you think that people only pay attention to the educated—those with PhDs? Never mind. The Lord loves us. We can have a degree too—a P. D.—a doctorate in prayer. If we will be faithful in our corner, praying for those who are on the front lines of battle, we will have a reward too.

When the soldiers went out to fight (1 Samuel 30:24), they may not have seen the need to divide the rewards with those who stayed behind. But, according to the regulations, those at the front and those who stayed behind to watch the baggage and provide the supplies had to share equally.

Let's be faithful in our little corner. The world may not see us, but the Lord does. We should be faithful in our prayer closets and pray earnestly for those who are witnessing for Him in more public ways. When the Lord comes, we will receive an equal reward.

Isn't that wonderful? I always check myself to see if I am not slack in my promise to pray for others. Many servants of God work day and night, witnessing and making disciples. We older folks cannot travel as they do, but we can be faithfully praying that the Holy Spirit might meet their needs. We should not get discouraged, but get to work by prayer.

Pray without ceasing [1 Thessalonians 5:17].

He who is faithful in a very little thing is faithful also in much [Luke 16:10].

Chapter 25

When I Am Wounded

Sometimes I, too, have hurt feelings. Through some offense or slight, imagined or real, my heart is wounded.

It is easy to become disheartened and even to hold a grudge. I have found that I must immediately lift my eyes to Jesus and keep them on Him, rather than on those who hurt me.

It matters not if I've been hurt,
It matters not at all
That sometimes from my weary eyes
The scalding teardrops fall.

What matters most is if I've erred
And not confessed my sin,
And through my lack some needy soul
Has failed to follow Him.

It matters not if cherished friends
On whom I lean in vain,
Have wounded me by word or deed,
And left me with my pain.
What matters is, can I forgive
Again and yet again?
It's not "Have they been true?" but
"Lord, have I been true to them?"

'Twill matter not, when evening comes,

How rough the road I've trod,
If only I have walked with Him
And led some soul to God.

—Source Unknown

Love...does not act unbecomingly; it does not seek its own, is not provoked, does not take into account a wrong suffered [1 Corinthians 13:5].

Chapter 26

The Gatekeeper

It is easy to reply too quickly to criticism, saying harsh words which one may later wish had not been spoken.

A certain lady who had a very pleasant disposition and patient spirit was known to have been formerly hot-tempered and irritable.

"What is the secret of your victory?" she was asked.

"I have a good gatekeeper," she replied. "When the devil comes to the door to tempt me, instead of going to open it myself, I send Jesus to the door. The devil bows and apologizes for coming to the wrong door."

I pray with the psalmist, "Set a guard, O Lord, over my mouth" (Psalm 141:3).

> For we all stumble in many ways. If anyone does not stumble in what he says, he is a perfect man, able to bridle his whole body as well [James 3.2].

Chapter 27

Tuning Up

I have seen many old years fade out and new years be born. Each brings renewed hope and faith that the Lord has not finished His work of perfecting me in His image.

I affirmed these words as my prayer on New Year's morning when I had already been bedridden for fifty years.

Dear Master, as the old year dieth,
Take Thou my harp
And prove if any string be out of tune,
Or flat or sharp.
Correct Thou, Lord, for me
What seemeth harsh to Thee,
That heart and life may sing
The new year long,
Thy perfect song.

—Source Unknown

For I am confident of this very thing, that He who began a good work in you will perfect it until the day of Christ Jesus [Philippians 1:6].

Chapter 28

Please Pass the Chocolates

Christians of considerable financial means have sometimes sat beside my bed, inquiring what they could do for the kingdom of God.

I grew up surrounded by wealth. I took for granted my family's lavish spending on feasts of a dozen courses, living in mansion-like homes with servants, jewels, and costly clothing. Until the Lord changed my heart to accept Him, I did not give such extravagance any thought. Suddenly I realized how much good could be done for the Lord's work with that same money, if it were not spent so foolishly.

Many young Christians have no idea how to use their money for the Lord. When I was traveling throughout China preaching the gospel, just such a group of wealthy Chinese girls invited me to a home high on the Hong Kong Peak, where one of the girls lived. We sat and gazed out over the jade green ocean, watching the huge ocean liners and small, picturesque junks bobbing in the waves. It was a breathtaking sight—we could see all the way across Kowloon and as far as China in the purple distance. We were having a good time with a great deal of polite small talk, all the while passing imported chocolates to one another.

Suddenly the tragic waste of the talents and spending money of these young new Christians overwhelmed me. I spoke up without any ceremony. "Girls, why don't you do something for the Lord with your money?"

They laughed and popped more chocolates into their mouths, declaring, "We would if we knew what to do." Their concept of

Christian work was very vague.

"I have an idea!" exclaimed one. "Why doesn't Miss Tsai become our missionary; we can all support her!"

I countered, "Why don't you girls rather pray and ask the Lord about starting a home missionary society, so that the good news of the gospel can go to unreached parts of China through Chinese missionaries?"

Apparently that chance remark planted a Holy Spirit-directed seed in the hearts of some of those very girls. They went to Kuling in 1918 and were instrumental in organizing the first Chinese Home Missionary Society. During the next year, enough support was raised that in 1919 six Chinese missionaries were sent to Yunnan Province under this society.

The names of the founders of the Home Missionary Society are:

Dr. Chen Ging-Ih

Dr. Yu-Reh Djang (Ambassador to America)

Dr. Chen Wei-Ping (Ambassador to Australia)

Dr. Mary Stone (First Chinese woman to receive a medical degree in America —Started first women's hospital in China)

President Katie Hu (President of St. Paul's Girls' High School in Hong Kong)

Miss Christiana Tsai

> But lay up for yourselves treasures in heaven, where neither moth nor rust destroys, and where thieves do not break in or steal; for where your treasure is, there will your heart be also [Matthew 6:19-21].

Chapter 29

Generation to Generation

The Lord is faithful to work in the hearts of the generations to come when there are Christian roots. Many times the situation of one's offspring or descendants looks hopeless, but the Lord answers prayer.

A certain Christian family named Ko, of Fukien province in China, was happy and prosperous. They had a son and a daughter. The father worked hard to build up a flourishing business. When he died, however, his son inherited the estate, and everything changed. Instead of working diligently at the business, the son began to use up the family wealth by gambling.

Day after day, night after night, like one possessed, he not only kept on gambling but kept on losing. Like all gamblers, he always hoped that the next time he would be lucky and win. So he kept on doubling his stakes. Becoming desperate, he refused to give up the hope that someday his luck would change, and he would win back more than he had lost. Soon the family savings were gone, then the business, then the household treasures, then the furniture, and then even their clothing.

Each time he lost, the son came home angry with himself, taking it out on his mother and sister. He slammed doors, stamped his feet, shouted, and abused them if they pleaded with him to stop gambling. They trembled every time they saw him, but they continued to pray for him.

One day when he was away, the mother, after hunting through the house, burst out crying. "There is no rice left in the bin, no oil in the jar, no food in the house, and no money to buy more! This is the end! There is nothing left for us to do but to jump into the river and drown ourselves!"

"Maybe brother will change now," the daughter pleaded. "When he sees we are reduced to starvation, certainly he will stop gambling. Wait until he comes home and then tell him the truth."

"Very well," the mother agreed. "I'll try just once more."

The next day, she spoke to her son about their desperate situation. "I have only one thing left—this gold ring which is a family heirloom, handed down from generation to generation. If you want us to stay alive a little longer, take it to the pawn shop and buy some food before we all die."

The son hung his head with remorse, realizing what he had done to his mother and sister. Even so, the gambling instinct was just as strong as before.

On the way to the pawn shop, he fingered the gold ring and thought to himself, *If I take it to the pawn shop, it will only bring ten dollars, and that will soon be gone. If I take it to the gambling house, I might get back double or triple—or I might lose everything. Shall I try my luck or do what Mother said?*

As he was debating within himself, the sound of singing came to his ears. Scarcely knowing what he was doing, he wandered toward the music. He came upon a little white-washed chapel. The door was open, and as he hesitated, a kindly voice invited him in. Not even noticing who spoke to him, he entered and sat down in the back. The group of people gathered inside were singing:

> What can wash away my sin?
> Nothing but the blood of Jesus.
> What can make me whole again?
> Nothing but the blood of Jesus.[1]

---

1 Robert Lowry, 1876

Soon he began to grasp the meaning of the words and decided they were singing just for him. Listening a little longer, he seemed to hear a voice inside, speaking to him. "Jesus!" he cried aloud. "Take away my sin—Make me whole!"

Immediately, a wonderful feeling of peace filled him, and the lust for gambling strangely left him. Some inner voice seemed to say that, from now on, everything would be changed. Not waiting to talk with anyone else, he rushed out and turned toward home, the gold ring still clutched in his hand.

When he entered the door, he was smiling. His mother and sister looked at his empty hands in despair, thinking he had gambled the ring away. He held out his hand and opened it to show the ring, still in his palm. "Here it is," he said. "Put it away."

"What happened to you?" his mother asked, trembling.

"Don't be afraid," he assured her. "From now on, I am going out to look for work, but today I will go and dig sweet potatoes for you to eat."

From that day forward, he was a changed man. Before long, he joined the church. Later, after marrying, his one desire was to have his children serve the Lord. Thus, the flame of the Christian faith was still passed on from father to son.

His true repentance was the unbroken link that kept the continuity of six generations of Christians. The bride in a wedding that took place in our home in Paradise, Pennsylvania, was the gambler's fifth generation; and her Christian children are now the sixth!

> One generation shall praise Thy works to another, and shall declare Thy mighty acts [Psalm 145:4].

Chapter 30

God Never Misdirects

Calamities, difficulties, and even sicknesses may seem to originate with the evil one. But I am learning not to judge too quickly, because the Lord is in control of all things to work them together for our good and for His glory.

Dr. James M. Gray, former president of the Moody Bible Institute in Chicago, was convalescing from a severe illness. His doctor, thinking that a change of scenery might bring the relaxation Dr. Gray needed, advised him to take an ocean voyage. But just when arrangements for the journey had been completed and the passage booked, Dr. Gray experienced an unexpected physical setback. He was greatly disappointed and began to wonder why his heavenly Father had allowed this new affliction.

About a week later, he picked up a newspaper. The front page story carried the tragic account of a steamer that had sunk after striking a coral reef in St. John's Harbor. There had been no survivors. Scanning the report more carefully, Dr. Gray learned that it was the very same ship he had planned to take!

How perfectly the Lord had directed his way after all. His temporary sickness was planned by God to deliver him from certain death.

And we know that God causes all things to work together for good to those who love God, to those who are called according to His purpose [Romans 8:28].

Chapter 31

The Unexpected Visitor

It is easy to lose our perspective in the matter of gifts and giving. Love should be our ultimate motivation and our Lord Himself the object.

I once heard a story about a certain family gathering on Christmas Eve. The parents had purchased a splendid, expensive Christmas tree and sent their children to bed early so that they could decorate it. The children eagerly anticipated receiving their gifts the next morning.

The wife commented that the tree seemed to need more ornaments, so the husband hurriedly went out and spent another fifty dollars for additional decorations. As they completed their task, the two parents stood back to admire the tree. "Our children will surely be pleased!" they agreed, as they piled the presents under the tree, each one elaborately wrapped with expensive Christmas paper and ribbons, and labeled with each person's name.

Suddenly, there was a knock on the door. The husband went to answer it. Instead of opening the door, he turned back, his face pale. "Oh, dear, the Master is here!" he called to his wife.

"Now? So early? Well, let Him in," his wife answered, flushing with embarrassment.

The husband objected. "What shall we do? We don't have any presents for Him. Shall we go to the bank and draw some money and wrap it up for Him?"

"Why, it's midnight! The bank is closed. Let Him come in anyway. Now I remember that last Sunday I did invite Him to come." The husband reluctantly opened the door, and the Master stepped in, wearing a beautiful white robe. Gently He spoke to the woman. "Thank you, dear lady, for the invitation to come to your home. So here I am. What a beautiful tree! Is it for your children?"

"Yes," the parents answered uneasily. Then the Master said, "Thank you for the present you gave me last Sunday. Shall I put it under the tree?" With His nail-scarred hands, He took out an envelope with fifty cents in it—their Sunday morning offering —and placed it under the tree with their other gifts.

> For where your treasure is, there will your heart be also [Luke 12:34].

> And now, little children, abide in Him, so that when He appears, we may have confidence and not shrink away from Him in shame at His coming [1 John 2:28].

Chapter 32

The Simplicity of Prayer

We are inclined to be too complicated in our relationship with the Lord. People tell us that we must understand systematic theology and have an advanced academic knowledge of the Bible in order to approach God correctly. Those are important. But a very common story has encouraged me to maintain a simple, childlike relationship with the Lord.

A man named Jim lived in a small village. He was poor, very shy, and stuttered. Every day at noon he would walk to a little whitewashed church and go in. After a couple of minutes, he would emerge again to quietly return to his home. The village people noticed his routine, and one day someone followed him. He watched Jim approach the pulpit and kneel down and say something.

"Jim, what do you do at the church every noon?" the people inquired.

Jim shyly answered, "I can't pray very fancy, so I just go there every day and say, 'Jesus, this is Jim.' "

After a time, Jim stopped going to the church. Some people of the village were concerned and went to his home to find out what had happened to him. Jim was sick in the hospital, they discovered.

Since Jim was poor, he had been placed in the ward of the hospital in which there were a number of noisy and complaining patients. The nurses disliked going into that ward because of the troublesome patients. But after Jim had been there for a few days, all of the difficult patients had become quiet and contented. The nurses asked the patients what had caused such a change in their attitudes.

They replied, "Jim has a friend who comes to see him every day at noon, and he helped us, too."

"What?" the nurses exclaimed. "Jim has no friend. We haven't seen anyone enter the hospital."

Jim timidly explained, "Every day, Jesus comes and stands at the foot of my bed and says, 'Jim, this is Jesus!' "

It is precious to me to remember that our Lord is no respecter of persons. He does not require us to be wealthy, eloquent, highly educated, or worthy. We need not be complicated in our approach to God, since Jesus has opened the way to the Father. Jesus appreciates our simple expressions of love and the sharing of our intimate daily concerns with Him.

> Let us therefore draw near with confidence to the throne of grace, that we may receive mercy and may find grace to help in time of need [Hebrews 4:16].

Chapter 33

Heed While You May

I have discovered that the Lord usually speaks to us quietly and gently at first, asking our obedience in something He has been revealing to us. If we do not listen, He speaks more loudly, often using hard trials or circumstances to get our attention.

A certain Christian millionaire had a schoolmate friend who went to Africa as a missionary. When he returned, he went to share his great burden for the many needs of the Africans. He asked his friend if he would consider giving some money to help. The millionaire answered that he was not at all interested in missions work and could spare no money.

The missionary explained to his friend how important it was to store wealth in heaven, rather than on earth. "When we go to heaven," he cautioned, "we can't take any money with us. It has to be there ahead of us." But the rich man's heart was not touched at all.

Later, the millionaire friend went to get something from his walk-in safe. He was careless about propping the door open and got locked inside the safe. He tried in vain to get out. The more he tried, the more confused he became, finally falling to the floor in exhaustion. He was on the verge of losing consciousness when one of his feet touched something that set off the alarm, calling the police.

His staff did not know why the police had arrived until they were told that the alarm had sounded inside the safe. "We don't have a key," the men explained. "Only the boss has it. His coat and hat are here, and we are waiting for him."

The policemen suspected the emergency and were able to force open the safe, finding the man nearly dead. He was taken to the hospital, where the doctors worked over him until he regained consciousness.

The first thing he said was, "Please call my missionary friend to come to see me." His family was puzzled, but they did as he said. He asked the missionary how much money he needed for the work in Africa. "Whatever amount is needed, I will write a check," he said.

I pray that I may never treasure worldly goods, since, by sharing them, I can store up riches in heaven.

> Do not lay up for yourselves treasures upon earth, where moth and rust destroy, and where thieves break in and steal. But lay up for yourselves treasures in heaven, where neither moth nor rust destroys, and where thieves do not break in or steal" [Matthew 6:19-20].

Chapter 34

Generation Gaps

I have often been asked, "At your advanced age, how can you relate to today's young people? Don't you feel some kind of generation gap?" Not at all, I'm happy to say! Chronological age has little to do with it.

I was encouraged by reading General Douglas MacArthur's comments on his seventy-fifth birthday (and I am far beyond that milestone!).

> Youth is not entirely a time of life—it is a state of mind. It is not wholly a matter of ripe cheeks, red lips, or supple knees. It is a temper of the will, a quality of the imagination, a vigor of the emotions. Nobody grows old by merely living a number of years.
>
> People grow old by deserting their ideals. You are as young as your faith, as old as your doubts; as young as your self-confidence, as old as your fear; as young as your hope, as old as your despair. In the central place of every heart there is a recording chamber; so long as it receives a message of beauty, hope, cheer, and courage, so long you are young. When the wires are all down, and your heart is covered with the snow of pessimism and the ice of cynicism, then, and only then, have you grown old.

I was not born at the age of ninety! I, too, passed through childhood, teen age, and the middle years. I know some of the problems of each stage. The Bible says that one generation shall declare the goodness of the Lord to another (Psalm 145:4)—that is not a one-way street! The old and the young can learn from each other and should listen to one another.

I love everyone and respect everyone, old and young. My greatest delight is to have young people come to visit me. I often find myself taking their part against the misunderstanding of their elders. I feel that God has put certain gifts and talents into each person; there are no two of us alike. And generation gaps are not necessary in God's family!

> Though youths grow weary and tired,
> And vigorous young men stumble badly,
> Yet those who wait for the Lord
> Will gain new strength;
> They will mount up with wings as eagles,
> They will run and not get tired,
> They will walk and not become weary
> [Isaiah 40:30-31].

Chapter 35

Purpose in Suffering

Some have asked me if I have seen any reasons for my sickness and sufferings. Surely, some have reasoned, a loving, heavenly Father would not allow suffering.

Dr. F. B. Meyer has discerningly written,

> The child of God is often called to suffer because there is nothing that will convince onlookers of the reality and power of true religion as suffering will do, when it is borne with Christian fortitude...not everyone can be trusted with trial. All could not stand the fiery ordeal. Even some who are Christians would speak rashly and complainingly. So the Master has to select with careful scrutiny the branches which can stand the knife, and the jewels which can stand the wheel. It is given to some to preach, to others to work, but to others to suffer. Just as a certain degree of the sun's heat is necessary to bring the finest fruit to perfection, so sickness, suffering, or fiery trials are indispensable for ripening the inner man.

> For to you it has been granted for Christ's sake, not only to believe in Him, but also to suffer for His sake [Philippians 1:29].

Chapter 36

A Finished Work

I have heard that many young people in the Western world are turning toward the Eastern religions. A friend asked me to compare Christianity with Buddhism, since I was on the verge of becoming a Buddhist nun when the Lord saved me.

Our whole family had been Buddhists. But, in later years, fifty-five of them became Christians. We have discovered that the difference between Buddhism and Christianity is that Christianity is a big *DONE*, and Buddhism is a big *DO*.

Buddhism depends upon a man's works. You have to "do it yourself," in order to go to the "West Heaven." In Christianity, we find that Christ's death on the cross is a completed work. The last words He spoke from the cross were "It is finished." Our salvation is accomplished when we believe and accept Him.

> He saved us, not on the basis of deeds which we have done in righteousness, but according to His mercy, by the washing of regeneration and renewing by the Holy Spirit [Titus 3:5].

Chapter 37

A Heart Lifted Up

We are not always able to pray long prayers in urgent times of need. We are not heard by God for our lengthy speaking, but only for a child's cry of need.

Often when I am very sick and cannot even sleep, read my Bible, or pray, I can only repeat the precious name of Jesus.

Sometimes I can only pray one sentence: "Jesus, I love You," or "Jesus, I need You," or "Jesus, come sit beside me."

We are human. We need companionship, don't we? I pray, "Jesus, come hold my hand."

Our Lord is "A very present help in trouble" (Psalm 46:1).

I love the Lord, because He hears
My voice and my supplications.
Because He has inclined His ear to me,
Therefore I shall call upon Him as long as I live.
[Psalm 116:1-2]

Chapter 38

Bearing the Cross

When our Lord Jesus was sentenced by Pilate to be crucified, He was forced to carry a heavy cross. On the way up the hill He fell. The soldiers forced a certain man named Simon to help Him carry the cross. I wondered, "Who was this Simon?"

Was he Simon the brother of Christ (Matthew 13:55)? No.

Was he Simon the Canaanite, one of the disciples (Matthew 10:4)? No.

Was he Simon the leper with whom Christ ate (Mark 14:3)? No.

Was he Simon the Pharisee who had a feast with Jesus (Luke 7:36, 44)? No.

Was he Simon called Peter by Christ, who said to the Lord, "I will lay down my life for Thy sake" (John 13:37)? No.

All of those Simons disappeared. Why did they run away? It is evident that they wanted to escape from the cross.

The Simon who carried the cross came from the country; he was the father of Alexander and Rufus (Romans 16:13). This Simon, inspired by Jesus' love, not only became His follower, but also led his family to serve the Lord. Simon did not shrink from bearing Jesus' cross.

Do we shrink from bearing our crosses? Those crosses may mean disgrace, suffering, long illness, persecution, or disappointment. Human nature wants to escape from the cross, but Jesus uses it as the sign of a true follower.

And He was saying to them all, "If anyone wishes to come after Me, let him deny himself, and take up his cross daily, and follow Me" [Luke 9:23].

Chapter 39

Of No Reputation

I search my own heart to see if I am willing to appear foolish in the eyes of man, for the sake of Christ, as I was in the youthful days of my conversion.

One of my sisters-in-law was a particularly strong Buddhist. She became very sick and prayed to Buddha for her healing. She made a vow at the temple that, if she recovered, she would publicly follow the parade of Buddha through the streets, regardless of the open spectacle she would make of herself. She promised that she would burn incense and dress in the red jacket and skirt of a prisoner for three years.

She actually did this, but as a rich lady accustomed to comfort, she arranged to have her sedan chair waiting for her when the parade came to an end.

After my conversion from Buddhism, she was persuaded to attend one of my meetings. She was very embarrassed to see that I was making a public spectacle of myself by standing up before common people and waving my arms around, directing the singing, and even preaching! She was so ashamed for me that, in order to escape from everyone's view, she hid her face in her arms, bowing her head.

Later, as a result of our family worship and seeing one after another of our family converted, she too became a most earnest Christian.

Am I indeed still willing to humble myself, as a loving prisoner of the Lord, to follow wherever He leads, regardless of public opinion?

For the word of the cross is to those who are perishing foolishness, but to us who are being saved it is the power of God [1 Corinthians 1:18].

For since in the wisdom of God the world through its wisdom did not come to know God, God was well-pleased through the foolishness of the message preached to save those who believe [1 Corinthians 1:21].

Chapter 40

Exchanging Crosses

Do I think that the cross I bear is greater than that of others? Would I want to exchange it? Do I ever reach the point where I think I can't carry it any longer? Many times I have been tempted with such thoughts.

I once read of a certain lady who thought her cross was the heaviest one in the whole world, until she had a dream in which she saw many, many crosses lying around.

She saw a beautiful, small cross, embedded with diamonds and jade and decided to exchange her cross for this one. But she found it heavier than her own.

Then she saw another one, carved with beautiful flowers and very attractive; it was also smaller than her own. She exchanged crosses again, but soon found that the new one had many thorns on the back that scratched her.

She tried this cross and that cross, but none suited her. Finally, she saw a plain and simple cross. She picked it up only to discover that it was her original cross.

Sometimes we think we would prefer the trials of others to our own. We think our own are too much to bear. But God has tailored our circumstances to accomplish His perfect purpose in our lives.

May I never try to exchange a cross that God, in His love, has especially prepared for me.

In this you greatly rejoice, even though now for a little while, if necessary, you have been distressed by various trials [1 Peter 1:6].

Chapter 41

As Unto Me

Simple, common acts done in the name of Christ often come back to us in blessing.

I heard a story about a certain poor student who went from door to door, selling books to earn his tuition. At one home, a girl answered the door. She had to tell the young man that her family could not afford to buy any books, because they were so poor.

He asked politely if he might have a glass of water. Instead, the young girl brought him a glass of milk, scarce as it was at that time.

Years passed, and the girl grew up. At one time, she became very ill. The famous doctor she consulted told her that she would need an expensive operation and a prolonged time of rest. Having little money, she asked for an estimated bill to see if she could afford the operation or not.

To her surprise, when the estimate was presented to her, the bill was already marked, "Paid in full by a glass of milk."

The noted doctor was the poor young student to whom she had given the glass of milk years ago.

> For whoever gives you a cup of water to drink because of your name as followers of Christ, truly I say to you, he shall not lose his reward [Mark 9:41].

Chapter 42

With Lowliness of Mind

I never wanted for my education and family status to become a stumbling block for my ministry to the country people. I am a debtor to all men (Romans 1:14), not only to the high but to the lowly as well.

I faced such a problem in village work with China Mary in China. "Don't let anyone know who I am," I instructed my co-workers. If I had let it become known that I was the daughter of a high official, we would have had a class gap between us; I could not have reached the poor and illiterate. I did not want my own social identity to hinder the gospel. But sometimes there was a slip beyond my control. When that happened, I prayed for the Lord to make use of even that.

While we were holding meetings in the far off countryside, I mailed a postcard to my home, telling of my safe arrival. Because it was not enclosed in an envelope, the eyes of the public fell upon it. The people noticed my educated writing of the Chinese characters, and the news spread fast.

Everyone became excited when they realized I could write beautiful scrolls for their walls. Immediately, people began streaming to my meetings, motivated by their desire to ask me to write scrolls for them. I wanted them to be attracted to my lovely Lord Jesus and not to myself. How was I to turn this unfortunate circumstance to His glory?

I bargained with the people: "If you will bring a dozen people to all three meetings, I will write a pair of Scripture scrolls for you."

Even though I had not brought along a proper Chinese brush or a table to write upon, I did the best I could—for the Lord's sake, writing the scrolls on the floor. The people kept their promise; the attendance exploded for the whole series of meetings, and many were saved!

> I know how to get along with humble means, and I also know how to live in prosperity; in any and every circumstance I have learned the secret of being filled and going hungry, both of having abundance and suffering need. I can do all things through Him who strengthens me [Philippians 4:12-13].

Chapter 43

Good Transmitters

How clearly can people see Jesus in me? How accurately can they hear the message from the Lord through me?

In the early days, while we were in a certain city in China, we heard a report that there was a radio nearby in a hospital. As it had been newly invented, I had not yet had occasion to see one in action.

"You can even hear Shanghai!" people cried excitedly.

We rushed to the hospital and crowded around the brown box, together with the doctors and nurses. Squeaks and howls came from the big loud speaker. Unfortunately, all we could hear that day was static.

I thought to myself that people often have great expectations of us as Christians. But sometimes all they get is static.

Lord, may I be a clear channel for Your Word to others. May they get the message from afar, directly from You, through me.

According to my earnest expectation and hope, that I shall not be put to shame in anything, but that with all boldness, Christ shall even now, as always, be exalted in my body, whether by life or by death [Philippians 1:20].

Chapter 44

The Book for Life

How precious is God's Book to me? Do I love to read my Bible as I do the letters of someone I love?

A mother was busy doing her household tasks one day, when her little daughter picked up a Bible from the bookshelf. She accidently let it fall to the floor.

Her mother cried in a distressed voice, "My dear, pick that book up at once! It is God's Book!"

The child looked earnestly into the face of her mother and said, "Well, if it's God's Book, let's give it right back to Him, Mother. We never use it anyway."

I ask myself: *Does my Bible remain on the shelf, or do I keep it in my hands as a useful and precious tool?* I can mentally determine to read it every day, but only through prayer, a love for the Lord, and an attitude of obedience can I know the hunger and thirst for it which comes from the Holy Spirit.

O how I love Thy law!
It is my meditation all the day.
[Psalm 119:97]

Chapter 45

Genuine Freedom and Peace

I once spoke to a group of prisoners who obviously felt that, if they were released, all of their problems would be answered.

I shared with them that God's way is not always to get us out of our difficult circumstances and then to give us joy; release from prison does not mean that a person will have freedom.

In the story of the storm in the New Testament (Mark 6:45-52), the disciples were out fishing, in the fourth watch of the night—at about 4 a.m. the darkest hour. The Chinese translation says that Jesus was on the shore, "watching" His disciples, who were having a hard time rowing against the wind. He came to them, walking on the water. When they saw Him, they were filled with fear.

Jesus *calmed His disciples* first; after that, He got into their boat and *calmed the wind*. That is exactly the opposite of what I probably would have done. But Jesus wants to deal with our inside problem first and then deal with our outside circumstances. What matters most is peace on the inside.

I heard a story about two artists who competed for a prize by painting a picture that was to represent peace. One painted on his canvas a tranquil and beautiful woodland scene with no disturbances—not a ripple on the creek, nor a leaf fluttering in the wind, nor a bird flying about. The other depicted a fierce storm, with lightning flashing and a swift running river. But at the base of a steep canyon, he painted a tree bent low, in the branches of which a mother bird had secured her nest. She was covering the baby birds with her wings. Which artist do you think received the prize?

In this world of trouble, the child of God can still have peace. True peace cannot be bought for any amount of money. We cannot command it; it is the gift of God. We face confusion and trials, but the Lord has offered us real and lasting peace as His last bequest. The peace Christ gives us is internal, rather than external. That kind of peace is undisturbed—no matter what happens to us.

> For they all saw Him and were frightened. But immediately He spoke with them and said to them, "Take courage; it is I, do not be afraid" [Mark 6:50].

Chapter 46

God's Hand on China

There is not a day that I have not prayed for China, my homeland, and the millions there who need Christ.

China's doors have been opened and closed to the gospel many times through different generations. My continued prayer is the last verse of this poem-hymn written more than fifty years ago in my home city of Nanking. The tune is "Jerusalem, the Golden."

O ancient land of China,
Four thousand years the same,
Whose glory lay in wisdom,
Whose scholars gave thee fame,
O China, we all love thee,
And pray that God may be
The source of all true knowledge,
And learning's deepest sea.

O beautiful for rivers,
High plains and mountains vast,
Whose voice of inspiration
Has sounded from the past;
Today God calls thee, China,
To stand with those who see
That problems of the future
Have also need of thee.

Though once thy gifted sages

Had seen a light afar,
They lost the purer radiance
Of Christ, the morning star,
His love, by faith illumined,
His peace awaiteth thee,
To teach thee God, the Father,
Whose truth sets all men free.

May every gate be open,
May every city wall
Behold the new world vision,
With Christ supreme o'er all;
Lord God, raise for us leaders
That China strong may be,
And through Thy Church triumphant,
Attain to unity.

—Source Unknown

I am telling the truth in Christ, I am not lying, my conscience bearing me witness in the Holy Spirit, that I have great sorrow and unceasing grief in my heart. For I could wish that I myself were accursed, separated from Christ for the sake of my brethren, my kinsmen according to the flesh [Romans 9:1-3].

Chapter 47

Only One Way

The human race is skilled at devising ways to enter heaven. Different religions have declared their own doors and even strange requirements to enter. But the Christian way is very narrow—only one door and one entrance requirement.

Chiang Kai-Shek, the president of the Republic of China on Taiwan, built a Christian church on that island. It was of sufficient size to enable those who worked in the government to attend the Sunday worship service. Anyone else who wanted to go to the services had to obtain an entrance permit.

Five missionaries I knew told me about their experience. They wanted to go to this church to worship. They asked a certain lady who knew Madam Chiang very well to get five tickets for them for a certain Sunday.

Most missionaries do not have much money to spare. These ladies shared the taxi fare and arrived in good time at the church. There they waited for the designated lady to provide them with the entrance tickets.

The service had already started, and they could hear singing, but still the lady with the tickets did not appear. One of the missionaries asked the usher at the door whether he would go in to see if their friend was in the church and had the tickets with her. The man went in and came out with a smile, declaring, "I couldn't find your friend, but your names are written in the guest book."

Then the ladies asked, "May we go in now?"

But the usher still insisted, "Sorry, you can't come in without tickets!"

That incident has been such a lesson to me. Our names may even be written on the church roles as church members. However, if we do not have the proper entrance ticket, we cannot enter heaven. Having accepted the Lord Jesus Christ as our Savior, trusting in His blood to cover our sins, we have received our entrance ticket.

> Jesus said to him, "I am the way, and the truth, and the life; no one comes to the Father, but through Me" [John 14:6].

Chapter 48

Just As I Am

The Lord wants us to come to Him just as we are, claiming no righteousness of ourselves. Doing good deeds or becoming famous does not gain us merit to enter heaven. We must come to God as sinners saved by grace.

A certain artist, at the closing of his studio one day, noticed a beggar boy standing outside his door. His face was very dirty and his hair was mussed up. His jacket was patched and repatched.

The artist was intrigued by his appearance. He asked the boy, "Do you want to earn two dollars?"

The boy was overjoyed. "Yes, sir!"

The artist instructed him, "Tomorrow, you come here very early. I would like to draw your picture. I will pay you two dollars."

The poor beggar boy was so pleased, he ran back to his mother, who helped him tidy up, wash his face, and comb his hair. He borrowed a jacket from a friend. The next day, he appeared at the artist's studio. He waited and waited nearly all day. Finally, the time came for the artist to leave his studio again. The boy rushed up to him, saying, "Sir, you told me to come here and you would draw my picture for two dollars." The artist looked the boy over carefully, from head to toe, and shook his head. "You are not the one I wanted to draw," he declared.

Upset, the boy insisted, "Yes, I am the one. I even borrowed a jacket."

The artist replied, "I'm sorry. I wanted to draw the picture as I saw you first, not as you are now."

How precious to me are the following lines from the familiar hymn:

> Just as I am, without one plea,
> But that Thy blood was shed for me,
> And that Thou bid'st me come to Thee,
> O Lamb of God, I come! I come! [1]

Once I heard evangelist Billy Graham on the radio, saying, "When I knock on the door of heaven, if I say, 'I'm Billy Graham. I wrote books and led thousands of people to believe in You. Please let me in,' then the door will not open. Yes, it is our obligation and joy to do what we can to lead others to follow the Lord. But that will not make us acceptable to God. We all must knock on the door and say only 'I am a sinner. By the precious blood of Christ, I appeal to come in.' Then we will be admitted."

> All our righteous deeds are like a filthy garment [Isaiah 64:6].

1 Charlotte Elliott, 1834.

Chapter 49

The Two Bears

In the family of God we are continually tested in getting along with each other. People who live together must have the same yoke. Two oxen can't go in different directions if they are under one yoke.

Our yoke is Christ. People who live and work together may see things differently. But they can pray that they will see alike on any major decisions and then act to the glory of God.

I heard about a couple who had only a tiny apartment and very meager means; even so, they seemed unusually happy. People commented that they acted as if they were on a continual honeymoon.

"That is because we have two bears with us," they laughed. Did they actually have bears living with them in that limited space? "We mean *bear* and *forbear*," they explained. "We are patient to forbear with each other's different viewpoints, and we also bear one another's burdens."

China Mary often reminded many friends of the story in Genesis 45:25, in which the brothers of Joseph went to Egypt to buy food. Joseph sent the brothers back to their father, after cautioning them, "Do not quarrel on the journey." The Chinese translation also implies that they were not to quarrel with one another.

We are pilgrims in God's way while on earth. Someday we too will go to our Father's house. Now we are fellow travelers, rubbing shoulders—sometimes roughly and uncomfortably—against others. We run into many potential misunderstandings and criticisms along the way, and we face the danger of "falling out" with each other. We need to ask the Lord to help us to bear one another's burdens, to understand each other, and to avoid quarreling on our journey homeward.

> Bear one another's burdens, and thus fulfill the law of Christ [Galatians 6:2].

> Bearing with one another, and forgiving each other, whoever has a complaint against anyone; just as the Lord forgave you, so also should you" [Colossians 3:13].

Chapter 50

The Outward Look

It is not easy to be outward-looking when one sees only the four walls of a room for decade after decade. One is tempted to dwell on one's own condition and needs in self-pity.

The story of the famous John D. Rockefeller is an example for me that I must always concern myself with the needs of others. By the age of thirty-three, this great man had made his first million dollars. At forty-three, he controlled the biggest business in the world. By fifty-three, he was the richest man on earth.

Despite his prosperity, he once confessed that he "wanted to be loved." Psychiatrists tell us that without love, a person loses his will to live.

Because he had worked so hard to get rich, Rockefeller lost his health and his happiness. He developed a condition that caused the hair on his head to fall out, along with his eyelashes and eyebrows. Because of poor digestion, the man who could have had anything in the world to eat had to restrict his diet to crackers and milk. At one time, he required bodyguards day and night because he was so hated by the men who had become poor because of his lust for riches. His weekly income was then reported to have been a million dollars.

When Rockefeller reached the age of fifty-three, people predicted that he would not live another year. Newspapers had his obituary ready in their files.

He began to do some serious thinking during his sleepless nights. He realized that he would not be able to take one thin dime with him into the next world. He decided not to hoard his money, but to use it to help others. With this resolve, he established the famous Rockefeller Foundation, which showered millions of dollars on universities, hospitals, religious organizations, and underprivileged people.

When he began to think *outwardly— about the needs of others*—a miracle happened. He began to sleep better, to eat normally, and to enjoy life. Instead of dying at fifty-three, Rockefeller lived a vital life until he was ninety-eight.

Rockefeller, after over half a century of sickly, wretched living, had learned one of the basic secrets to real life—the hard way. It is pathetic indeed that he did not heed earlier the admonitions in God's Book to evaluate true treasures.

> But those who want to get rich fall into temptation and a snare and many foolish and harmful desires which plunge men into ruin and destruction. For the love of money is a root of all sorts of evil, and some by longing for it have wandered away from the faith, and pierced themselves with many a pang. But flee from these things, you man of God; and pursue righteousness, godliness, faith, love, perseverance and gentleness [1 Timothy 6:9-11].

Chapter 51

Thanks — in Everything?

We should give thanks in all things. That is easy to say, but it is difficult to face the test.

Two missionary ladies were living not far from our home in Nanking. One had a quiet, calm disposition; the other was hot-tempered and easily upset. As they faced a particular new year, they decided, "No matter what happens to us this year, we shall give thanks to the Lord in everything." They both prayed, "Lord, help us."

One day they received an unexpected amount of money, designated to buy something personal. They went out to shop and bought a very lovely and expensive Peking rug, with a blue background and a beautiful flower pattern. The rug was delivered very late that night, so they put it next to their desk to spread it out in the morning.

The hot-tempered woman was the first to awaken in the morning and went downstairs to admire their new rug. She nearly jumped with rage at the huge ink spot she discovered, right in the center of the rug.

"Who could have done such a terrible thing?" Her shouts brought her more reserved companion to the room. When she saw the ruin, she recalled their intention before the Lord to give thanks in all things.

"But we have spent a lot of money on this rug!"

"We promised to give thanks. If someone sent us a box of chocolate candy, wouldn't we have said, 'Thank you'? Now this thing has happened too, because the Lord allowed it."

Finally, they both agreed to keep their promise to the Lord. They bowed their heads, praying in Chinese to practice the language. The hot-tempered missionary prayed aloud very emphatically. "Thank You, Lord, for this big ink spot on our Peking rug!"

After their prayer, their Chinese servant came out from behind the curtains, trembling. "Ladies, I've been serving you for seven years, and I never wanted to accept Christ because of you, lady. You scolded me and lost your temper at every little thing. Today I came early to clean your room and dust the tables, and the ink bottle accidentally fell on your new rug. I was so scared! I was sure you would dismiss me, so I hid behind the curtains when I heard you coming. I could hardly believe it when you both thanked God instead of scolding me. If that is how your God can change you, I have decided to follow Jesus as my Savior too!"

> In everything give thanks; for this is God's will for you in Christ Jesus [1 Thessalonians 5:18].

Chapter 52

The Grip of Fear

There are few things as paralyzing to our thoughts and emotions as fear. It damages our spiritual lives and makes us ineffective as channels to lift others nearer to God. We fall into fear when we doubt that God is with us. We are afraid when we are alone. But He has promised to be with us, "even to the end of the age" (Matthew 28:20b).

A certain song has been a great encouragement to me. Let us pray for one another when we read or sing it, so that we may all follow the Lord and not be afraid.

I will not be afraid.
I will not be afraid.
I will look upward,
And travel onward,
And not be afraid.

He says He will be with me.
He says He will be with me.
He goes before me,
And is beside me,
So I'm not afraid.
So we go singing onward.
So we go singing onward.
We're pressing upward,
We're marching Homeward,
To Him, unafraid.

He Himself has said, "I will never desert you, nor will I ever forsake you" [Hebrews 13:5].

Chapter 53

To Each Its Season

God's creation graphically illustrates spiritual truth with the change of every season.

All summer long, the robins busily hop around on our lawn, pulling up worms and insects for their food. Then they fly to the sunny South, as the gusty autumn wind blows the dead leaves here and there. I recall how my godmother, China Mary, sometimes wheeled me to the parlor to have a look at our lawn. The glow of the sunset was beautifully reflected in the remaining bright leaves, after the dead leaves had silently dropped off the maple tree.

Oh, Master of the universe, help me to drop off the profitless thoughts and desires of my life, like the dead leaves on the maple tree, at this sunset of my life.

I have come to realize that the thing that matters most to God is not the works that I have done, or the books that I have written, but the life that I have lived and the thoughts of my mind.

My single desire is to please the heart of God in every detail of my life. May I not go to my Lord Jesus as a shopper would go to the supermarket, selecting only what I want. Instead, may I eagerly accept whatever He chooses and desires for me.

For,
All flesh is like grass,
And all glory like the flower of grass.
The grass withers,
And the flower falls off,
But the word of the Lord abides forever [1 Peter 1:24].

Chapter 54

Where I Must Look

On days of special commemoration, on birthdays, at the dividing line between the old year and the new, I have offered these words of prayer and rededication to God:

1. I dare not look backward.

Lord, You know how I wasted time and bore no fruit and failed You many times with regret. I want to put all my failures under Your cross, Lord Jesus Christ. You are a merciful and forgiving God. You not only erase all of the records of my failures, but You forget them.

2. I dare not look forward.

My Lord, only You know the future and whether the road ahead is long and difficult or short and easy. You will help me to go forward, step by step. When trials come to me, You will help me to overcome them. When heavy burdens come, You, Lord, will carry them for me. Oh, my precious Lord, I deeply believe that You will lead me peacefully to reach my homeland.

3. I will look upward.

When I see Your glorious, exquisite, kind face, my Lord, my heart is at rest, and my fear disappears. The darkness turns to light, and the inside of my heart is filled with Your love and joy. Then I really enter into Your perfect peace and rest.

Brethren, I do not regard myself as having laid hold of it yet; but one thing I do: forgetting what lies behind and reaching forward to what lies ahead, I press on toward the goal for the prize of the upward call of God in Christ Jesus [Philippians 3:13-14].

Chapter 55

Master of the Tempest

Sometimes it takes a seemingly worse calamity to relieve us from our immediate dangerous situation. We need only to trust God with every storm that arises.

The Lord gave China Mary Leaman and me the privilege of witnessing for Him in many places in America in the early 1920s. Three years later, we left San Francisco to return again to our homeland, China, on the S.S. Pierce.

The boat sailed along smoothly and quietly for about three weeks. In one more day, we were to reach our destination. During the night, the fog horn blew without ceasing. Alarmed, I asked China Mary what that meant.

She answered, "Just trust and believe. God will take care of us."

At about 4 p.m. on the following day, I was writing some short choruses for the Chinese women to learn. I was suddenly startled to hear a very loud crash. The noise made me jump off my seat. Looking out through the porthole, I could see a precipice practically pressing against our ship. Then I heard footsteps running up to the higher deck, followed by the sound of a key locking all the doors, to keep the second and third class passengers from going up on deck.

China Mary and I knelt down and prayed. "Lord, help us!" We grabbed our coats and Bibles, forgetting even our bags and life-jackets, and followed the panicking crowds to the deck.

About three hundred passengers had gathered on the deck. The fog was so thick that one could hardly see his hand in front of him. Women were crying, and some sobbed, "I will never see my husband or mother again!"

I could dimly make out the captain's face, pale as a sheet. He was wringing his hands and calling, "Pray, pray, pray!" China Mary and I were standing by the railing, trying to peer through the fog, but we couldn't even see the sky.

Not too much later, the captain shouted, "The boat is going down! All passengers get into your lifeboats!" Our lifeboat was number eleven.

I could hear the sailors shouting, "The fog is so thick. How can we even let down the lifeboats?"

Just then, a big storm suddenly blew in upon us, with thunder, lightning, and pouring rain. The fog lifted. The captain could immediately see the location of the boat. The bow was wedged between two precipices. The sailors worked hard to plug the gaping hole and to bail out the water that had flowed into the boat. The captain ordered the boat to back out slowly. We were saved from danger!

It took that other storm, a seemingly worse calamity, to rescue us from the immediate dangerous predicament.

God has full control over winds and waves of the material world, as well as our "life storms." We can trust Him with both.

> And being aroused, He rebuked the wind and said to the sea, "Hush, be still." And the wind died down and it became perfectly calm [Mark 4:39].

Chapter 56

Certain Destination

Out of a smooth sea, a sudden storm may rise; on an ordinary day, a great calamity might happen; a short walk may turn out to be a long journey. No matter what life brings, God, the author of life, plans only good for His children.

I remember January 11, fifty-one years ago in China, as clearly is if it were today. The weather was crisp and clear. I was enjoying perfect health, serving the Lord with joy in public ministry and many travels. That day, I kept an appointment at the mayor's office to sign an important paper, attended to a few errands, and wearily made my way home in late afternoon.

China Mary greeted me with the surprise that she had moved me from a big room in the house we shared to a cozy, smaller one, which would be warmer and more convenient for me. She was always lovingly looking out for my welfare.

I remember the vivid details of the lovely supper we shared that evening. Our cook had made delicious biscuits as a special treat, and I ate two of them. Then I drank the steaming cup of Ovaltine and finished with some fruit. As soon as my head hit the pillow that night, I sank into an exhausted sleep.

At about four in the morning, I woke with a start. My head throbbed and the house was whirling. I was both feverish and chilled at the same time, and my eyes were painfully sensitive to light. For seventeen days, I was so ill that I could not move. That first day commenced my fifty-one years as a bedridden invalid.

But I look back upon more than half a century in bed as no

accident; rather, it has been God's plan to bring me through His school of training. My life started smoothly, as a calm voyage would. As the years progressed, the waters became deeper and more troubled. But I had trusted my life to the Lord, my Captain, to hold the compass and steer my life steadily, because He has chosen the direction I should go. And I have trusted Him with the time schedule.

My story of the boat in the storm had a happy ending—we reached our destination, though much delayed. I know that I will reach my eternal home as well, though later than I would ever have imagined. My Lord promised that it would be ready for me when I got there.

On that long ago occasion of the boat catastrophe, my precious mother had been waiting at home to receive a telegram announcing my safe arrival. Day after day passed, and she grew anxious—even ill—because no word had come. When our boat finally reached the wharf, we were overwhelmed by the kindness and relief of members of my family and friends from Nanking who had waited there so long. They showered us with beautiful flowers to greet us. My brothers had prepared a feast for our friends and us, but we passed it up with the urgency to catch the first train to our home to see Mother. When our carriage was almost there, we could see our family members and servants waiting outside to greet us. They had firecrackers and beautiful red candles burning to welcome us home.

When I reach my certain destination, the home in heaven that the Lord has waiting for me, then—as much as I want to see China Mary again, along with my mother, my precious family, and those believers who have preceded me into His presence—the *first* thing I want to do is to behold the face of the Lord Jesus, my King of Light. Everything else will take second place. My destination will be reached!

Let not your heart be troubled; believe in God, believe also in Me. In My Father's house are many dwelling places; if it were not so, I would have told you; for I go to prepare a place for you [John 14:1-2].

Queen of the Dark Chamber :
The Complete works of Christiana Tsai

Author Christiana Tsai
Chief Editor Timothy Su
Publisher Ambassadors For Christ, In.
21 Ambassador Dr.
Paradise, PA 17562
Tel: (717)687-0537 · (717)687-8564
Fax: (717)687-6178
E-mail: book@afcinc.org
Website: http://www.afcinc.org
U. S. Order line: (800)624-3504
First Edition April, 2015
Printed in Taiwan, R. O. C. @2015

ISBN: 978-1-63420-027-1

www.afcinc.org

Reaching Chinese intellectuals for Christ in this generation

Ambassadors For Christ Inc.